Pass CISSP CAT Exam in First Attempt

ARUN E THOMAS

About the Author

Arun E Thomas With over 16 years of experience as Information Security Professional, Arun holds Multiple Information Security patents and 28+ Professional IT certifications including CISSP concentrations, SSCP, CASP, ECSA/LPT and CCSE. He is the author of several books and is the Chief Security Architect & CTO of NetSentries Technologies (UAE and India) and CISO of GreenSentries DMCC. Arun holds his dual Engineering Degree from Institution of Engineers (India) and has held a number of positions during his professional career including Chief Security Architect, CTO, SOC SME, Security Analyst, Consultant and Security Practice Lead.

Technical Editor

Renjith Gopalakrishnan An Enterprise Architect and Technology Evangelist with 13 years of success leading all phases of IT and Security projects and designing diverse portfolio of solutions. Renjith holds numerous professional IT certification including PRINCE2, COBIT, TOGAF, ITILv3, SE1 (Splunk) and other technical certification credentials. He holds a Bachelor's degree in Computer Science and Executive MBA in IT. Known for designing usable solutions understanding the business and its requirements with customer satisfaction as a priority and carry the experience of understanding what business/various stakeholder's demands from ITaaS (IT as a Service) and Security services. He is Director – Customer Success at NetSentries Technologies and GreenSentries DMCC, and experienced in Infrastructure and Security Architecture Design, Enterprise Architecture Design, Service Delivery Management, Infrastructure Management, Solution Designing, Security Project Management and Systems Integrations.

INDEX

Introduction 1
   Launch of Computerized Adaptive Testing (CAT) for CISSP Exams 5
   How will it work? 5

Introduction to CISSP 7
   History of CISSP Certification 7
   Topical Domains 9
   The CISSP Exam 11
   Ongoing certification 12

Chapter 1 13
Security Governance Through Principles and Policies

Chapter 2 27
Personnel Security and Risk Management Concepts

Chapter 3 39
Business Continuity Planning

Chapter 4 48
Laws, Regulations, and Compliance

Chapter 5   67   D2
Protecting Security of Assets

Chapter 6   90
Cryptography and Symmetric Key Algorithms

Chapter 7   103
PKI and Cryptographic Applications

Chapter 8   117   D3
Principles of Security Models, Design, and Capabilities

Chapter 9   139
Security Vulnerabilities, Threats, and Countermeasures

Chapter 10   165
Physical Security Requirements

Chapter 11   184
Communication and Network Security

Chapter 12   251   D4
Identity and Access Management

Chapter 13   326
Security Assessment and Testing

Chapter 14   360
Security Operations

Chapter 15   437
Software Development Security

Chapter 16   486
Preventing and Responding to Incidents

Chapter 17   510
Disaster Recovery Planning

Chapter 18   531
Incidents and Ethics

Chapter 19   553
Malicious Code and Application Attacks

Glossary   579

An Introduction to the Pass CISSP CAT Exam in First Attempt

Welcome to the Pass CISSP CAT Exam in First Attempt practice questions exam cram! This question bank is a companion volume to the Certified Information Systems Security Professional (CISSP) Official Study Guide. This material is specially designed for readers and students pursuing CISSP certification. If you wish to test your knowledge before taking up the CISSP exam, this question bank will help you by providing a combination of 1,000 questions with answers and explanations. However, this will help you learn, drill, and review for the CISSP certification exam.

Pass CISSP CAT Exam in First Attempt question bank is designed to be equivalent to taking the new CAT based CISSP exam. It contains complex scenarios as well as standard multiple-choice questions related to the ones you may encounter in the main certification exam itself. The question bank itself is broken up into 19 chapters: 5 domain- centric chapters with more than 100 questions about each domain and remaining chapters contain lesser number of questions to simulate taking the exam itself.

Pass CISSP CAT Exam in First Attempt question bank covers 19 domains of information security knowledge. These domains are intended to serve as the comprehensive knowledge foundation necessary to succeed in the new CAT based CISSP exam. The chapters include:

Chapter 1 - Security Governance Through Principles and

Policies

Chapter 2 - Personnel Security and Risk Management Concepts

Chapter 3 - Business Continuity Planning

Chapter 4 - Laws, Regulations, and Compliance

Chapter 5 - Protecting Security of Assets

Chapter 6 - Cryptography and Symmetric Key Algorithms

Chapter 7 - PKI and Cryptographic Applications

Chapter 8- Principles of Security Models, Design, and Capabilities

Chapter 9 - Security Vulnerabilities, Threats, and Countermeasures

Chapter 10 - Physical Security Requirements

Chapter 11 - Communication and Network Security

Chapter 12 - Identity and Access Management

Chapter 13 - Security Assessment and Testing

Chapter 14- Security Operations

Chapter 15 - Software Development Security

Chapter 16 - Preventing and Responding to Incidents

Chapter 17: Disaster Recovery Planning

Chapter 18: Incidents and Ethics

Chapter 19: Malicious Code and Application Attacks

Each chapter covers a domain, with a range of questions that can help you test your security knowledge of real-world, scenarios, and best practices. Some chapters carry more exam weight than others. The question bank covers questions related to applications, network and system threats; what exploits them; and how to counter these vulnerabilities. Besides, questions related to operational security, physical security, U.S. and international security criteria, computer crimes, forensics, are also covered.

Pass CISSP CAT Exam in First Attempt question bank covers many of the crucial topics in each of these domains. The key purpose of this question bank is to effectively prepare you to take the CAT based CISSP exam. This material provides several questions that you might come across while taking the CISSP exam so you need to properly prepare for all kinds of questions and question formats. Most of the questions on the CISSP question bank are four option, multiple choice questions with a single correct answer and an explanation to justify the answer. Use this explanation to learn why an answer is correct and reinforce the content in your mind for main CISSP exam. Some questions are straightforward, such as asking you to select a definition. While some questions are bit more intricate, asking you to select the right concept or best practice. And some present you with a situation or scenario and ask you to choose the best response from four options.

In some cases, the right answer will be very clear to you. While in other cases, many answers may seem correct. In such circumstances, you must select the best answer for the question asked. Lookout for general, precise, universal, superset, and subset answer selections. In certain instances, none of the answers seems to be correct. In these cases, you'll need to choose the least incorrect answer. Usage of FIRST, LAST, EXCEPT and NOT words in many questions seems to be confusing so be careful while answering such questions.

To successfully pass the CISSP exam, you can even use plenty of different study materials and use this question bank as a drill, review, and practice session. Make sure to read each question and its answer choices along with explanations thoroughly rather than reading a few words and immediately assuming you know what the question is all about.

Remember the CISSP exam is:

- Truly international, not specific to any country

- Vendor Neutral, does not cover any product knowledge

- Not specific to your organization or any other organization

- Not specific to any particular industry

- Not specific to your way of thinking or your style of working

Launch of Computerized Adaptive Testing (CAT) for CISSP Exams

(ISC)² has changed the format of its CISSP exam from linear, fixed-form to Computerized Adaptive Testing (CAT). The new format will be introduced for all English versions of CISSP exams worldwide. The CAT format for CISSP Exams will offer a remarkably different test-taking experience. This new adaptive aspect creates more opportunities for exam administration as it is more precise and efficient at evaluating competency, and has shorter test administration sessions.

The CISSP CAT offers a unique testing approach for each candidate. It is a variable-length adaptive test where the number of questions presented to each candidate will vary based on their previous answers. In case of CAT formats, the computer will adapt to your answers and determine your competence level based on that. The application of CAT reinforces (ISC)²'s promise to meet the vital demand of cyber security pros worldwide by delivering an unbiased, valid, effective and reliable exam administration process.

How will it work?

Each candidate taking the CAT based CISSP exam will begin with a question that is well below the passing standard. Depending on your answer, the scoring algorithm will decide what question to feed you next, all in real-time. If you have answered the previous question correctly then the scoring algorithm will bestow you with a more complex question. On the other hand, if you have answered the previous question incorrectly, the computer will present you with an easy question.

The scoring algorithm will try to judge the candidate's ability and knowledge based on their answers and therefore presents a more accurate and clear picture to the ISC². Each question affects the next question and there is no option of changing your answer to a previously answered question. If you reach an extent where it is no longer possible to make a passing score, then the CISSP exam will terminate in prior to the completion of all other questions.

CISSP exam is highly difficult and challenging and therefore, this question bank can act as a main source for your CISSP study. To successfully complete the CISSP exam, you'll just need to be conversant with every domain but not essentially be a master of each domain. While this question bank is mainly intended to be used as a study guide for the CAT based CISSP exam, it is also a handy reference guide for use after your certification.

Introduction to CISSP

International Information Systems Security Certification Consortium, also known as (ISC)² developed the well-known and highly regarded professional credential - Certified Information Systems Security Professional (CISSP). In the realm of security certifications, the CISSP is considered to be the "gold standard" and vendor-neutral IT security credentials. Also, it is one amongst the IT security certifications to meet the stern requirements of ISO/IEC Standard 17024 – an international criterion for appraising and certifying personnel.

CISSP is the information security certification for those who are engaged in designing, developing and managing the complete security posture of an organization, from cyber security policy to practical implementation. This globally recognized certification has been adopted as a baseline for the U.S. National Security Agency's ISSEP program. As of 1st January 2018, there are around 122,289 (ISC)² members holding the CISSP certification worldwide, in 166 countries. United States holds the record of highest member count with total of 79,617 members.

The U.S. Department of Defense and NSA have adopted the CISSP certification and embedded it as an essential requirement for government personnel who deal with sensitive data and computer systems. And thus, CISSP is the most sought-after certification in the information security domain.

History of CISSP Certification

CISSP is an independent vendor neutral credentials granted and governed by International Information Systems Security Certifications Consortium (ISC)². This non-profit organization came into existence by a group of few industry associations in 1988. And since then it has been famous for providing standardized information security certifications. The main aim of the consortium is to standardize the knowledge and flairs required in information security domain. After a series of brainstorming meetings, the crew finalized the curriculum widely popular as Common Body of Knowledge (CBK). The first version of the CBK was finalized by 1992, while the CISSP certification was launched by 1994.

(ISC)² supports and provides a wide range of certifications, including CISSP, CAP, SSCP, CCFP, HCISPP, CSSLP and CCSP. Ever since its inception, the CISSP certification has gained much deserved respect amongst the professionals and organizations looking for a comprehensive information security exposure. CISSP emerged as the first certification in the industry to be accredited under the American National Standards Institute (ANSI) ISO/IEC Standard 17024:2003.

Why become a CISSP?

In today's ever-changing landscape, the need for security and technology advancements continues to grow. Most organizations are desperate to identify and employ veteran and endowed security professionals to help safeguard the resources. As a Certified Information Systems Security Professional (CISSP), you will be regarded as a security expert who has effectively met a predefined standard of knowledge and experience.

Key reasons for attaining a CISSP certification:

- To propel your career

- To expand your current knowledge of security concepts and practices

- To demonstrate your ability as a veteran security professional

- To become more marketable in today's highly competitive workforce

- To upsurge your salary and be qualified for more employment opportunities

- To bring enhanced security expertise to your present occupation

- To show dedication to the security discipline

The CISSP certification enables organizations to discover which individuals have the talent, knowledge, and experience required to implement robust security practices, identify necessary countermeasures, and execute risk analysis. Also, the certification indicates that an esteemed third-party organization has acknowledged an individual's theoretical and technical knowledge, and differentiates that individual from those who lack this expertise.

Topical Domains

The curriculum of the CISSP certification deals with concepts from a comprehensive array of information security subjects. The CISSP exam mainly covers 8 individual subject areas, which are referred to as domains. The examination is completely based on what (ISC)² terms the Common Body of Knowledge (CBK). Typically, the 8 domains make up (ISC)²'s Common Body of Knowledge, which are referred as a framework and collection of information security best practices, technologies, methodologies and concepts. The complete CISSP curriculum can be divided into eight topical domains:

- Security and Risk Management
- Asset Security
- Security Engineering
- Communications and Network Security
- Identity and Access Management
- Security Assessment and Testing
- Security Operations
- Software Development Security

These eight domains offer a vendor-independent outline of a common security context. This context is the base for a conversation on security practices that can be supported in all kind of organizations worldwide. The topical domains were subjected to a major revision as of April 2015. The domains were shortened from ten to eight, and many concepts and topics were re-organized.

The CISSP Exam

The CISSP exam tests your know-how on best practices, concepts and standards. The exam is truly international and is not focused on a specific country, organization or industry. The CISSP exam consists of 250 standard multiple-choice questions, which a candidate should answer in six hours. Only 225 questions are rated, while remaining 25 are used for research purposes. The 25 research questions are incorporated into the exam, but you won't know what questions are not rated. To pass the CISSP exam, you must score at least 700 points out of 1,000. Not all questions are worth the same number of points. Some questions are weighted more based on their difficulty. No questions will be specific to a certain products or vendors. Instead, you will be tested on the security models, concepts, practices and methodologies.

Concentrations

CISSP certification holder can earn additional credentials in areas of specialty. The three concentrations offered by (ISC)2 include:

- Information Systems Security Architecture Professional (CISSP-ISSAP)

- Information Systems Security Management Professional (CISSP-ISSMP)

- Information Systems Security Engineering Professional (CISSP-ISSEP)

Ongoing certification

The (ISC)2 CISSP credential is valid only for three years. The CISSP certification holders have to renew the credential either by retaking the CISSP exam or by submitting CPE credits. The accredited professionals need to gain 20 CPE each year, and total of 120 CPE credit at the end of third year. In addition to it, you're required to pay the annual maintenance fee to further hold your CISSP certification.

Passing the CISSP exam is not an easy task. It requires a lot of effort, dedication and hard work. A combination of CISSP training, appraising, studying, and practice tests can help you reach this pinnacle of professional success. CISSP is a certification with great demand across organizations and industries globally. A CISSP certification holder is on every recruiter's radar. If you are looking to take your career to its peak level, then strive for the most demanding CISSP certification!!

Chapter 1
Security Governance Through Principles and Policies

1. .... comprises of the primary goals and objectives of security.

a. A network's border perimeter

b. A stand-alone system

c. The CIA Trend

d. The internet

Ans. c. The CIA Trend

(The primary goals and objectives of security are confidentiality, integrity, and availability, commonly referred to as the CIA Triad)

2. An act of hiding or preventing disclosure is known as .....

a. Seclusion

b. Criticality

c. Concealment

d. Sensitivity

Ans. c. Concealment

(Concealment is an act of hiding something or preventing it from being known)

3. Availability, the third principle of CIA Trend, includes efficient uninterrupted access to objects

and prevention of ………………

a. Virus

b. Trojan Horse

c. Malware

d. Denial-of-service (DOS) attacks

Ans. d. Denial-of-service (DOS) attacks

(A common form of attack on availability is a Denial of Service (DoS) which prevents authorized individuals from accessing the required data.)

4. **Storing something in an out-of-the-way location is known as…….**

a. Seclusion

b. Criticality

c. Sensitivity

d. Isolation

Ans. a. Seclusion

(Seclusion is the act of secluding, i.e. storing something in an isolated location)

5. **…….. is the process of verifying or testing whether the claimed identity is valid.**

a. Authorization

b.   Authentication

c.   Auditing

d.   Accounting

Ans. b. Authentication

(Authentication is the process of proving or showing something to be valid.)

6.   .... is an act of decision where an operator can influence or control disclosure in order to minimize harm or damage.

a.   Concealment

b.   Isolation

c.   Discretion

d.   Secrecy

Ans. c. Discretion

(Discretion can be defined as a right or power where an operator can act according to his own judgment in order to lessen harm or damage)

7.   .... is ultimately dependent on the strength of the authentication process.

a.   Auditing

b.   Human accountability

c. Nonrepudiation

d. Accounting

Ans. b. Human accountability

(Human associated with a specific user account is the actual entity controlling that user account when the undesired action took place)

8. Use of multiple controls in a series is known as ....

a. Protection Mechanism

b. Layering

c. Abstraction

d. Encryption

Ans. b. Layering

(Layering also known as defense-in-depth is simply the application of multifarious layers in a series)

9. .... is a key element in security controls as well as in programming?

a. Data Hiding

b. Encryption

c. Layering

d. Abstraction

Ans. a. Data Hiding

(Data hiding plays a vital role in security controls as well as in programming)

10. The art and science of hiding the meaning or intent of a communication from unintended recipients.

a. Concealment

b. Encryption

c. Defense-in-depth

d. Layering

Ans. b. Encryption

(Encryption is an important element in security control, especially in regard to hiding the intention of a communication from inadvertent recipients)

11. .... is the collection of practices related to supporting, defining, and directing the security efforts of an organization.

a. Security Governance

b. Business case

c. Security policy

d. Protection mechanism

Ans. a. Security Governance

(Security Governance is a process of establishing and maintaining a framework to provide assurance that information security strategies are aligned with and support business objectives)

12. The information security team should be spearheaded by a designated ……… who is entitled to report directly to the senior management.

a.   Chief Security Officer (CSO)

b.   Chief executive officer

c.   Board of Directors (BOD)

d.   Chief information officer

Ans. a. Chief Security Officer (CSO)

(Chief Security Officer is always entitled to report directly to the senior management regarding security issues within an organization)

13.   ………….. is a documented argument or stated position in order to define a need to make a decision or take some form of action?

a.   Argumentation

b.   Security Governance

c.   Business case

d. Security Plan

Ans. c. Business case

(A business case is a formal, written argument intended to convince a decision maker to approve some kind of action)

14. .... is a long-term plan that is fairly stable and defines the organizations security purpose?

a. Tactical Plan

b. Operational Plan

c. Strategic Plan

d. Technical Plan

Ans. c. Strategic Plan

(Strategic Plan is long term plan that helps to understand the security functions of the organization)

15. Who will be held liable for the overall success or failure of a security solution as well as for exercising due care and due intelligence in establishing security for an organization?

a. Auditor

b. Senior Manager

c. Security Professional

d.   User

Ans. b. Senior Manager

(Senior Manager is ultimately responsible for the security maintained by an organization)

16.   The role of security professionals can be labeled as ……. function role.

a.   CIRT Role

b.   IS/IT Role

c.   Data Owner Role

d.   Data Custodian Role

Ans. b. IS/IT Role

(The security professional role is filled by a dynamic team of IS/IT, who is responsible for designing and implementing security solutions)

17.   The data owner is typically a high-level manager who is ultimately responsible for ………..

a.   Data Dissemination

b.   Data Analysis

c.   Data Protection

d.   Data filtration

Ans. c. Data Protection

(Usually data owner is responsible for classifying data for placement and protection within the security solutions)

18. The .... performs all activities necessary to provide adequate protection for the CIA Triad of data.

a. Data Custodian

b. Data owner

c. Auditor

d. Security Professionals

Ans. a. Data Custodian

(Data Custodian performs all necessary activities and fulfills the requirements and responsibilities delegated from upper managements)

19. .... is a documented set of best IT Security practices crafted by the Information Systems Audit and Control Association (ISACA).

a. COBIT

b. ITIL

c. COSO

d. TOGAF

Ans. a. COBIT

(COBIT prescribes goals and requirements for security controls and encourages mapping of IT security deals to Business objectives)

20. A document that defines the scope of security needed by the organization and discusses the assets that require protection is known as ....

a. Security Policy

b. Business case

c. Argumentation

d. Security Standards

Ans. a. Security Policy

(Security Policy defines the main security objectives and outlines the security framework of an organization)

21. .... is a specialized dynamic testing technique that provides many diverse types of input to software to stress its limit and find previously undetected flaws.

a. Black Box Testing

b. Beta Testing

c. Penetration testing

d. Fuzz testing

Ans. d. Fuzz testing

(Fuzz testing is a technique used to discover coding errors, and security loopholes in software, operating systems or networks)

22. .... is a security procedure where potential threats are identified, categorized and scrutinized.

a. Threat modeling

b. Attack Modeling

c. Architectural Risk Analysis

d. Security Development lifecycle

Ans. a. Threat modeling

(Threat modeling is process that identifies the potential harm, the probability of occurrences, the priority of concern and the means to eradicate and reduce threat)

23. Who developed the threat categorization scheme called STRIDE?

a. SAP

b. ORACLE

c. Microsoft

d. Red Hat

Ans. c. Microsoft

(Microsoft developed a threat categorization scheme known as STRIDE i.e., Spoofing, Tampering, Repudiation, Information disclosure, Denial of Service attack, Elevation of privilege)

24. ………………….. is used to falsify communication or alter static information.

a. Spoofing

b. Tampering

c. Repudiation

d. Elevation of privilege

Ans. b. Tampering

(In order to misrepresent communication or amend static information, Tampering is used)

25. Which of the following is the first step toward designing defenses to help eliminate downtime, compromise or loss?

a. Diagramming potential attacks

b. Prioritization and response

c. Identifying Threats

d. Performing Reduction Analysis

Ans. c. Identifying Threats

(Identifying Threats is the first and foremost step toward designing defenses to help eradicate downtime, compromise or loss)

Chapter 2
Personnel Security and Risk Management Concepts

26. .... are the weakest element in any security solution.

a. Software products

b. Security policies

c. Humans

d. Internet connections

Ans. c. Humans

(Regardless of the specifics of a security solution, humans are the weakest element. No matter what physical or logical controls are deployed, humans can discover ways to avoid them.)

27. What is the first step in defining security needs related to personnel and being able to seek out new hires?

a. Screen candidates

b. Craft a job description

c. Set position classification

d. Request resumes

Ans. b. Create a job description

(The first step in defining security needs and hiring new employees is to create a job description. Without a job description, there is no consensus on what type of individual needs to be found and hired)

28.   Working together to penetrate a crime is called as ………

a.   Illegal agreement

b.   Collusion

c.   Candidate Screening

d.   Compliance

Ans. b. Collusion

(When several people work together to commit a crime or fraud is called as collusion)

29.   What is the main purpose of an exit interview?

a.   To analyze the exiting employee's performance

b.   To review the nondisclosure agreement

c.   To cancel the exiting employee's network access accounts

d.   To return the exiting employee's personal stuffs

Ans. b. To review the nondisclosure agreement

(The primary purpose of an exit interview is to review the nondisclosure agreement (NDA) and other liabilities and restrictions placed on the former employee, based on the employment agreement and any other security-related documentation)

30. The act of conforming to or adhering to rules, regulations, standards, or requirements is known as ....

a. Security Governance

b. Compliance

c. Hybrid assessment

d. Risk aversion process

Ans. b. Compliance

(Compliance means adhering to a rule, such as a specification, policy, standard or law. In general, compliance describes the goal that organizations aspire to achieve in their efforts to ensure that they are aware of and take steps to comply with relevant laws, polices and regulations)

31. .... is a process by which the goals of risk management are achieved.

a. Risk Terminology

b. Risk Analysis

c. Risk Mitigation

d. Risk Identification

Ans. b. Risk Analysis

(Risk analysis is the assessment of the risks associated with a particular event or action. It is applied to projects, information technology, security issues and any action where risks may be analyzed on a quantitative and qualitative basis.)

32. …………….. is a flaw, loophole, oversight, error, limitation, frailty, or susceptibility in the IT infrastructure or any other aspect of an organization.

a. Exposure

b. Threat

c. Vulnerability

d. Attack

Ans. c. Vulnerability

(Vulnerability is a flaw in code or design that creates a potential point of security compromise for an endpoint or network. If a vulnerability is exploited, loss or damage to assets can occur.)

33. The process of reading the exchanged materials and verifying them against standards and expectations is known as ……………..

a. Third-party governance

b. Documentation review

c. Risk management

d.   Assets valuation

Ans. b. Documentation review

(Documentation review is the process of evaluating the exchanged materials and authenticating them against standards and expectations. The documentation review is typically performed before any on-site inspection takes place)

34.   .... is an assessment of probability, possibility, or chance.

a.   Risk

b.   Attack

c.   Threat

d.   Breach

Ans. a. Risk

(When we appraise the probability, possibility, or chance, a risk may occur)

35.   An occurrence where a security mechanism is being bypassed would be known as a ....

a.   Exposure

b.   Vulnerability

c.   Breach

d.   Safeguards

Ans. c. Breach

(A breach is the occurrence of a security mechanism being bypassed or thwarted by a threat agent. When a breach is combined with an attack, a penetration, or intrusion, can result)

36.   How is Annualized Loss Expectancy (ALE) calculated?

a.   Threat + vulnerability

b.   Asset value($)*exposure factor

c.   SLE*ARO

d.   ARO* vulnerability

Ans. c. SLE*ARO

(The Annualized Loss Expectancy (ALE) that occurs due to a threat can be calculated by multiplying the Single Loss Expectancy (SLE) with the Annualized Rate of Occurrence (ARO)

37.   The …………….. represent the percentage of loss that an organization would experience if a specific asset were violated by a realized risk.

a.   Exposure factor

b.   Annualized Loss Expectancy

c. Single Loss Expectancy

d. Annualized Rate of Occurrence

Ans. a. Exposure factor

(Exposure factor (EF) is the subjective, potential percentage of loss to a specific asset, if a specific threat is realized. The exposure factor is a subjective value that the person assessing risk must define)

38. ………………….. is an anonymous feedback-and-response process used to enable a group to reach an anonymous consensus.

a. The Delphi technique

b. The Fuzz testing

c. Penetration testing

d. Hybrid assessment

Ans. a. The Delphi technique

(The Delphi technique is a widely used and accepted method for gathering data from respondents within their domain of expertise. The technique is designed as a group communication process which aims to achieve a convergence of opinion on a specific real-world issue.)

39. The method of combining quantitative and qualitative analysis into a final assessment of organizational risk is known as …………..

a. Risk Analysis

b. Assets valuation

c. Hybrid Analysis

d. Documentation review

Ans. c. Hybrid Analysis

(Under the Hybrid Analysis method, both qualitative and quantitative assessment techniques are combined for the final appraisal of organizational risk.

40. How is residual risk calculated?

a. Total risk – controls gap

b. Threat * vulnerability * asset value

c. Threat + vulnerability

d. Asset value($)*exposure factor

Ans. a. Total risk – controls gap

(The difference between Total risk and controls gap is known as residual risk)

41. A .... access control is deployed to discourage violation of security policies.

a. Preventive

b. Compensating

c. Directive

d. Deterrent

Ans. d. Deterrent

(A deterrent access control picks up where prevention leaves off. The deterrent control doesn't stop with trying to prevent an action; instead, it goes further to exact consequences in the event of an attempted or successful violation)

42. A detective access control is deployed to …………….. unwanted or unauthorized activity.

a. Discover or detect

b. Thwart or stop

c. Control

d. Analyze

Ans. a. Discover or detect

(Detective access control operates after the fact and can discover the unwanted or unauthorized activity only after it has occurred.)

43. ……………… is a guideline for how a risk is to be assessed, resolved and monitored.

a. Risk frameworks

b. Business impact analysis

c. Information security strategy

d. Qualitative risk analysis

Ans. a. Risk frameworks

(Risk frameworks promotes the concept of near real-time risk management and ongoing information system authorization, through the implementation of robust continuous monitoring processes)

44. Which of the following is a prerequisite to security training?

a. Security basic

b. Awareness

c. Security literacy

d. Education

Ans. b. Awareness

(Security Awareness is a criterion to security training. The goal of creating awareness is to bring security to the forefront and make it a recognized entity for users)

45. A portion of the .... is the logical and practical analysis of business procedures and organizational policies.

a. Hybrid assessment

b. Risk aversion process

c. Countermeasure selection

d. Documentation review

Ans. d. Documentation review

(The documentation review process ensures that the stated and implemented business tasks, systems, and methodologies are practical, efficient, cost-effective but most of all they support security through the reduction of vulnerability and the avoidance, reduction, or mitigation of risk.)

46. **What is the formula to calculate Single Loss Expectancy (SLE)?**

a. Asset value (AV) * Exposure factor (EF)

b. Threat * vulnerability * asset value

c. Total risk – controls gap

d. SLE*ARO

Ans. a. Asset value (AV) * Exposure factor (EF)

(Single-loss expectancy (SLE) is the monetary value expected from the occurrence of a risk on an asset. However, SLE is calculated by multiplying the Asset value with the Exposure factor.)

Chapter 3
Business Continuity Planning

47. The top priority of Business Continuity Planning (BCP) and Disaster Recovering Planning (DRP) is ....

a. People

b. Resources

c. Capital

d. Infrastructure

Ans. a. People

(The top priority of BCP and DRP is always people. However, the primary concern is to get people out of harm's way; then one can address IT restoration or recovery issues)

48. .... is the first Business Impact Assessment (BIA) task facing the BCP team.

a. Risk identification

b. Identification of business priorities

c. Resource prioritization

d. Impact assessment

Ans. b. Identification of business priorities

(The first BIA task is to ascertain the business priorities. Depending upon the line of business, there will be certain activities that are most essential for day-to-day operation when disasters strikes)

49. The risk identification portion of the BIA process is purely .... in nature.

a. Quantitative

b. Qualitative

c. Technical

d. Cognitive

Ans. b. Qualitative

(The risk identification portion is purely qualitative in nature and the BCP team should not be concerned about likelihood or the amount of damage in this phase)

50. Mention the phase that bridges the gap between the business impact assessment and the continuity planning phases of BCP development.

a. Provisions and processes

b. Strategic development

c. Plan approval

d. Plan implementation

Ans. b. Strategic development

(The strategy development task bridges the gap between business impact assessment and continuity planning by analyzing the prioritized list of risks developed during the BIA and determining which risks will be addressed by the BCP)

51. Mention the first step in developing a business continuity plan (BCP)

a. Determine the critical recovery time period.

b. Classify the importance of systems.

c. Establish a disaster recovery strategy.

d. Execute a risk ranking.

Ans. b. Classify the importance of systems.

(Determining the classification of systems is the first and foremost step in a BCP exercise. Without determining the classification of the systems, the other steps cannot be performed. Choices A, C and D are carried out later in the process)

52. Disaster recovery planning (DRP) for a company's computer system typically focuses on:

a. Strategic long-term planning

b. Operations turnover procedures

c. alternative procedures to process transactions

d. The probability that a disaster will occur

Ans. c. Alternative procedures to process transactions

(It is important that disaster recovery planning identifies alternative processes that can be put in place while the system is not available.)

53.   A disaster recovery plan (DRP) for an organization should:

a.   Increase the length of the recovery time and the cost of recovery

b.   Reduce the length of the recovery time and the cost of recovery

c.   Reduce the duration of the recovery time and increase the cost of recovery

d.   not affect the recovery time nor the cost of recovery

Ans. b. Reduce the length of the recovery time and the cost of recovery

(One of the main objectives of a DRP is to reduce the duration and cost of recovering from a disaster. DRP would increase the cost of operations before and after the disaster occurs, but should reduce the time to return to normal operations and the cost that could result from a disaster)

54.   .... has the highest priority in a business continuity plan (BCP)?

a.   Restoring the site

b.   Resuming critical processes

c. Recovering sensitive processes

d. Relocating operations to an alternative site

Ans. b. Resuming critical processes

(The resumption of critical processes has the highest priority as it allows business processes to begin immediately after the interruption and not later than the declared mean time between failures (MTBF).)

55. After incorporation of a disaster recovery plan (DRP), pre-disaster and post-disaster operational cost for an organization will ....

a. Increase

b. Decrease

c. Remain constant

d. Increase or decrease depending upon the nature of the business

Ans. a. Increase

(There are costs associated with all activities and disaster recovery plan is not an exception. Although there are costs associated with a DRP, there are unknown costs that are incurred if a DRP is not implemented)

56. .... is not an element of the risk analysis process?

a. Analyzing an environment for risks

b.   Selecting appropriate safeguards and implementing them

c.   Evaluating each threat event as to its likelihood of occurring and cost of the resulting damage

d.   Creating a cost/benefit report for safeguards to present to upper management

Ans. b. Selecting appropriate safeguards and implementing them

(Risk analysis includes analyzing an environment for risks, appraising each threat event as to its likelihood of occurring and the cost of the damage it would cause, and creating a cost/benefit report for safeguards to present to upper management)

57.   .... cannot be considered as an asset in a risk analysis?

a.   A development process

b.   A proprietary system resource

c.   An IT infrastructure

d.   Users' personal files

Ans. d. Users' personal files

(The personal files of users are not usually considered as assets of the organization and thus are not considered in a risk analysis.)

58. .... represents accidental or intentional exploitations of vulnerabilities.

a. Threat events

b. Threat agents

c. Breaches

d. Risks

And. a. Threat events

(Threat events are accidental or intentional exploitations of vulnerabilities)

59. The major resource consumed by the BCP process during the BCP phase is ....

a. Hardware

b. Software

c. Personnel

d. Processing time

Ans. c. Personnel

(During the BCP phase, the most significant resource utilization will be the time dedicated by members of the BCP team to the planning process itself. This represents a significant use of business resources and is another reason that buy-in from senior management is essential.)

60. Disaster recovery planning addresses the ....

a. technological aspect of BCP

b. functional aspect of BCP

c. operational piece of BCP

d. overall coordination of BCP

Ans. a. technological aspect of BCP

(Disaster recovery planning is the technological aspect of business continuity planning (BCP). Business resumption planning addresses the operational part of BCP).

61. Which of the following would best support 24/7 availability?

a. Offsite storage

b. Daily backup

c. Mirroring

d. Periodic testing

Ans. c. Mirroring

(Mirroring of critical elements is a tool that facilitates immediate recoverability. Daily backup implies that it is reasonable for restoration to take place within a number of hours but not immediately. Offsite storage and periodic testing of systems do not support continuous availability)

Chapter 4
Laws, Regulations, and Compliance

62. Which law forms the bedrock of the body of laws that preserve the peace and keep our society safe?

a. Civil law

b. Criminal law

c. Administrative law

d. Patents law

Ans. b. Criminal law

(Criminal law forms the bedrock of the body of laws that preserve the peace and keep our society safe. Laws that police concern themselves with murder, assault, robbery, arson, etc.)

63. ……………. are used to create the framework of government that the executive branch uses to carry out its responsibilities.

a. Civil law

b. Criminal law

c. Administrative law

d. Patents law

Ans. a. Civil law

(Civil laws form the bulk of our body of laws. Also, it is used to create the framework of government that the executive branch uses to carry out its responsibilities.)

64. **The Computer Fraud and Abuse Act (CFAA) was enacted in the year ...., as an amendment to the first federal computer fraud law, to address hacking.**

a. 1966

b. 1976

c. 1986

d. 1956

Ans. c. 1986

(The Computer Fraud and Abuse Act (CFAA) was enacted by Congress in 1986 as an amendment to existing computer fraud law)

65. **Who proposed significant changes to the Computer Fraud and Abuse Act (CFAA) in 2015?**

a. Barack Obama

b. George W. Bush

c. Joe Biden

d. Hillary Clinton

Ans. a. Barack Obama

(In January 2015 Barack Obama proposed expanding

the CFAA and the RICO Act in his Modernizing Law Enforcement Authorities to Combat Cyber Crime proposal.)

66. The Federal Sentencing Guidelines released in ……… provided punishment guidelines to help federal judges interpret computer crime laws.

a. 1991

b. 1990

c. 1992

d. 1993

Ans. a. 1991

(The Federal Sentencing Guidelines are rules that set out a uniform sentencing policy for individuals and organizations convicted of felonies and serious misdemeanors in the United States federal courts system. In 1991, The Federal Sentencing Guidelines was released to provide punishment guidelines to help federal judges interpret computer crime laws.)

67. Mention the act that primarily addresses the program management and evaluation aspects of information security.

a. The Government Information Security Reform Act (GISRA) of 2000

b. Paperwork Reduction Act (PRA) of 1995

c. Federal Information Security Management Act (FISMA) of 2002

d. National Information Infrastructure Protection Act (NIIPA) of 1996

Ans. a. The Government Information Security Reform Act (GISRA) of 2000

(The Government Information Security Reform Act (GISRA) of 2000, established information security program, evaluation, and reporting requirements for federal agencies)

68. Who was responsible for developing the FISMA implementation guidelines?

a. National Institute of Standards and Technology (NIST)

b. National Research Council

c. Office of Management And Budget (OMB)

d. National security agency

Ans. a. National Institute of Standards and Technology (NIST)

(In accordance with FISMA, NIST is responsible for developing standards, guidelines, and associated methods and techniques for providing adequate information security for all agency operations and assets, excluding national security systems)

69. Which act was created as an updated version of copyright laws to deal with the special challenges of regulating digital material?

a. Computer Security Act

b. Uniform Computer Information Transactions Act

c. Digital Millennium Copyright Act

d. Gramm-Leach-Bliley Act

Ans. c. Digital Millennium Copyright Act

(The Digital Millennium Copyright Act of 1998 forms the legal framework for rights management in digital works, such as copyrights)

70. The Digital Millennium Copyright Act (DMCA) is a US copyright law that implements two 1996 treaties of ………………………..

a. World Intellectual Property Organization (WIPO)

b. Anti-Counterfeiting Trade Agreement (ACTA)

c. Trade-Related Aspects of Intellectual Property Rights (TRIPS)

d. World Health Organization (WHO)

Ans. a. World Intellectual Property Organization (WIPO)

(The Digital Millennium Copyright Act (DMCA) is a U.S. copyright law that implements two 1996 treaties of the

WIPO. It also criminalizes the act of circumventing an access control, whether or not there is actual infringement of copyright itself.)

71. ………….. protects the intellectual property rights of inventors.

a. Trademarks

b. Patents

c. Trade secrets

d. Copyrights

Ans. b. Patents

(Patents protect the intellectual property rights of inventors. In the technology field, patents have been used to protect hardware devices and manufacturing processes.)

72. …………………… is a federal law designed for adoption by each of the 50 states to provide a common framework for the conduct of computer-related business transactions.

a. Uniform Computer Information Transactions Act (UCITA)

b. Anti-Counterfeiting Trade Agreement (ACTA)

c. Federal Information Security Management Act (FISMA)

d. The Government Information Security Reform

Act (GISRA)

Ans. a. Uniform Computer Information Transactions Act (UCITA)

(The Uniform Computer Information Transactions Act (UCITA) is a proposed law to create a clear and uniform set of rules to govern areas such as software licensing, online access, and other transactions in computer information)

73. Which law protects the right of citizens to privacy by placing restrictions on the authority granted to government agencies to search private residences and facilities?

a. Privacy Act

b. Fourth Amendment

c. Second Amendment

d. Gramm-Leach-Bliley Act

Ans. b. Fourth Amendment

(The Fourth Amendment to the U.S. Constitution sets the "probable cause" standard that law enforcement officers must follow when conducting searches and/or seizures of private property. It also states that those officers must obtain a warrant before gaining involuntary access to such property.)

74. .... is a federal law that places restrictions on the federal government's collection, use, and dissemination of personal information.

a. Electronic Communications Privacy Act of 1986

b. Privacy Act of 1974

c. Communications Assistance for Law Enforcement Act (CALEA) of 1994

d. Economic and Protection of Proprietary Information Act of 1996

Ans. b. Privacy Act of 1974

(Privacy Act of 1974 is the most significant piece of privacy legislation restricting the way the federal government may deal with private information about individual citizens)

75. ………………… Act was intended to preserve the ability of law enforcement officials to conduct electronic surveillance effectively and efficiently in the face of rapid advances in telecommunications technology.

a. Communications Assistance for Law Enforcement Act of 1994

b. Electronic Communications Privacy Act of 1986

c. Health Information Technology for Economic and Clinical Health Act of 2009

d. USA PATRIOT Act of 2001

Ans. a. Communications Assistance for Law Enforcement Act of 1994

(The Communications Assistance For Law Enforcement Act (CALEA) is a U.S. wiretapping law passed by Congress in 1994. CALEA requires all communications carriers to make wiretaps possible for law enforcement with an appropriate court order, regardless of the technology in use.)

76. The Health Insurance Portability and Accountability Act (HIPAA) was enacted by the United States Congress in the year ....

a.   1992

b.   1996

c.   1994

d.   1990

Ans. b. 1996

(In 1996, the Health Insurance Portability and Accountability Act was enacted by the United States Congress and signed by President Bill Clinton)

77. What law formalizes many licensing arrangements used by the software industry and attempts to standardize their use from state to state?

a.   Computer Security Act

b.   Digital Millennium Copyright Act

c.   Gramm-Leach-Bliley Act

d. Uniform Computer Information Transactions Act

Ans. d. Uniform Computer Information Transactions Act

(The Uniform Computer Information Transactions Act (UCITA) attempts to implement a standard framework of laws regarding computer transactions to be adopted by all states. One of the issues addressed by UCITA is the legality of various types of software license agreements)

78. Which law was passed to protect the privacy of children below 13 years of age?

a. Gramm-Leach-Bliley Act of 1999 *(GLBA)*

b. Children's Online Privacy Protection Act of 1998 *(COPPA)*

c. Family Educational Rights and Privacy Act *(FERPA)*

d. USA PATRIOT Act of 2001

Ans. b. Children's Online Privacy Protection Act of 1998

(The Children's Online Privacy Protection Act (COPPA) is a law passed by the U.S. Congress in 1998 to specifically protect the privacy of children under 13 years)

79. The European Union (EU) Parliament passed a sweeping directive outlining privacy measures on ……….. to protect personal data processed by information systems.

a. October 24, 1995

b. September 24, 1998

c. October 2, 1994

d. November 24. 1998

Ans. a. October 24, 1995

(On October 24, 1995, the European Union (EU) Parliament passed a sweeping directive outlining privacy measures that must be in place for protecting personal data processed by information systems)

80. Who should conduct reviews of the security controls put in place by vendors, both during the initial vendor selection and evaluation process.

a. Data Custodian

b. Data owner

c. Security Professionals

d. User

Ans. c. Security Professionals

(During the initial vendor selection and evaluation process, Security Professionals should conduct reviews of the security controls as a part of ongoing vendor governance reviews)

81. Government agencies use ………….. to promulgate the day-to-day regulations that interpret existing law.

a. Civil law

b. Criminal law

c. Administrative law

d. Patents law

Ans. c. Administrative law

(Many government agencies promulgate administrative law, such as the HIPAA Security Rule, that affects specific industries and data type)

82. Mention the Act that outlines the steps the government must take to protect its own systems from attack.

a. The Computer Fraud and Abuse Act

b. The Digital Millennium Copyright Act

c. The Economic Espionage Act

d. The Uniform Computer Information Transactions Act

Ans. a. The Computer Fraud and Abuse Act

(The Computer Fraud and Abuse Act protects computers used by the government or in interstate commerce from a variety of abuses)

83. ………………… protect original works of authorship, such as books, articles, poems, and songs.

a. Trademarks

b. Patents

c. Copyrights

d. Trade secret law

Ans. c. Copyrights

(Copyright is a legal right created by the law of a country that grants the creator of an original work exclusive right for its use and distribution)

84. Mention the Act that prohibits the circumvention of copy protection mechanisms placed in digital media and limits the liability of Internet service providers for the activities of their users.

a. Digital Millennium Copyright Act

b. Computer Security Act

c. The Economic Espionage Act

d. The Uniform Computer Information Transactions Act

Ans. a. Digital Millennium Copyright Act

(DMCA prohibits the manufacture, importation, or distribution of "devices, products, components" or services used for circumvention of copy-protection technologies)

85. Which Act provides penalties for individuals found guilty of the theft of trade secrets?

a. The Computer Fraud and Abuse Act

b. The Digital Millennium Copyright Act

c. The Economic Espionage Act

d. The Uniform Computer Information Transactions Act

Ans. c. The Economic Espionage Act

(Conviction of the theft of trade secrets under the Economic Espionage Act can result in a fine of up to $250,000 for an individual (up to $5 million for corporations), imprisonment up to ten years, or both.)

86. Written agreement between a software vendor and a user is termed as ....

a. Contractual license agreements

b. Click-wrap agreements

c. Shrink-wrap agreements

d. Mutual agreements

Ans. a. Contractual license agreements

(Contractual license agreements are written agreements between a software vendor and user)

87. Which federal government agency is liable for ensuring the security of government computer systems that are not utilized to process sensitive and/or classified information?

a. Federal Bureau of Investigation

b. National Security Agency

c. National Institute of Standards and Technology

d. Secret Service

Ans. c. National Institute of Standards and Technology

(The National Institute of Standards and Technology (NIST) is charged with the security management of all federal government computer systems that are not used to process sensitive national security information.)

88. Which one of the following laws is not designed to protect the privacy rights of Internet users and consumers?

a. Health Insurance Portability and Accountability Act

b. USA PATRIOT Act

c. Identity Theft Assumption and Deterrence Act

d. Gramm-Leach-Bliley Act

Ans. b. USA PATRIOT Act

(The USA PATRIOT Act was adopted in the wake of the September 11, 2001, terrorist attacks. While the other laws contain provisions designed to enhance individual privacy rights.)

89. Which one of the following industry was most directly impacted by the provisions of the Gramm-Leach-Bliley Act?

a. Law enforcement

b. Health care

c. Defense contractors

d. Banking

Ans. d. Banking

(The Gramm-Leach-Bliley Act provides regulations regarding the way financial institutions can handle private information belonging to their customers)

90. In the United States, the standard duration of patent protection is

a. 20 years from the application date

b. 20 years from the date the patent is granted

c. 14 years from the application date

d. 14 years from the date the patent is granted

Ans. a. 20 years from the application date

(In the United States, the term of the patent is 20 years from the earliest filing date of the application on which the patent was granted and any prior U.S. or Patent Cooperation Treaty (PCT) applications from which the patent claims priority)

91. What compliance obligation relates to the processing of credit card information?

a. SOX

b. HIPAA

c. PCI DSS

d. FERPA

Ans. c. PCI DSS

(The Payment Card Industry Data Security Standard (PCI DSS) is a set of security standards designed to ensure that all companies that accept, process, store, or transmit credit card information maintain a secure environment.)

92. Mention the act that updated the privacy and security requirements of the Health Insurance Portability and Accountability Act (HIPAA)?

a. HITECH

b. CALEA

c. CFAA

d. CCCA

Ans. a. HITECH

(Health Information Technology for Economic and Clinical Health Act (HITECH) updated many of the HIPAA's privacy and security requirements and was implemented through the HIPAA Omnibus Rule in 2013)

Chapter 5
Protecting Security of Assets

93. **The first and foremost step in asset security process is ……………..**

a. Identifying data roles

b. Classifying and labeling assets

c. Protecting Privacy

d. Determining data security controls

Ans. b. Classifying and labeling assets

(The first step in asset security is classifying and labeling assets. Organizations often include classification definitions within a security policy. Personnel then label assets appropriately based on the security policy requirements.)

94. **Any information that can identify an individual is known as ……………**

a. Personally identifiable information (PII)

b. Protected health information (PHI)

c. Proprietary data

d. Personal data

Ans. a. Personally, identifiable information (PII)

(Personally, identifiable information (PII), or sensitive personal information (SPI), as used in information security and privacy laws, is information that can be used on its own or with other information to identify, contact, or locate a single person, or to identify an individual in context.)

95. Any data that helps an organization maintain a competitive edge is termed as ……..

a. Proprietary data

b. Protected health information (PHI)

c. Personally identifiable information (PII)

d. Personal data

Ans. a. Proprietary data

(Proprietary data is a data that contains technical or other types of information controlled by a firm to safeguard its competitive edge. It could be software code it developed, technical plans for products, internal processes, intellectual property, or trade secrets)

96. Data stored on media such as external USB drives, system hard drives, storage area networks (SANs), and backup tapes are termed as

a. Data in motion

b. Data in transit

c. Data at rest

d. Data in use

Ans. c. Data at rest

(In information technology, Data at rest means inactive data that is stored physically in any digital form e.g. databases, data warehouses, spreadsheets, archives, tapes, off-site backups, mobile devices etc.)

97. Any data that is transmitted over an internet is known as ……….

a.   Data in transit

b.   Data in use

c.   Sensitive data

d.   Private data

Ans. a. Data in transit

(Data in transit includes those data that is transmitted over an internal network using wired or wireless methods and data transmitted over public networks such as the Internet.

98. Users can easily identify the classification level of any data by ……………….

a.   Marking Sensitive Data

b.   Handling Sensitive Data

c.   Storing Sensitive Data

d.   Destroying Sensitive Data

Ans. a. Marking Sensitive Data

(Marking sensitive information ensures that users can easily identify the classification level of any data. The most important information that a mark or a label provides is the classification of the data)

99. ………….. is the data that remains on a hard drive as residual magnetic flux.

a. Purging

b. Data remanence

c. Degaussing

d. Sanitization

Ans. b. Data remanence

(Data remanence is the residual representation of digital data that remains on a hard drive even after attempts have been made to remove or erase the data.)

100. The main objective of managing a sensitive data is to prevent ………..

a. Data breaches

b. Threat events

c. Risk

d. Intellectual properties

Ans. a. Data breaches

(A key goal of managing sensitive data is to prevent data breaches. A data breach is any event in which an unauthorized entity is able to view or access sensitive data)

101. ……………. is a process of preparing media for reuse and assuring that the cleared data cannot be recovered using traditional recovery tools.

a. Clearing

b. Erasing

c. Purging

d. Declassification

Ans. a. Clearing

(Clearing is the removal of sensitive data from storage devices in such a way that there is assurance that the data may not be reconstructed using normal system functions or software file/data recovery utilities)

102. …………….. is the final stage in the life cycle of media and is the most secure method of sanitizing media.

a. Destruction

b. Degaussing

c. Declassification

d.   Sanitization

Ans. a. Destruction

(Destruction is the ultimate stage in the life cycle of media and is the most secured method of sanitizing media)

103.   Which one of the following is not a sensitive data?

a.   Personally identifiable information (PII)

b.   Protected health information (PHI)

c.   Proprietary data

d.   Data posted on a website

Ans. d. Data posted on a website

(Data posted on a website is not sensitive, but PII, PHI, and proprietary data all are sensitive data)

104.   The process of determining the impact of the loss of CIA of the information to an organization is known as …………

a.   Categorization

b.   Overwriting

c.   Classification

d.   Data Policy

Ans. a. Categorization

(Categorization includes a process of determining the impact of the loss of CIA (confidentiality, integrity and availability) of the information to an organization)

105. What is the primary purpose of information classification processes?

a.   Define the requirements for protecting sensitive data.

b.   Define the requirements for backing up data.

c.   Define the requirements for storing data.

d.   Define the requirements for transmitting data.

Ans. a. Define the requirements for protecting sensitive data.

(A primary purpose of information classification processes is to identify security classifications for sensitive data and define the requirements to protect sensitive data. Information classification processes will typically include requirements to protect sensitive data at rest (in backups and stored on media), but not requirements for backing up and storing any data.)

106. Which one of the following is the most important consideration while determining the classification of data?

a.   Processing system

b.   Value

c. Storage media

d. Accessibility

Ans. b. Value

(Data is classified based on its value to the organization. In some cases, it is classified based on the potential negative impact if unauthorized personnel can access it, which represents a negative value. It is not classified based on the processing system, but the processing system is classified based on the data it processes. Similarly, the storage media is classified based on the data classification, but the data is not classified based on where it is stored. Accessibility is affected by the classification, but the accessibility does not determine the classification. Personnel implement controls to limit accessibility of sensitive data)

107. State the most vital aspect of marking media?

a. Data labeling

b. Content description

c. Electronic labeling

d. Classification

Ans. d. Classification

(Classification is the most important aspect of marking media because it clearly identifies the value of the media and users know how to protect it based on the classification. Including information such as the date and a description of the content isn't as important as marking the classification. Electronic labels or marks can be used, but when they are used, the most important information is still the classification of the data.)

108. Any information that isn't public or unclassified is known as ....

a. Sensitive data

b. Private data

c. Data in transit

d. Data in use

Ans. a. Sensitive data

(Sensitive data is any information that isn't public or unclassified. It can include confidential, proprietary, protected, or any other type of data that an organization needs to protect due to its value to the organization, or to comply with existing laws and regulations)

109. Which one of the following is not a government data classification?

a. Top secret

b. Confidential

c. Unclassified

d. Public

Ans. d. Public

(Government data classifications include top secret, secret, confidential, and unclassified whereas Non-Government Classifications include proprietary, private, sensitive, and public)

110. An act of performing a delete operation against a file, a selection of files, or the entire media is known as ……………

a. Erasing media

b. Clearing

c. Overwriting

d. Purging

Ans. a. Erasing media

(Erasing media is simply performing a delete operation against a file, a selection of files, or the entire media. In most cases, the deletion or removal process removes only the directory or catalog link to the data)

111. …………… is the most reliable method of destroying data on a solid state drive?

a. Erasing

b. Degaussing

c. Deleting

d. Purging

Ans. d. Purging

(Purging is the most reliable method of the given choices. Purging overwrites the media with random bits multiple times and includes additional steps to ensure data is removed. While not an available answer choice, destruction of the drive is a more reliable method. Erasing or deleting processes rarely remove the data from media, but instead mark it for deletion.)

112. The most secure method of deleting data on a DVD is ……………………..

a. Formatting

b. Deleting

c. Destruction

d. Degaussing

Ans. c. Destruction

(Physical destruction is the most secure method of deleting data on optical media such as a DVD. Formatting and deleting processes rarely remove the data from any media. DVDs do not have magnetic flux so degaussing a DVD doesn't destroy data.)

113. Which one of the following options mentioned below does not erase data?

a. Clearing

b. Purging

c.   Overwriting

d.   Remanence

Ans. d. Remanence

(Data remanence refers to data remnants that remain on a hard drive as residual magnetic flux. Clearing, purging, and overwriting are valid methods of erasing data.)

114.   A combination of processes that removes data from a system or from media is termed as ……..

a.   Sanitization

b.   Degaussing

c.   Declassification

d.   Purging

Ans. a. Sanitization

(Sanitization can refer to the destruction of media or using a trusted method to purge classified data from the media without destroying it. It is a blend of processes that removes data from a system or from media. It ensures that data cannot be recovered by any means)

115.   ………………… is the person or entity that controls processing of the data.

a.   Data controller

b.   System owner

c. Data owner

d. Data administrator

Ans. a. Data controller

(The Data Controller is the person or organization that has full authority to decide how and why personal data is to be processed. This includes using, storing and deleting the data.)

116. Which one of the following is the most important element of asset retention?

a. Record Retention

b. Data Retention

c. Customer Retention

d. Personnel retention

Ans. a. Record Retention

(Record retention and media retention is the most vital element of asset retention. Record retention involves retaining and maintaining important information as long as it is needed and destroying it when it is no longer needed.)

117. Which is the most popular symmetric encryption algorithm?

a. Advanced Encryption Standard (AES)

b. Data Encryption Standard (DES)

c. Microsoft Encrypting File System (EFS)

d. Transport Encryption

Ans. a. Advanced Encryption Standard (AES)

(The Advanced Encryption Standard (AES) is one of the most popular symmetric encryption algorithms. While the Microsoft Encrypting File System uses AES for file and folder encryption)

118. 3DES is used by Microsoft OneNote and System Center Configuration Manager to protect ....

a. Classified data

b. Rainbow table attacks

c. Content and passwords

d. Data in transit

Ans. c. Content and passwords

(Developers created Triple DES (or 3DES) as a possible replacement for DES. Microsoft OneNote and System Center Configuration Manager use 3DES to protect some content and passwords)

119. Which of the following key size do not support Advanced Encryption Standard (AES)?

a. 128 bits

b. 192 bits

c. 256 bits

d. 320 bits

Ans. d. 320 bits

(Advanced Encryption Standard supports key sizes of 128 bits, 192 bits, and 256 bits, and the US government has approved its use to protect classified data up to top secret. Larger key sizes add additional security, making it more difficult for unauthorized personnel to decrypt the data.)

120. Who developed Blowfish as a possible alternative to Advanced Encryption Standard (AES).

a. Bruce Schneier

b. Myriam Dunn Cavelty

c. Stefano Mele

d. Patrick C. Miller

Ans. a. Bruce Schneier

(Security expert Bruce Schneier developed Blowfish as an alternative to DES. Also, it can use key sizes of 32 bits to 448 bits and is a strong encryption protocol.

121. .... is based on Blowfish and helps

protect against rainbow table attacks?

a. 3DES

b. AES

c. Bcrypt

d. SCP

Ans. c. Bcrypt

(Linux systems use bcrypt to encrypt passwords, and bcrypt is based on Blowfish. Bcrypt adds 128 additional bits as a salt to protect against rainbow table attacks.)

122. Administrators use .... to connect to a remote server securely for administration.

a. Telnet

b. Secure File Transfer Protocol (SFTP)

c. Secure Copy (SCP)

d. Secure Shell (SSH)

Ans. d. Secure Shell (SSH)

(SSH is a secure alternative to Telnet because it encrypts data transmitted over a network. In contrast, Telnet transmits data in cleartext. SFTP and SCP are good methods for transmitting sensitive data over a network, but not for administration purposes.)

123. **Which one of the following tasks would a data custodian most likely perform?**

a. Access the data

b. Classify the data

c. Assign permissions to the data

d. Back up data

Ans. d. Back up data

(A data custodian performs day to day tasks to protect the integrity security of data and this includes backing it up. Whereas users access the data, owners classify the data and administrators assign permissions to the data.)

124. **Who is responsible for granting appropriate access to personnel?**

a. Data administrator

b. User

c. Custodian

d. System owner

Ans. a. Data administrator

(The administrator assigns permissions based on the principles of least privilege and need to know. A custodian protects the integrity and security of the data. System Owners have ultimate responsibility for the data and ensure that it is classified properly, and owners provide guidance to administrators on who can have access, but owners do not assign permissions. Users simply access the data.)

125. Which of the following best describes "rules of behavior" set by a data owner?

a.   Ensuring users are granted access to only what they need

b.   Determining who has access to a system

c.   Identifying appropriate use and protection of data

d.   Applying security controls to a system

Ans. c. Identifying appropriate use and protection of data

(The rules of behavior identify the rules for appropriate use and protection of data. Least privilege ensures users are granted access to only what they need. A data owner determines who has access to a system, but that is not rules of behavior. Rules of behavior apply to users, not systems or security controls)

126. The EU Data Protection law defines a data processor as ....

a.   The entity that processes personal data on behalf of the data controller

b.   The entity that controls processing of data

c.   The computing system that processes data

d. The network that processes data

Ans. a. The entity that processes personal data on behalf of the data controller

(The EU Data Protection law defines a data processor as "a natural or legal person which processes personal data solely on behalf of the data controller." The data controller is the entity that controls processing of the data and directs the data processor. Within the context of the EU Data Protection law, the data processor is not a computing system or network)

127. In which year did Google discover that Secure Sockets Layer (SSL) is susceptible to the POODLE attack (Padding Oracle On Downgraded Legacy Encryption).

a. 2014

b. 2015

c. 2016

d. 2013

Ans. a. 2014

(In 2014, Google discovered that SSL is susceptible to the POODLE attack. As a result, many organizations have disabled SSL in their applications.)

128. Which agreement prevents employees from leaving the job and sharing proprietary data with others?

a. Nondisclosure agreements (NDAs)

b. Non-Compete agreement

c. Personnel retention agreement

d. Record retention agreement

Ans. a. Nondisclosure agreements (NDAs)

(Organizations include nondisclosure agreements (NDAs) when hiring new personnel. These NDAs prevent employees from leaving the job and sharing proprietary data with others)

129. To capture traffic sent over a network, attackers use ....

a. Sniffer analyzer

b. Blowfish

c. Triple DES

d. AES

Ans. a. Sniffer analyzer

(Attackers can use a sniffer or protocol analyzer to capture traffic sent over a network. The sniffer allows attackers to read all the data sent in cleartext. However, attackers are unable to read data encrypted with a strong encryption protocol.)

130. Which one of the following is a secure protocol

used to transfer encrypted files over a network?

a. HTTP

b. SFTP

c. TCP

d. FTP

Ans. b. SFTP

(SCP and SFTP are secure protocols that are used to transfer encrypted files over a network. Protocols such as File Transfer Protocol (FTP) transmit data in cleartext and so are not appropriate for transmitting sensitive data over a network.)

131. Which of the following methods help business owners and mission owners to balance security control requirements with business or mission needs?

a. COBIT

b. ITIL

c. COSO

d. TOGAF

Ans. a. COBIT

(Organizations often implement IT governance methods such as Control Objectives for Information and Related Technology (COBIT). These methods help business owners and mission owners balance security control requirements with business or mission needs.)

132. Organizations that wish to transfer data to and from EU countries must abide by the principles of ……..

a. PCI DSS

b. Data Encryption Standard

c. Safe Harbor standard

d. Advanced Encryption Standard

Ans. c. Safe Harbor standard

(Organizations that want to transfer data to and from EU countries must abide by the principles in the Safe Harbor standard. Similarly, organizations that do not transfer data to and from EU countries do not need to comply with the Safe Harbor standard)

Chapter 6
Cryptography and Symmetric Key Algorithms

133. In Cryptography, encrypted message is called as

a. Plain text

b. Cipher Text

c. Secret Text

d. clear-text

Ans. b. Cipher Text

(In cryptography, cipher text is the result of encryption performed on plaintext using an algorithm, called a cipher)

134. Which is the most commonly used public-key cryptography algorithms?

a. RSS

b. RAS

c. RSA

d. RAA

Ans. c. RSA

(Several algorithms in common employ public-key cryptography, probably the best known being the RSA algorithm named after its inventors, Ronald Rivest, Adi Shamir and Leonard Adleman.)

135. How many keys exist in a 4-bit key space?

a. 4

b. 8

c. 16

d. 128

Ans. c. 16

(To determine the number of keys in a key space, raise 2 to the power of the number of bits in the key space. In this example, 24 = 16)

136. Mention the length of the cryptographic key implemented in the Data Encryption Standard (DES) cryptosystem?

a. 56 bits

b. 128 bits

c. 192 bits

d. 256 bits

Ans. a. 56 bits

(DES uses a 56-bit key. This is considered to be one of the major weaknesses of cryptosystem)

137. Which of the following types of cipher rely on changing the location of characters within a message

to achieve confidentiality?

a. Stream cipher

b. Transposition cipher

c. Block cipher

d. Substitution cipher

Ans. b. Transposition cipher

(Transposition ciphers use a variety of techniques to reorder the characters within a message)

138. A set of rules that dictates how enciphering and deciphering processes are to take place is known as ......

a. Encryption

b. Decryption

c. Algorithm

d. Cipher text

Ans. c. Algorithm

(An algorithm is a specific set of instructions for carrying out a procedure or solving a problem, usually with the requirement that the procedure terminate at some point.)

139. .... algorithm transforms cipher text to plaintext.

a. Encryption

b. Decryption

c. Substitution

d. Transposition

Ans. b. Decryption

(Decryption algorithm transforms cipher text to plaintext while Encryption algorithm transforms plaintext to cipher text)

140. The art of creating and implementing secret codes and ciphers is known as ……..

a. Cryptography

b. Kerchoff's assumption

c. Hieroglyphics

d. Algorithm

Ans. a. Cryptography

(Cryptography is an art of writing a secret code that defend the data getting exchanged between two communicating parties from external attack)

141. …………….. defines the rules used for the bits and bytes that form the nervous system of any computer?

a. Cryptanalysis

b. Cryptography

c. Boolean mathematics

d. Cryptosystems

Ans. c. Boolean mathematics

(Boolean mathematics defines the rules used for the bits and bytes that form the nervous

system of any computer)

142. ……………….. is a study of methods to defeat codes and ciphers.

a. Cryptanalysis

b. Cryptography

c. Cryptosystems

d. Hieroglyphics

Ans. a. Cryptanalysis

(Cryptanalysis is the decryption and analysis of codes, ciphers or encrypted text. Cryptanalysis uses mathematical formulas to search for algorithm vulnerabilities and break into cryptography or information security systems.)

143. Which one of the following is not a possible key length for the Advanced Encryption Standard

Rijndael cipher?

a. 56 bits

b. 128 bits

c. 192 bits

d. 256 bits

Ans. a. 56 bits

(The Rijndael cipher allows users to select a key length of 128, 192, or 256 bits, depending on the specific security requirements of the application)

144. The output value of the mathematical function 16 mod 3 is ....

a. 0

b. 1

c. 3

d. 5

Ans. b. 1

(Option B is correct because 16 divided by 3 equals 5, with a remainder value of 1.)

145. Mention the type of cipher that operates on large pieces of a message rather than individual characters or bits of a message?

a. Stream cipher

b. Caesar cipher

c. Block cipher

d. ROT3 cipher

Ans. c. Block cipher

(Block ciphers operate on message "chunks" rather than on individual characters or bits. The other ciphers mentioned operate on individual bits or characters of a message)

146. Mention the number of keys required to fully implement a symmetric algorithm, with 10 participants?

a. 10

b. 20

c. 45

d. 100

Ans. c. 45

(The number of keys required for a symmetric algorithm is dictated by the formula $(n*(n-1))/2$, which in this case, where n = 10, is 45.)

147. Which of the following attack makes the Caesar cipher virtually unusable?

a. Meet-in-the-middle attack

b. Escrow attack

c. Frequency analysis attack

d. Transposition attack

Ans. c. Frequency analysis attack

(Frequency analysis attack is a kind of attack that makes the Caesar cipher virtually unusable)

148. In Cipher Block Chaining (CBC) mode, ………………….. is the streaming cipher version.

a. Output Feedback (OFB) Mode

b. Cipher Feedback (CFB) mode

c. Counter (CTR) Mode

d. Direct Mode

Ans. b. Cipher Feedback (CFB) mode

(Cipher Feedback (CFB) mode is the streaming cipher version of CBC. In other words, CFB operates against data produced in real time.)

149. Who developed the Twofish algorithm?

a. Bruce Schneier

b. Diffie-Hellman

c. Stefano Mele

d. Patrick C. Miller

Ans. a. Bruce Schneier

(The Twofish algorithm developed by Bruce Schneier, was one of the AES finalists. Also, it makes use of both prewhitening and postwhiteneing techniques)

150. One of the major goals of cryptography is ……………...

a. Confidentiality

b. Integrity

c. Nonrepudiation

d. Availability

Ans. a. Confidentiality

(Confidentiality is one of the major goals of cryptography. It protects the secrecy of data while it is both at rest and in transit)

151. Which of the following mode is considered the least secure and is used only for short messages?

a. ECB mode

b. OFB mode

c. CBC mode

d.   CFB mode

Ans. a. ECB mode

(ECB mode is considered the least secure and is used only for short messages)

152.   Which of the following method provides a one-time session key for two parties?

a.   Diffie-Hellman

b.   RSA

c.   DES

d.   AES

Ans. a. Diffie-Hellman

(Diffie-Hellman is an algorithm used to establish a shared secret between two parties. It is primarily used as a method of exchanging cryptography keys for use in symmetric encryption algorithms)

153.   A mathematical operation that easily produces output values for each possible combination of inputs is known as ....

a.   Modulo Function

b.   Zero-Knowledge Proof

c.   split knowledge

d.   One-Way Functions

Ans. d. One-Way Functions

(A one-way function is a function that is easy to compute on every input, but hard to invert given the image of a random input)

154.   A random number that acts as a placeholder variable in mathematical functions is known as ………

a.   Ciphers

b.   Nonce

c.   Array name

d.   User-defined random number

Ans. b. Nonce

(A nonce is an arbitrary number used only once in a cryptographic communication, in the spirit of a nonce word. They are often random or pseudo-random numbers.)

155.   The US government published the Data Encryption Standard in the year ………

a.   1967

b.   1986

c.   1977

d.   1957

Ans. c. 1977

(The Data Encryption Standard was published in 1977 by the US government as a proposed standard cryptosystem for all government communications)

156. ……………………….. is an encryption algorithm developed by the US National Security Agency (NSA) for the transmission of information.

a.   Blowfish

b.   Twofish

c.   Skipjack

d.   Double DES

Ans. c. Skipjack

(In cryptography, Skipjack is a block cipher—an algorithm for encryption—developed by the U.S. National Security Agency (NSA).)

Chapter 7
PKI and Cryptographic Applications

157. The Secure Hash Algorithm (SHA) and its successors, SHA-1 and SHA-2, was developed by the ....

a. National Research Council

b. National Institute of Standards and Technology (NIST)

c. Office of Management And Budget (OMB)

d. National security agency

Ans. b. National Institute of Standards and Technology

(The Secure Hash Algorithm (SHA) and its successors, SHA-1 and SHA-2, are government standard hash functions developed by the National Institute of Standards and Technology (NIST) and are specified in an official government publication)

158. Which one of the following numbers will always be the largest, in the RSA public key cryptosystem?

a. e

b. n

c. p

d. q

Ans. b. n

(The number n is generated as the product of the two

large prime numbers, p and q. Therefore, n must always be greater than both p and q. Furthermore, it is an algorithm constraint that e must be chosen such that e is smaller than n. Therefore, in RSA cryptography, n is always the largest of the four variables shown in the options to this question.)

159. Who developed the Message Digest 2 (MD2) hash algorithm in 1989?

a. Nathalie Rogier

b. Pascal Chauvaud

c. Ronald Rivest

d. Frederic Mueller

Ans. c. Ronald Rivest

(The Message Digest 2 (MD2) hash algorithm was developed by Ronald Rivest in 1989 to provide a secure hash function for 8-bit processors)

160. Which of the following algorithms reduces the speed of message digest production significantly?

a. MD4

b. MD5

c. MD2

d. SHA

Ans. b. MD5

(In 1991, Rivest released the next version of his message digest algorithm, called MD5. MD5 implements additional security features that reduce the speed of message digest production significantly.)

161. Which of the following cryptographic algorithm forms the basis of the El Gamal cryptosystem?

a. RSA

b. Diffie-Hellman

c. 3DES

d. IDEA

Ans. b. Diffie-Hellman

(The El Gamal cryptosystem extends the functionality of the Diffie-Hellman key exchange protocol to support the encryption and decryption of messages.)

162. ………………… has emerged as a de facto standard for encrypted email.

a. Online Certificate Status Protocol (OCSP)

b. Secure Multipurpose Internet Mail Extensions (S/MIME) protocol

c. Hypertext Transfer Protocol (HTP)

d. Transmission Control Protocol (TCP)

Ans. b. Secure Multipurpose Internet Mail Extensions (S/MIME) protocol

(The Secure Multipurpose Internet Mail Extensions (S/MIME) protocol has emerged as a de facto standard for encrypted email. S/MIME uses the RSA encryption algorithm and has received the backing of major industry players, including RSA Security)

163. Secure Sockets Layer (SSL) was developed by ....

a.   Microsoft

b.   Swiss developers

c.   Netscape

d.   Mozilla

Ans. c. Netscape

(Secure Sockets Layer (SSL) is a protocol developed by Netscape for transmitting private documents via the Internet. SSL uses a cryptographic system that uses two keys to encrypt data – a public key known to everyone and a private or secret key known only to the recipient of the message.)

164. Which one of the following algorithms does not support Digital Signature Standard?

a.   Digital Signature Algorithm

b.   RSA

c. El Gamal DSA

d. Elliptic Curve DSA

Ans. c. El Gamal DSA

(The Digital Signature Standard allows federal government to use the Digital Signature Algorithm, RSA, or the Elliptic Curve DSA in conjunction with the SHA-1 hashing function to produce secure digital signatures.)

165. Which of the following protocol eliminates the latency inherent in the use of certificate revocation lists?

a. Secure File Transfer Protocol (SFTP)

b. Secure Multipurpose Internet Mail Extensions (S/MIME) protocol

c. Hypertext Transfer Protocol (HTP)

d. Online Certificate Status Protocol (OCSP)

Ans. d. Online Certificate Status Protocol (OCSP)

(Online Certificate Status Protocol (OCSP) eliminates the latency inherent in the use of certificate revocation lists by providing a means for real-time certificate verification)

166. The art of using cryptographic techniques to embed secret messages within another message is known as ....

a. Topography

b. Electrocardiography

c. Steganography

d. Cryptography

Ans. c. Steganography

(Steganography is the act of hiding a secret message within an ordinary message and the extraction of it at its destination)

167. Which one of the following protects the entire communications circuits by creating a secure tunnel between two points?

a. End-to-end encryption

b. Link encryption

c. DES

d. 3DES

Ans. b. Link encryption

(Link encryption protects entire communications circuits by creating a secure tunnel between two points using either a hardware solution or a software solution that encrypts all traffic entering one end of the tunnel and decrypts all traffic entering the other end of the tunnel)

168. .... is a standard architecture set forth by the Internet Engineering Task Force (IETF) for setting up a secure channel to exchange

information between two entities.

a. IPsec

b. ISAKMP

c. WPA

d. WPA

Ans. a. IPsec

(Internet Protocol security (IPSec) is a framework of open standards for helping to ensure private, secure communications over Internet Protocol (IP) networks through the use of cryptographic security services)

169. Which one of the following technologies is considered flawed and should never be used on a wireless network?

a. SHA-2

b. PGP

c. WEP

d. TLS

Ans. c. WEP

(The WEP algorithm has documented flaws that make it trivial to break. It should never be used to protect wireless networks)

170. An algebraic manipulation that attempts to reduce the complexity of the algorithm is termed as ......

a. Implementation Attack

b. Statistical Attack

c. Analytic Attack

d. Brute Force

Ans. c. Analytic Attack

(Analytic Attack is an algebraic manipulation that attempts to reduce the complexity of the algorithm. Analytic attacks focus on the logic of the algorithm itself.)

171. .... is a random value that is added to the end of the password before the operating system hashes the password.

a. Ciphertext

b. Pepper cryptography

c. Cryptographic salt

d. Random bytes

Ans. c. Cryptographic salt

(Cryptography salt is random data that is used as an additional input to a one-way function that "hashes" a password or passphrase. Salts are closely related to the concept of nonce.)

172. The encryption technique which WPA use to protect wireless communications is

a. TKIP

b. DES

c. 3DES

d. AES

Ans. a. TKIP

(WiFi Protected Access (WPA) uses the Temporal Key Integrity Protocol (TKIP) to protect wireless communications. WPA2 uses AES encryption.)

173. Which of the following International Telecommunications Union (ITU) standard governs the creation and endorsement of digital certificates for secure electronic communication?

a. X.500

b. X.509

c. X.900

d. X.905

Ans. b. X.509

(X.509 governs digital certificates and the public key

infrastructure (PKI). It defines the appropriate content for a digital certificate and the processes used by certificate authorities to generate and revoke certificates.)

174. ………………….. cryptosystem provides the encryption/decryption technology for the commercial version of Phil Zimmerman's Pretty Good Privacy secure email system?

a.   IDEA

b.   ROT13

c.   ECC

d.   El Gamal

Ans. a. IDEA

(Pretty Good Privacy uses a "web of trust" system of digital signature verification. The encryption technology is based on the IDEA private key cryptosystem.)

175. Which of the following attack pattern uses a series of sequential or combinatorial inputs in an attempt to test every possible combination against some security feature?

a.   Denial of service attack

b.   Distributed attack

c.   Brute-force attack

d. Buffer overflow attack

Ans. c. Brute-force attack

(A brute-force attack is an attempt to discover passwords for user accounts by systematically attempting every possible combination of letters, numbers, and symbols)

176. In which of the following types of attack does the intruder initiate connections to both a client and a server?

a. Replay attack

b. Chosen plain-text attack

c. Meet-in-the-middle attack

d. Man-in-the-middle attack

Ans. d. Man-in-the-middle attack

(In the man-in-the-middle attack, a malicious individual sits between two communicating parties and intercepts all communications (including the setup of the cryptographic session).)

177. .... can be used to improve the effectiveness of a brute-force password cracking attack?

a. Rainbow tables

b. Hierarchical screening

c. TKIP

d. Random enhancement

Ans. a. Rainbow tables

(Rainbow tables contain pre-computed hash values for commonly used passwords and may be used to increase the efficiency of password cracking attacks)

178. Which of the following protocol allows a certificate's authenticity to be immediately verified?

a. OCSP

b. FTP

c. SNMP

d. SMTP

Ans. a. OCSP

(Online Certificate Status Protocol (OCSP) can be used to immediately verify a certificate's authenticity.)

179. The major disadvantage of using certificate revocation lists is ………………..

a. Key management

b. Latency

c. Record keeping

d. Vulnerability to brute-force attacks

Ans. b. Latency

(The major disadvantage to certificate revocation lists is that they must be downloaded and cross-referenced periodically, i.e., introducing a period of latency between the time a certificate is revoked and the time end users are notified of the revocation)

180. Which of the following types of attacks can be used to find collisions in a cryptographic hash function?

a. Meet-in-the-middle attack

b. Man-in-the-middle attack

c. Birthday attack

d. Chosen Ciphertext Attack

Ans. c. Birthday attack

(The birthday attack, also known as a collision attack or reverse hash matching attack seeks to find flaws in the one-to-one nature of hashing functions)

Chapter 8
Principles of Security Models, Design, and Capabilities

181. A combination of hardware, software, and controls that work together to enforce a security policy is termed as ……………..

a. Trusted Computing Base

b. Untrusted Computing Base

c. Timely Computing Base

d. Untimely Computing Base

Ans. a. Trusted Computing Base

(The Orange Book describes a trusted computing base (TCB) as a combination of hardware, software, and controls that work together to form a trusted base to enforce a security policy. The TCB is a subset of a complete information system)

182. What is system accreditation?

a. A functional evaluation of the manufacturer's goals for each hardware and software component to meet integration standards

b. The process to specify secure communication between machines

c. Formal acceptance of a stated system configuration

d. Acceptance of test results that prove the computer system enforces the security policy

Ans. c. Formal acceptance of a stated system configuration

(Accreditation is the formal acceptance process. Option 'a' is not an appropriate answer because it addresses manufacturer standards. Options b and d are incorrect because there is no way to prove that a configuration enforces a security policy and accreditation does not entail secure communication specification)

183. An imaginary boundary that separates the TCB from the rest of the system is known as ....

a.   Security token

b.   Security label

c.   Security perimeter

d.   Security model

Ans. c. Security perimeter

(The security perimeter of your system is an imaginary boundary that separates the TCB from the rest of the system. This boundary ensures that no insecure communications or interactions occur between the TCB and the remaining elements of the computer system)

184. A trusted path is a channel that allows necessary communication to occur without exposing the TCB to ....

a.   Risk

b.   Security vulnerabilities

c.   Threat

d. Malware

Ans. b. Security vulnerabilities

(A trusted path is a channel established with strict standards to allow necessary communication to occur without exposing the TCB to security vulnerabilities)

185. The collection of components in the TCB that work together to implement reference monitor functions is called ....

a. Security token

b. Security label

c. Security perimeter

d. Security kernel

Ans. d. Security kernel

(The security kernel is made up of hardware, software, and firmware components that fall within the TCB and implements and enforces the reference monitor concept. The security kernel is the core of the TCB and is the most commonly used approach to building trusted computing systems)

186. According to the state machine model, ... is a snapshot of a system at a specific moment in time.

a. State

b. Transition

c. Token

d. Label

Ans. a. State

(The state machine model describes 'state' as a snapshot of a system at a specific moment in time)

187. Which of the following model is concerned with preventing information flow from a high security level to a low security level?

a. Biba model

b. Bell-LaPadula

c. Clark-Wilson model

d. Sutherland model

Ans. b. Bell-LaPadula

(The Bell-LaPadula Model is a state machine–based multilevel security policy. Bell-LaPadula is concerned with preventing information flow from a high security level to a low security level)

188. Which one of the following is not a type of composition theory?

a. Cascading

b. Feedback

c. Hookup

d. State transition

Ans. d. State transition

(There are three recognized types of composition theory which include: Cascading, Feedback and Hookup while State transition does not come under the types of composition theory)

189. Why was Bell-LaPadula model developed?

a. To thwart threat or attack

b. To create new rights

c. To protect classified information

d. To protect unclassified information

Ans. c. To protect classified information

(The Bell–LaPadula model focuses on data confidentiality and controlled access to classified information)

190. Which of the following security models are built on a state machine model?

a. Bell-LaPadula and Take-Grant

b. Biba and Clark-Wilson

c. Clark-Wilson and Bell-LaPadula

d.   Bell-LaPadula and Biba

Ans. d. Bell-LaPadula and Biba

(The Bell-LaPadula and Biba models are built on the state machine model)

191. Which of the following security model addresses data integrity?

a.   Bell-LaPadula

b.   Clark-Wilson

c.   Brewer and Nash

d.   Goguen-Meseguer Model

Ans. b. Clark-Wilson

(Only the Clark-Wilson model addresses data integrity. While Bell-LaPadula model addresses data confidentiality. The Brewer and Nash model prevents conflicts of interest)

192. Biba Model primarily protects ………..

a.   Data confidentiality

b.   Data integrity

c.   Data validity

d.   Information flow

Ans. b. Data integrity

(The Biba model was designed after the BellLaPadula model. Where the Bell-LaPadula model addresses confidentiality, the Biba model addresses integrity)

193. In which year, was the Clark-Wilson Model developed?

a. 1987

b. 1997

c. 1967

d. 1957

Ans. a. 1987

(Clark-Wilson Model was developed in 1987 specifically for the commercial environment. The Clark-Wilson model uses a multifaceted approach to enforcing data integrity)

194. A data item whose integrity is protected by the security model is known as ....

a. Unconstrained data item (UDI)

b. Constrained data item (CDI)

c. Integrity verification procedure (IVP)

d. Transformation procedures (TPs)

Ans. b. Constrained data item (CDI)

(Constrained data items (CDI) are data for which integrity

must be preserved.)

195. Which model was created to permit access controls to change dynamically based on a user's previous activity?

a. Graham-Denning Model

b. Brewer and Nash Model

c. Goguen-Meseguer Model

d. Clark-Wilson Model

Ans. b. Brewer and Nash Model

(The Brewer and Nash model was constructed to provide information security access controls that can change dynamically. This security model, also known as the Chinese wall model, was designed to provide controls that mitigate conflict of interest in commercial organizations, and is built upon an information flow model)

196. Mention the model that is focused on the secure creation and deletion of both subjects and objects.

a. Graham-Denning model

b. Bell-LaPadula model

c. Biba model

d. Goguen-Meseguer Model

Ans. a. Graham-Denning model

(The Graham-Denning model is a computer security model that shows how subjects and objects should be securely created and deleted)

197. Trusted Computer System Evaluation Criteria (TCSEC) was developed by …………………

a.   National Institute of Standards and Technology (NIST)

b.   National Computer Security Center (NCSC)

c.   National Research Council

d.   National security agency

Ans. b. National Computer Security Center (NCSC)

(In 1985, the National Computer Security Center (NCSC) developed the TCSEC, usually called the Orange Book because of the color of this publication's cover)

198. Which of the following systems provide more security controls than category C or D systems?

a.   Discretionary protection systems

b.   Mandatory protection systems

c.   Controlled access protection systems

d.   Verified protection systems

Ans. b. Mandatory protection systems

(Mandatory protection systems provide more security controls than category C or D systems. This category of systems is based on the Bell-LaPadula model)

199. In a labeled security system, each subject and each object has a …………..

a. Security token

b. Security label

c. Security perimeter

d. Security model

Ans. b. Security label

(Each subject and each object has a security label in labeled security system)

200. Which of the following systems are difficult to attack successfully and provide sufficient secure controls for very sensitive or secret data?

a. B3 systems

b. B2 systems

c. B1 systems

d. B4 systems

Ans. a. B3 systems

(B3 systems are difficult to attack successfully and provide sufficient secure controls for very sensitive or secret data)

201. The Trusted Network Interpretation of the TCSEC (TNI), was published as the .... in 1987.

a.	Orange Book

b.	Red Book

c.	Green Book

d.	Violet Book

Ans. b. Red Book

(Red books also called Trusted Network Interpretation (TNI) of the TCSEC, addresses security evaluation topics for networks and network components.)

202. Which of the following is not the function of the Red Book?

a.	Rates confidentiality and integrity

b.	Addresses communications integrity

c.	Addresses denial of service protection

d.	Rates availability

Ans. d. Rates availability

(The red book performs functions such as rating confidentiality and integrity, addressing communications integrity, and addressing denial of service protection)

203. Which one of the following books provides guidelines for the password creation and management?

a. Orange Book

b. Red Book

c. Green Book

d. Tan Book

Ans. c. Green Book

(The Green Book, or the Department of Defense Password Management Guidelines, provides guidelines for the password creation and management)

204. The .... guidelines evaluate the functionality and assurance of a system using separate ratings for each category.

a. TCSEC

b. ITSEC

c. PPs

d. STs

Ans. b. ITSEC

(The ITSEC represents an initial attempt to create

security evaluation criteria in Europe. It was developed as an alternative to the TCSEC guidelines. The ITSEC guidelines evaluate the functionality and assurance of a system using separate ratings for each category)

205. An intermediate grouping of security requirement components that can be added or removed from a TOE is known as …………..

a.   Package

b.   Security targets

c.   Protection profiles

d.   System

Ans. a. Package

(A package is an intermediate grouping of security requirement components that can be added or removed from a TOE (like the option packages when purchasing a new vehicle))

206. ……………….. is a collection of requirements for improving the security of electronic payment Transactions.

a.   PCI-DSS

b.   TCSEC

c.   ITSEC

d.   CC

Ans. a. PCI-DSS

(PCI-DSS is a collection of requirements for improving the security of electronic payment transactions. These standards were defined by the PCI Security Standards Council members, who are primarily credit card banks and financial institutions)

207. Which one of the following defines standards for industrial and commercial equipment, software, protocols, and management, among others?

a.   DIN

b.   ISO

c.   BS EN

d.   IEEE

Ans. b. ISO

(ISO is a worldwide standards-setting group of representatives from various national standards organizations. ISO defines standards for industrial and commercial equipment, software, protocols, and management, among others.)

208. ……………….. is the formal declaration by the designated approving authority (DAA) that an IT system is approved to operate in a particular security mode.

a.   Certification

b. Authentication

c. Validation

d. Accreditation

Ans. d. Accreditation

(Accreditation is a formal declaration provided by an approved body to individuals or organizations in order to perform certain tasks.)

209. .... is a core security component that must be designed and implemented into an operating system.

a. Virtualization

b. Hardware security module

c. Memory protection

d. Software security module

Ans. c. Memory protection

(Memory protection is a core security component that must be designed and implemented into an operating system. The main purpose of memory protection is to prevent a process from accessing memory that has not been allocated to it.)

210. Which technology is used to host one or more operating systems within the memory of a single host computer?

a. Virtualization technology

b. Multitenant Technology

c. Hardware technology

d. Hyper-V Technology

Ans. a. Virtualization technology

(Virtualization technology is used to host one or more operating systems within the memory of a single host computer. This mechanism allows virtually any OS to operate on any hardware.)

211. What is used to store and process cryptographic keys for the purposes of a hardware supported/ implemented hard drive encryption system?

a. USB token

b. Virtualization technology

c. TPM chip

d. Hyper-V Technique

Ans. c. TPM chip

(A Trusted Platform Module (TPM) is a specialized chip on an endpoint device that stores RSA encryption keys specific to the host system for hardware authentication. Each TPM chip contains an RSA key pair called the Endorsement Key)

212. .... is a cryptoprocessor used to manage/store digital encryption keys, accelerate crypto operations, support faster digital signatures, and improve authentication.

a.   OES Security Module

b.   Hardware security module (HSM)

c.   Software security module (SSM)

d.   Trusted Platform Module

Ans. b. Hardware security module (HSM)

(A hardware security module (HSM) is a physical computing device that safeguards and manages digital keys for strong authentication and provides cryptoprocessing. These modules traditionally come in the form of a plug-in card or an external device that attaches directly to a computer or network server.)

213. What is the main purpose of a constrained interface?

a.   To host one or more operating systems

b.   To prevent an attack

c.   To limit or restrict the actions of users

d.   To classify data

Ans. c. To limit or restrict the actions of users

(The purpose of a constrained interface is to limit or restrict the actions of both authorized and unauthorized users)

214. The ability of a system to suffer a fault but continue to operate is known as ....

a. Fault tolerance

b. Restricted Interfaces

c. Constrained Interfaces

d. Disaster Recovery

Ans. a. Fault tolerance

(Fault tolerance is the property that enables a system to continue operating properly in the event of the failure of (or one or more faults within) some of its components.)

215. A table of subjects and objects that indicates the actions or functions that each subject can perform on each object is known as ....

a. Access control matrix

b. Take-Grant model

c. Access control list

d. Capabilities list

Ans. a. Access control matrix

(An Access Control Matrix or Access Matrix is an abstract, formal security model of protection state in computer systems that characterizes the rights of each subject with respect to every object in the system)

216. How many major categories do the TCSEC criteria define?

a. Two

b. Three

c. Four

d. Five

Ans. c. Four

(TCSEC defines four major categories: Category A is verified protection, Category B is mandatory protection, Category C is discretionary protection, and Category D is minimal protection)

217. In the Biba model, what does * (star) integrity axiom mean?

a. No read up

b. No write down

c. No read down

d. No write up

Ans. d. No write up

(Biba has two integrity axioms - Simple Integrity Axiom and Integrity Axiom. The * (star) Integrity Axiom (* Axiom) states that a subject at a specific classification level cannot write data to a higher classification level. This is often shortened to "no write up.)

218. .... is a KEY responsibility for the "Custodian of Data"?

a. Data content and backup

b. Integrity and security of data

c. Authentication of user access

d. Classification of data elements

Ans. b. Integrity and security of data

(Data custodians have a number of 'rights and responsibilities' related to the release of, and access to, source datasets for data integration projects. It is the responsibility of data custodians to ensure they are authorized by legislation or consent to release identifiable data to an integrating authority)

219. Which one of the following factor is critical in all systems to protect data integrity?

a. Data classification

b. Information ownership

c. Change control

d. System design

Ans. a. Data classification

(Integrity is dependent on confidentiality, which relies on data classification. Also Biba integrity model relies on data classification)

220. According to the Orange Book, trusted facility management is not required for which security levels?

a. B1

b. B2

c. B3

d. A1

Ans. a. B1

(B1 does not provide trusted facility management, the next highest level that does is B2)

Chapter 9
Security Vulnerabilities, Threats, and Countermeasures

221. The use of two or more central processing units (CPUs) within a single computer system is known as ....

a. Multiprogramming

b. Multithreading

c. Multitasking

d. Multiprocessing

Ans. d. Multiprocessing

(Multiprocessing refers to the ability of a system to support more than one processor or the ability to allocate tasks between them)

222. .... mode is designed to give the operating system access to the full range of instructions supported by the CPU.

a. Privileged mode

b. Supervisory mode

c. System mode

d. Kernel mode

Ans. a. Privileged mode

(Privileged mode is typically the mode in which the operating system runs, because it has access to all the resources in the computer)

223. The part of an operating system that always remains resident in memory (so that it can run on demand at any time) is called as ……………..

a. Thread

b. Kernel

c. Processor

d. Program

Ans. b. Kernel

(The 'kernel' is the central component of most computer operating systems; it is a bridge between applications and the actual data processing done at the hardware level. The kernel's responsibilities include managing the system's resources)

224. Which of the following mode is used by the CPU when executing user applications?

a. Privileged Mode

b. Supervisory mode

c. Applications mode

d. User Mode

Ans. d. User Mode

(User mode is the basic mode used by the CPU when executing user applications)

225. Which one of the following is the second major hardware component of a system?

a. Memory

b. Processor

c. Secondary Storage

d. Input/Output Devices

Ans. a. Memory

(The second major hardware component of a system is memory, the storage bank for information that the computer needs to keep readily available)

226. .... provide software developers with an opportunity to store information permanently on a high-speed, customized memory chip.

a. PROM chips

b. EPROM chips

c. EEPROM chips

d. ROM Chips

Ans. a. PROM chips

(PROMs are used in digital electronic devices to store permanent data, usually low level programs such as firmware (microcode))

227. .... is a programmable read-only memory that can be erased and re-used.

a. RAM

b. Flash Memory

c. EPROM

d. ROM

Ans. c. EPROM

(An EPROM, or erasable programmable read-only memory, is a type of memory chip that retains its data when its power supply is switched off. It can be erased and re-used.)

228. .... is readable and writable memory that contains information a computer uses during processing.

a. Random access memory (RAM)

b. Programmable Read-Only Memory (PROM)

c. Read-Only Memory (ROM)

d. Flash Memory

Ans. a. Random access memory (RAM)

(Random-access memory is a form of computer data storage which stores frequently used program instructions to increase the general speed of a system)

229. Which of the following is the largest RAM storage resource available to a computer?

a. Cache RAM

b. Real Memory

c. Dynamic RAM

d. Static RAM

Ans. b. Real Memory

(Real memory (also known as main memory or primary memory) is typically the largest RAM storage resource available to a computer)

230. The CPU includes a limited amount of onboard memory, known as ....

a. Registers

b. Chips

c. Thread

d. Kernel

Ans. a. Registers

(The CPU includes a limited amount of onboard memory, known as registers, that provide it with directly accessible memory locations that the brain of the CPU, the arithmetic-logical unit (ALU), uses when performing calculations or processing instructions)

231. Which one of the following is the primary advantage of ROM?

a. It can't be modified

b. It is part of the ALU itself

c. Operates in lockstep with the CPU

d. It can be used to store massive amounts of information

Ans. a. It can't be modified

(ROM's primary advantage is that it can't be modified.)

232. Which of the following types of memory might retain information after being removed from a computer and, therefore, represent a security risk?

a. Static RAM

b. Dynamic RAM

c. Secondary memory

d. Real memory

Ans. c. Secondary memory

(Secondary memory is a term used to describe magnetic, optical, or flash media. These devices will retain their contents after being removed from the computer and may later be read by another user)

233. …………….. serves as the primary building block for dynamic RAM chips?

a. Capacitor

b. Resistor

c. Flip-flop

d. Transistor

Ans. a. Capacitor

(Dynamic RAM chips are built from a large number of capacitors, each of which holds a single electrical charge. These capacitors must be continually refreshed by the CPU in order to retain their contents. The data stored in the chip is lost when power is removed)

234. A technology that allows the electronic emanations that every monitor produces to be read from a distance is ……………..

a. Analog Rytm

b. Van Eck radiation

c. Van Eck phreaking

d. TEMPEST

Ans. d. TEMPEST

(TEMPEST is a technology that allows the electronic emanations that every monitor produces (known as Van

Eck radiation) to be read from a distance (this process is known as Van Eck phreaking) and even from another location)

235. A technique for assigning specific signal lines to specific devices through a special interrupt controller is known as ………….

a. Memory-mapped I/O

b. Interrupt (IRQ)

c. Direct Memory Access (DMA)

d. Firmware

Ans. b. Interrupt (IRQ)

(Interrupt (IRQ) is an abbreviation for interrupt request, a technique used for assigning specific signal lines to specific devices through a special interrupt controller.)

236. Which one of the following storage devices requires encryption technology to maintain data security in a networked environment?

a. Hard disk

b. Backup tape

c. Removable drives

d. RAM

Ans. c. Removable drives

(Removable drives are easily taken out of their authorized physical location, and it is often not possible to apply operating system access controls to them. Therefore, encryption is often the only security measure short of physical security that can be afforded to them.)

237. Java, a platform-independent programming language was developed by ....

a. Microsoft

b. Swiss developers

c. Sun Microsystems

d. Netscape

Ans. c. Sun Microsystems

(Java was developed by James Gosling at Sun Microsystems and released in 1995 as a core component of Sun Microsystems' Java platform)

238. A data mining technique performed by analyzing data in order to illegitimately gain knowledge about a subject or database is known as ....

a. Inference attacks

b. Aggregation attacks

c. Direct attack

d. Indirect attack

Ans. a. Inference attacks

(Inference attacks involve combining several pieces of non-sensitive information to gain access to information that should be classified at a higher level)

239. ………….. is a computation system designed to perform numerous calculations simultaneously?

a. Data Analytics

b. Distributed Systems

c. Parallel data systems

d. Cloud Computing

Ans. c. Parallel data systems

(Parallel computing is a type of computation in which many calculations or the execution of processes are carried out simultaneously. Large problems can often be divided into smaller ones, which can then be solved at the same time)

240. …………… is a form of parallel distributed processing that loosely groups a significant number of processing nodes to work toward a specific processing goal.

a. Cloud Computing

b. Grid Computing

c. Peer-to-peer (P2P) technology

d.   Parallel computing

Ans. b. Grid Computing

(Grid computing is the collection of computer resources from multiple locations to reach a common goal. The grid can be thought of as a distributed system with non-interactive workloads that involve a large number of file)

241. In which of the following addressing scheme is the data actually supplied to the CPU as an argument to the instruction?

a.   Direct addressing

b.   Immediate addressing

c.   Base + offset addressing

d.   Indirect addressing

Ans. b. Immediate addressing

(In immediate addressing, the CPU does not need to actually retrieve any data from memory. The data is contained in the instruction itself and can be immediately processed.)

242. ………………….. is often used to provide a web-based SSO (single sign-on) Solution

a.   OWASP

b.   SAML

c. XML

d. PMD

Ans. b. SAML

(Security Association Markup Language (SAML) is an XML framework for exchanging authentication and authorization information. SAML is often used to provide a web-based SSO (single sign-on) solution.)

243. **A nonprofit security project that is focused on improving security for online or web-based applications is ....**

a. OWASP

b. ASP

c. NTI

d. NSGP

Ans. a. OWASP

(The Open Web Application Security Project (OWASP) is a not-for-profit group that helps organizations develop, purchase, and maintain software applications that can be trusted)

244. **What attribute is designed to prevent someone from casually picking up and being able to use your phone or mobile device?**

a. Lockout

b. Screen lock

c. GPS

d. Application Control

Ans. b. Screen lock

(Screen lock is a security feature for computers and mobile devices that help prevent unauthorized access to the device. Also known as a screenlock or lock screen, a screen lock requires a specific action or sequence of actions to be correctly performed by anyone attempting to use a lockscreen-protected device)

245. A standard to establish radio communications between devices in close proximity is known as ....

a. Near field communication (NFC)

b. Device Access Control

c. Mobile Device Management

d. Remote Wiping

Ans. a. Near field communication (NFC)

(Near Field Communication (NFC) is a short-range wireless connectivity standard that uses magnetic field induction to enable communication between devices when they're touched together, or brought within a few centimeters of each other)

246. .... is a form of computer-management device that controls industrial processes and machines.

a. Distributed control systems (DCSs)

b. Programmable logic controllers (PLCs)

c. Industrial control system (ICS)

d. Supervisory control and data acquisition (SCADA)

Ans. c. Industrial control system (ICS)

(Industrial control system is a form of computer-management device that controls industrial processes and machines whereas option a, b, d are forms of Industrial control system)

247. Which one of the following security feature lets you delete all data and possibly even configuration settings from a device remotely?

a. Asset Tracking

b. Storage Segmentation

c. Geotagging

d. Remote Wiping

Ans. d. Remote Wiping

(Remote wipe is a security feature that allows a network administrator or device owner to send a command to a computing device and delete data)

248. .... is the **RAM** that a computer uses to keep necessary information readily available to the CPU while the computer is running.

a. Primary memory

b. Secondary memory

c. Flash memory

d. Auxiliary memory

Ans. a. Primary memory

(Primary storage, also known as main storage or memory, is the area in a computer in which data is stored for quick access by the computer's processor)

249. Which one of the following is a common example of a sequential storage device?

a. Hard disk drive

b. CD

c. Magnetic tape drive

d. Internal RAM

Ans. c. Magnetic tape drive

(In computing, sequential access memory (SAM) is a class of data storage devices that read stored data in a sequence. Magnetic tape is the only type of sequential access memory still in use; historically, drum memory has also been used)

250. .... allow an operating system to read (and sometimes write) immediately from any point within the device by using some type of addressing system.

a. Random access storage devices

b. Sequential storage device

c. Tertiary Storage

d. Off-line Storage

Ans. a. Random access storage devices

(Random-access memory is a form of computer data storage which stores frequently used program instructions to increase the general speed of a system. Also, it allows an operating system to read (and sometimes write) immediately from any point within the device by using some type of addressing system)

251. .... is used to artificially compartmentalize various types or values of data on a storage medium.

a. Application Control

b. Storage segmentation

c. Inventory Control

d.   Asset Tracking

Ans. b. Storage segmentation

(Storage segmentation is used to artificially compartmentalize various types or values of data on a storage medium)

252. .... is a security practice that blocks or restricts unauthorized applications from executing in ways that put data at risk.

a.   Application control

b.   Full Device Encryption

c.   Remote Wiping

d.   Device Access Control

Ans. a.   Application control

(Application control is a device-management solution that limits which applications can be installed onto a device. It can also be used to force specific applications to be installed or to enforce the settings of certain applications, in order to support a security baseline or maintain other forms of compliance)

253. Which one of the following is not the objective of Mobile Device Management?

a.   To improve security

b.   To reduce unauthorized access

c. To provide monitoring

d. To support troubleshooting

Ans. b. To reduce unauthorized access

(The goals of Mobile Device Management (MDM) are to improve security, provide monitoring, enable remote management, and support troubleshooting)

254. A security option that prohibits unauthorized software from being able to execute is known as ....

a. Application whitelisting

b. Geotagging

c. Credential Management

d. Encryption

Ans. a. Application whitelisting

(Application whitelisting is the practice of specifying an index of approved software applications that are permitted to be present and active on a computer system. The goal of whitelisting is to protect computers and networks from potentially harmful applications)

255. Who should evaluate the legal concerns of BYOD?

a. Managers

b.   Users

c.   Security professionals

d.   Company attorneys

Ans. d. Company attorneys

(Company attorneys should evaluate the legal concerns of BYOD)

256. ……………..is a system that has software embedded into hardware, designed for specific application.

a.   Static systems

b.   Industrial Control Systems

c.   Distributed control systems

d.   Embedded system

Ans. d.   Embedded system

(An embedded system is some combination of computer hardware and software, either fixed in capability or programmable, that is designed for a specific function or for specific functions within a larger system)

257. Which one of the following is the key element in robotics and sensor networks?

a.   Cyber-physical systems

b. Modern in-vehicle systems

c. Embedded systems

d. Static systems

Ans. a. Cyber-physical systems

(Cyber-physical devices and systems are essentially key elements in robotics and sensor networks.)

258. A hardware device typically designed for general network filtering is ....

a. Web application firewall

b. Network firewall

c. Proxy firewall

d. Secure Web gateway

Ans. b. Network firewall

(A network firewall is a hardware device, typically called an appliance, designed for general

Network filtering)

259. What kind of memory device is generally used to contain a computer's motherboard BIOS?

a. PROM

b. EEPROM

c. ROM

d. EPROM

Ans. b. EEPROM

(BIOS and device firmware are often stored on EEPROM chips to facilitate future firmware updates.)

260. What is the most effective method of protecting the data on your mobile device, such as a notebook computer?

a. Defining a strong logon password

b. Minimizing sensitive data stored on the mobile device

c. Using a cable lock

d. Encrypting the hard drive

Ans. b. Minimizing sensitive data stored on the mobile device

(The risk of a lost or stolen notebook is the data loss, not the loss of the system itself. Thus, keeping minimal sensitive data on the system is the only way to reduce the risk and protect the data on your mobile device. Hard drive encryption, cable locks, and strong passwords, although good ideas, are preventive tools, not means of reducing risk.)

261. A method that is used to pass information over a path that is not normally used for communication is

known as ....

a. Trusted paths

b. Covert channel

c. Wireless Channels

d. Overt Channel

Ans. b. Covert channel

(A covert channel is a type of computer security attack that creates a capability to transfer information objects between processes that are not supposed to be allowed to communicate by the computer security policy)

262. Which of the following channel conveys information by altering the performance of a system component or modifying a resource's timing in a predictable manner?

a. Covert Storage Channel

b. Covert Timing Channel

c. Overt Channel

d. Fibre Channel

Ans. b. Covert Timing Channel

(A covert timing channel conveys information by altering the performance of a system component or modifying a resource's timing in a predictable manner)

263. The time at which the subject checks on the status of the object is known as ………

a. Time of check (TOC)

b. Time of use (TOU)

c. Time of availability

d. Time of accessibility

Ans. a.   Time of check (TOC)

(The time of check (TOC) is the time at which the subject checks on the status of the object. There may be several decisions to make before returning to the object to access it)

264. …………… is a special enclosure that acts as an EM capacitor.

a. White noise

b. Control zones

c. Faraday cage

d. Jamming

Ans. c. Faraday cage

(A Faraday cage is a metallic enclosure that prevents the entry or escape of an electromagnetic field (EM field))

265. Firmware is software stored on a …………. chip

a. RAM

b. ROM

c. PROM

d. EPROM

Ans. b. ROM chip

(Firmware is software stored on a non-volatile ROM chip)

266. .... prevents information from being read from a different security level.

a. Data hiding

b. Hardware segmentation

c. Abstraction

d. Process isolation

Ans. a. Data hiding

(Data hiding is a software development technique specifically used in object-oriented programming to hide internal object details (data members). Data hiding ensures exclusive data access to class members and protects object integrity by preventing unintended or intended changes)

267. Which one of the following technology provides an organization with the best control over BYOD equipment?

a. Application whitelisting

b. Mobile device management

c. Encrypted removable storage

d. Geotagging

Ans. b. Mobile device management

(Mobile device management (MDM) is a software solution to the challenging task of managing the myriad mobile devices that employees use to access company resources. The goals of MDM are to improve security, provide monitoring, enable remote management, and support troubleshooting. Not all mobile devices support removable storage, and even fewer support encrypted removable storage)

Chapter 10
Physical Security Requirements

268. .... is the most vital aspect of security?

a. Physical security

b. Intrusion detection

c. Logical security

d. Awareness training

Ans. a. Physical security

(Physical security is the most important aspect of overall security. Without physical security, none of the other aspects of security are sufficient)

269. What method can be used to identify relationships between mission-critical applications, processes, and operations and all the necessary supporting elements?

a. Log file audit

b. Critical path analysis

c. Risk analysis

d. Inventory

Ans. b. Critical path analysis

(A critical path analysis is the process of identifying relationships between mission-critical applications, processes, and operations and all of the supporting elements. Critical path analysis can be used to map out the needs of an organization for a new facility.)

270. Which of the following agreement clearly defines the response time a vendor will provide in the event of an equipment failure emergency?

a.   Record retention agreement

b.   Service-level agreement (SLA)

c.   Anti-Counterfeiting Trade Agreement (ACTA)

d.   Contractual license agreements

Ans. b. Service-level agreement (SLA)

(A Service-level agreement (SLA) clearly defines the response time a vendor will provide in the event of an equipment failure emergency)

271. .... is the act of gathering information from a system by observing the monitor or the use of the keyboard by the operator.

a.   Web surfing

b.   Palm surfing

c.   Shoulder surfing

d.   Secure web surfing

Ans. c. Shoulder surfing

(Shoulder surfing refers to the act of obtaining personal or private information through direct observation. Shoulder surfing involves looking over a person's shoulder to gather pertinent information while the victim is oblivious)

272. A mechanism by which the communication pathway is either constantly or periodically checked with a test signal is known as ....

a.   Heartbeat sensor

b.   Locking Mechanisms

c.   Signal-transduction pathway

d.   Direct sensor

Ans. a. Heartbeat sensor

(A heartbeat sensor is a mechanism by which the communication pathway is either constantly or periodically checked with a test signal. If the receiving station detects a failed heartbeat signal, the alarm triggers automatically)

273. The act of using someone else's security ID to gain entry into a facility is ....

a.   Piggybacking

b.   Masquerading

c.   Emanations

d.   Critical path analysis

Ans. b. Masquerading

(Masquerading is an act where the attacker pretends to be an authorized user of a system in order to gain access to it or to gain greater privileges than they are authorized for)

274. **Broadcasting false traffic at all times to mask and hide the presence of real emanations is known as ....**

a. Control zone

b. Emanation cage

c. White noise

d. Faraday cage

Ans. c. White noise

(White noise is a false traffic used to mask or hide the presence of a true signal emanation)

275. **An act of following someone through a secured gate or doorway without being identified or authorized personally is known as ....**

a. Piggybacking

b. Masquerading

c. Impersonating

d. Mimicking

Ans. a. Piggybacking

(Piggybacking is gaining access to restricted communication channel by using session that another user has already established)

276. Which one of the following is not the type of Water Suppression Systems?

a. Wet pipe system

b. Dry pipe system

c. Action system

d. Deluge system

Ans. c. Action system

(There are four main types of water suppression systems which include Wet pipe system, Dry pipe system, Deluge system and Preaction system)

277. Which one of the following water-based system is most appropriate for environments that house both computers and humans together?

a. Wet pipe system

b. Dry pipe system

c. Deluge system

d. Preaction system

Ans. d.   Preaction system

(Preaction systems are the most appropriate water-based system for environments that house both computers and humans together)

278. What is the most common cause of failure for a water-based fire suppression system?

a. System error

b. Human error

c. Water shortage

d. Ionization detectors

Ans. b. Human error

(The most common cause of failure for a water-based system is human error, such as turning off a water source when a fire occurs or triggering water release when there is no fire)

279. .... is a perimeter-defining device used to deter casual trespassing.

a. Fences

b. Gates

c. Turnstiles

d. Mantraps

Ans. a. Fences

(A fence is a perimeter-defining device. Fences are used to clearly differentiate between areas that are under a specific level of security protection and those that aren't.)

280. ……………….. is a double set of doors that is often protected by a guard and is used to contain a subject until their identity and authentication is verified?

a. Gate

b. Turnstile

c. Mantrap

d. Proximity detector

Ans. c. Mantrap

(A mantrap is a physical access control method that consists of a double set of locked doors or turnstiles)

281. Which one of the following is the most common form of perimeter security devices or mechanisms?

a. Security guards

b. Fences

c. CCTV

d. Lighting

Ans. d. Lighting

(Lighting is the most common form of perimeter security devices or mechanisms. Entire site should be clearly lit. This provides for easy identification of personnel and makes it easier to notice intrusion)

282. ………….. is the most common and inexpensive form of physical access control device?

a. Lighting

b. Security guard

c. Key locks

d. Fences

Ans. c. Key locks

(Key locks are the most common and inexpensive form of physical access control device. Lighting, security guards, and fences are all much more costly)

283. What is the ideal humidity range for a computer room?

a. 20–40%

b. 40–60%

c. 60–75%

d. 80–95%

Ans. b. 40–60%

(The humidity in a computer room should preferably be from 40 to 60 percent.)

284. Which one of the following is not the type of fire detection systems?

a. Heat sensing

b. Flame sensing

c. CO2 sensing

d. Smoke sensing

Ans. c. CO2 sensing

(CO2 sensing is not a valid type of fire detection system. The three categories of fire detection systems include heat sensing, flame sensing, and smoke sensing)

285. Above what concentrations is Halon considered toxic when inhaled?

a. 5%

b. 6%

c. 10%

d. 15%

Ans. c. 10%

(Halon is considered toxic in concentrations above 10%)

286. Which one of the following is considered to be

the best replacement for Halon?

a. Argon

b. FM-200

c. Inergen

d. FM-300

Ans. b. FM-20

(The EPA considers FM-200 the replacement of choice for Halon systems. It is similar to Halon but does not affect the ozone system. Argon and Inergen will work but are not effective. FM-300 does not exist)

287. Which one of the following fits in the category of a power excess?

a. Faults and blackouts

b. Spikes and surges

c. Sags and brownouts

d. Noise and EMIst

Ans. b. Spikes and surges

(A power excess can quickly damage sensitive electronic equipment. The best way to guard against this type of problem is through the use of surge protectors. Brownouts occur when power companies experience an increasingly high demand for power, and blackouts are associated with power loss)

288. .... is a critical part of physical security.

a. Guard dogs

b. Layered access control

c. Fences

d. CCTV

Ans. b. Layered access control

(Access control is the key to physical security, and it works best when deployed in layers. Each layer acts as a physical barrier. At a minimum, a system should have three physical barriers: entrance to the building, entrance to the computer center, and entrance to the computer room itself. These barriers can include guards, biometric access control, locked doors, CCTV, and alarm systems)

289. Which of the following statements is not true with regard to CCTV?

a. CCTV is a perfect example of a deterrent system.

b. CCTV is a good example of an automated intrusion- detection system.

c. CCTV is effective in deterring security violations.

d. CCTV is an ideal example of a detection system.

Ans. b. CCTV is a good example of an automated

intrusion- detection system

(Although CCTV (closed-circuit TV) systems are good deterrents and detection systems, they are not automatic. CCTV requires individuals to watch the captured video, detect the malicious activity, and respond accordingly)

290. Which one of the following water suppression systems contains compressed air?

a. Wet pipe

b. Dry pipe

c. Deluge system

d. Preaction system

Ans. b. Dry pipe

(Dry pipe systems contain compressed air until fire suppression systems are triggered, and then the pipe is filled with water)

291. ……………….. is considered as a gas-discharge fire extinguishing system.

a. Wet pipe

b. Dry pipe

c. Flame activated sprinkler

d. Handheld CO2 fire extinguisher

Ans. d. Handheld CO2 fire extinguisher

(A handheld CO2 fire extinguisher is considered a gas-discharge fire extinguishing system. Wet pipe systems are filled with water. Dry pipe systems contain compressed air until fire suppression systems are triggered, and then the pipe is filled with water; and flame activated sprinklers trigger when a predefined temperature is reached)

292. A specification that defines a software interface between an operating system and platform firmware is known as ....

a. Basic Input/Output System (BIOS)

b. Unified Extensible Firmware Interface (UEFI)

c. Extensible Firmware Interface (EFI)

d. Virtual Machine (VM)

Ans. b. Unified Extensible Firmware Interface (UEFI)

(Unified Extensible Firmware Interface (UEFI) is a specification for a software program that connects a computer's firmware to its operating system)

293. What type of computer attack affects the firmware of embedded system, computers and networking devices?

a. Phlashing

b. Piggybacking

c. Espionage

d. Masquerading

Ans. a. Phlashing

(Phlashing is a type of computer attack that affects the firmware of embedded system, computers and networking devices. It is designed to affect firmware and software of computing devices that have embedded firmware operating system and applications)

294. Which of the following can be used to isolate static environments in order to prevent changes and/or exploits from reaching them?

a. Storage segmentation

b. Hardware segmentation

c. Memory segmentation

d. Network segmentation

Ans. d. Network segmentation

(Network segmentation in computer networking is the act or profession of splitting a computer network into sub-networks, each being a network segment. Advantages of such splitting are primarily for boosting performance and improving security)

295. What level of static discharge is required for the destruction of data stored on hard drives?

a. 100 static volts

b. 500 static volts

c. 1,000 static volts

d. 1,500 static volts

Ans. d. 1,500 static volts

(In low-humidity environments, it's not impossible to create static charges in excess of 20,000 volts. It takes only about 1,500 static volts to damage a hard drive or cause destruction of data. Sensitive electronic components can be damaged by less than 100 static volts)

296. What type of attack depends upon the trusting nature of employees and the art of deception?

a. Hijacking

b. Social engineering

c. Spoofing

d. Deception

Ans. b. Social engineering

(Social engineering is a type of attack in which intruders may attempt to gain physical access to your facility by exploiting the generally trusting nature of people. A social engineering attack may come from someone posing as a vendor or as someone coming to the facility to repair a problem. Regardless of how they appear, social engineering can be hard to detect)

297. ……………….. is a type of intrusion detection system that is capable of sensing changes in vibration and noise level in an area.

a. Wave pattern

b. Proximity detection

c. Passive infrared system

d. Acoustical system

Ans. d. Acoustical system

(Acoustical systems are sensitive to changes, sound, and vibration. Proximity detection works by detecting changes to the magnetic field. Passive infrared systems look for the rise of heat waves. Wave pattern bounces various frequency waves around a room while verifying that the pattern is undisturbed)

298. Which one of the following is not a valid intrusion detection system?

a. Wave pattern

b. Proximity detection

c. Geometric system

d. Acoustical system

Ans. c. Geometric system

(Geometric system is not a valid intrusion detection system whereas wave pattern, proximity detection and acoustical system are forms of intrusion detection system)

299. .... is the best type of water-based fire suppression system for a computer facility?

a.   Wet pipe system

b.   Dry pipe system

c.   Preaction system

d.   Deluge system

Ans. c. Preaction system

(A Preaction system is the best type of water-based fire suppression system for a computer facility)

300. Which policy allows employees to bring their own personal mobile devices to work and then use those devices to connect to the company network to business resources and/or the Internet?

a.   BYOD policy

b.   Security policy

c.   EISP policy

d.   SPP Policy

Ans. a. BYOD policy

(Bring Your Own Device (BYOD) refers to the policy of permitting employees to bring personally owned devices (laptops, tablets, and smart phones) to their workplace, and to use those devices to access privileged company information and applications)

Chapter 11
Communication and Network Security

301. .... is a standard set of rules that determines how systems will communicate across networks.

a.　Network protocol

b.　File Transfer Protocol

c.　Secure Protocol

d.　Encryption Protocol

Ans. a. Network protocol

(Network protocols are formal standards and policies comprised of rules, procedures and formats that define communication between two or more devices over a network. Network protocols govern the end-to-end processes of timely, secure and managed data or network communication)

302. At which OSI model layer, does the IPSec protocol function?

a.　Presentation

b.　Network

c.　Physical

d.　Data Link

Ans. b. Network

(IPSec is a suite of protocols that provide security services at IP layer of TCP/IP stack i.e. Network Layer in OSI model. AH provides authentication, integrity and anti-replay services at Network Layer and above)

303. Which one of the following layer formats data into a standardized format and deals with the syntax of the data, not the meaning?

a.   Presentation layer

b.   Application layer

c.   Transport layer

d.   Physical layer

Ans. a. Presentation layer

(The presentation layer, i.e., layer 6, formats data into a standardized format and deals with the syntax of the data, not the meaning)

304. The protocols, technologies, and computers that operate within the OSI model are considered as ....

a.   Closed Systems

b.   Network architecture

c.   Open system

d.   TCP Model

Ans. c. Open system

(The protocols, technologies, and computers that operate within the OSI model are considered open systems. Open systems are capable of communicating with other open systems because they implement international standard protocols and interfaces)

305. Which of the following OSI model layer convert bits into voltage for transmission?

a.   Data link layer

b.   Transport layer

c.   Presentation layer

d.   Physical layer

Ans. d. Physical layer

(The physical layer i.e., layer 1, provides physical connections for transmission and performs the electrical encoding of data. This layer transforms bits to electrical signals)

306. Which one of the following is the function of a Session Layer?

a.   Provides end-to-end transmission

b.   Establishes connection between two applications

c.   Transforms bits to electrical signals

d.   Formats data

Ans. b. Establishes connection between two applications

(The session layer - layer 5, is responsible for establishing a connection between the two applications, maintaining it during the transfer of data, and controlling the release of this connection)

307. Which of the following protocols doesn't work at Session Layer?

a.   Password Authentication Protocol (PAP)

b.   Point-to-Point Tunneling Protocol (PPTP)

c.   Network Basic Input Output System (NetBIOS)

d.   Temporal Key Integrity Protocol (TKIP)

Ans. d. Temporal Key Integrity Protocol (TKIP)

(Some protocols that work at Session layer are the Password Authentication Protocol (PAP), Point-to-Point Tunneling Protocol (PPTP), Network Basic Input Output System (NetBIOS), and Remote Procedure Call (RPC).)

308. Communication between a computer and a keyboard involves .... transmission.

a.   Half-duplex

b.   Simplex

c.   Full-duplex

d.   Automatic

Ans. b. Simplex

(In Simplex transmission, communication between a computer and a keyboard takes place)

309. The protocols that function at transport layer are ………………….

a. PAP and PPTP

b. TCP and UDP

c. NetBIOS and RPC

d. OSPF and BGP

Ans. b. TCP and UDP

(The main protocols that work at transport layer are TCP and UDP)

310. At which layer of the OSI Model, is Encryption protocols and JPEG found?

a. Presentation Layer - Layer 6

b. Application Layer - Layer 7

c. Network Layer - Layer 3

d. Transport Layer - Layer 4

Ans. a. Presentation Layer - Layer 6

(Encryption protocols and JPEG are found at the Presentation Layer of the OSI Model)

311. Internet layer in TCP/IP is equivalent to what layers in OSI Model?

a.   Data link layer

b.   Transport layer

c.   Presentation layer

d.   Network Layer

Ans. d. Network Layer

(Internet layer in TCP/IP is equivalent to Network layers of OSI Model)

312. Which of the following protocol is session oriented and provides either 40bit or 128 bit encryption?

a.   SSL

b.   TCP

c.   UDP

d.   JPEG

Ans. a. SSL

(Secure Sockets Layer (SSL) is a session-oriented protocol that provides confidentiality and integrity. SSL is deployed using a 40-bit key or a 128-bit key)

313. The protocols at the ………….. layer convert data into LAN or WAN frames for transmission and

define how a computer accesses a network.

a. Physical layer

b. Presentation layer

c. Data link layer

d. Network Layer

Ans. c. Data link layer

(Data link layer is the protocol layer that transfers data between adjacent network nodes in a wide area network (WAN) or between nodes on the same local area network (LAN) segment)

314. …………….. is a communications protocol that is specially designed for use in SCADA systems.

a. Controller Area Network bus (CAN bus)

b. Distributed Network Protocol 3 (DNP3)

c. Transmission Control Protocol (TCP)

d. Internet Protocol (IP)

Ans. b. Distributed Network Protocol 3 (DNP3)

(The Distributed Network Protocol 3 (DNP3) is a communications protocol designed for use in SCADA systems, particularly those within the power sector)

315. A connectionless protocol that does not send

or receive acknowledgments when a datagram is received is known as ……………..

a. UDP

b. TCP

c. IP

d. DNP3

Ans. a. UDP

(User Datagram Protocol (UDP) is considered a connectionless protocol as it does not send or receive acknowledgments when a datagram is received)

316. Which of the following protocols convert the IP address into a MAC address?

a. Reverse Address Resolution Protocol (RARP)

b. Address Resolution Protocol (ARP)

c. Internet Control Message Protocol (ICMP)

d. Open Shortest Path First (OSPF)

Ans. b. Address Resolution Protocol (ARP)

(Address Resolution Protocol (ARP) converts an Internet Protocol (IP) address to its corresponding physical network address. IP networks including those that run on Ethernet and Wi-Fi require ARP in order to function)

317. Mention the method that is used to disconnect a TCP session?

a. Data encapsulation

b. FIN (finish) flagged packets

c. Supernetting

d. SYN (synchronization) flagged packets

Ans. b. FIN (finish) flagged packets

(Two common methods are used to disconnect a TCP session. One is FIN (finish) flagged packets and the other one is RST (reset) flagged packets)

318. ……………….. **is a terminal emulation network application that supports remote connectivity for executing commands and running applications but does not support transfer of files.**

a. Telnet

b. Routers

c. Secure Shell

d. Ping

Ans. a. Telnet

(Telnet is a terminal emulation program for TCP/IP networks such as the Internet. The Telnet program runs on your computer and connects your PC to a server on the network)

319. Fibre Channel (FC) was developed by ANSI in the year ………

a.   1968

b.   1978

c.   1988

d.   1998

Ans. c. 1988

(FC was developed by ANSI in 1988 as a way to connect supercomputers using optical fibers)

320. Multiprotocol Label Switching (MPLS) was originally developed to ………………

a.   Connect supercomputers

b.   Transmit data

c.   Improve routing performance

d.   Integrate security protection

Ans. c. Improve routing performance

(MPLS was originally developed to improve routing performance, but is frequently used for its ability to create VPNs over a variety of layer 2 protocols)

321. A set of technologies that allows peripherals to

be connected to computers is termed as ……….

a. MPLS

b. FCoE

c. SCSI

d. Converged protocols

Ans. c. SCSI

(The Small Computer System Interface (SCSI) is a set of parallel interface standards developed by the American National Standards Institute (ANSI) for attaching printers, disk drives, scanners and other peripherals to computers)

322. **Which version of Internet Protocol is most widely used around the world?**

a. IPv4

b. IPv3

c. IPv1

d. IPv2

Ans. a. IPv4

(IPv4 is the version of Internet Protocol that is most widely used around the world, while IP versions 1, 2, 3 were experimental versions)

323. **……………………….. is used to determine the**

health of a network or a specific link.

a. Classless Inter-Domain Routing (CIDR)

b. Internet Group Management Protocol (IGMP)

c. Address Resolution Protocol (ARP)

d. Internet Control Message Protocol (ICMP)

Ans. d. Internet Control Message Protocol (ICMP)

(Internet Control Message Protocol (ICMP) is used to determine the health of a network or a specific link. ICMP is utilized by ping, traceroute, pathping, and other network management tools)

324. The act of transmitting data to multiple specific recipients is known as ....

a. Multicasting

b. Unicasting

c. Broadcasting

d. Anycasting

Ans. a. Multicasting

(In computer networking, multicast is group communication where data transmission is addressed to a group of destination computers simultaneously)

325. A network application that supports an exchange

of files that does not require authentication is known as ……………

a. File Transfer Protocol (FTP)

b. Simple Mail Transfer Protocol (SMTP)

c. Trivial File Transfer Protocol (TFTP)

d. Internet Message Access Protocol (IMAP)

Ans. c. Trivial File Transfer Protocol (TFTP)

(Trivial File Transfer Protocol (TFTP) is primarily used to exchange configuration or bootfiles between machines in an environment. It is relatively simple and provides no authentication mechanism)

326. ……………… is a connection-oriented protocol that sends and receives acknowledgments.

a. Distributed Network Protocol 3 (DNP3)

b. Transmission Control Protocol (TCP)

c. User Datagram Protocol (UDP)

d. Sequenced Packet Exchange (SPX)

Ans. b. Transmission Control Protocol (TCP)

(TCP is connection oriented protocol i.e., once a connection is established, data can be sent bidirectional)

327. ……………………. is an open network

architecture guide for network product vendors.

a. OSI model

b. TCP model

c. IP model

d. Business model

Ans. a. OSI model

(The Open Systems Interconnection model (OSI model) is a conceptual model that characterizes and standardizes the communication functions of a telecommunication or computing system without regard to their underlying internal structure and technology)

328. Which one of the following serve as an alternative to IP at the OSI Network layer (3)?

a. Socket

b. Non-IP protocols

c. TCP Handsake

d. IPSec

Ans. b. Non-IP protocols

(Non-IP protocols serve as an alternative to IP at the OSI Network - layer 3)

329. Which of the following is the most effective

technique described in RFC 4987?

a. Use of cookies

b. Sampling technique

c. Use of SYN caches

d. Filtering technique

Ans. c. Use of SYN caches

(One of the most effective techniques described in RFC 4987 is the use of SYN caches, which delays the allocation of a socket until the handshake is completed)

330. **Which of the following is used to pull email messages from an inbox on an email server down to an email client?**

a. Simple Mail Transfer Protocol (SMTP)

b. Post Office Protocol version 3 (POP3)

c. Dynamic Host Configuration Protocol (DHCP)

d. Hypertext Transport Protocol (HTTP)

Ans. b. Post Office Protocol version 3 (POP3)

(Post Office Protocol version 3 (POP3) is a message access protocol that enables the client to fetch an e-mail from the remote mail server)

331. **…………… is a network service that is used to**

support file sharing between dissimilar systems.

a. Simple Network Management Protocol (SNMP)

b. X Window

c. Network File System (NFS)

d. Bootstrap Protocol

Ans. c. Network File System (NFS)

(NFS allows a system to share directories and files with others over a network. By using NFS, users and programs can access files on remote systems almost as if they were local files)

332. Which of the following network service is used to spool print jobs and to send print jobs to printers?

a. Bootstrap Protocol (BootP)

b. Line Print Daemon (LPD)

c. Internet Message Access Protocol (IMAP)

d. Secure Sockets Layer (SSL)

Ans. b. Line Print Daemon (LPD)

(Line Print Daemon (LPD) is a network service that is used to spool print jobs and to send print jobs to printers)

333. Which one of the following is not an ideal example of network segmentation?

a. Intranet

b. DMZ

c. Extranet

d. VPN

Ans. d. VPN

(A VPN is a secure tunnel used to establish connections across a potentially insecure intermediary network. Intranet, extranet, and DMZ are examples of network segmentation)

334. The arrangement of computers and devices is called a ....

a. Token Ring technology

b. Network topology

c. Ethernet technology

d. Socket

Ans. b. Network topology

(Network topology is the arrangement of the various elements (links, nodes, etc.) of a communication network. Essentially, it is the topological structure of a network and may be depicted physically or logically)

335. .... is a protocol that encapsulates the Extensible Authentication Protocol (EAP) within

an encrypted and authenticated Transport Layer Security (TLS) tunnel.

a. LEAP

b. WEP

c. MAC Filter

d. PEAP

Ans. d. PEAP

(PEAP (Protected Extensible Authentication Protocol) encapsulates EAP methods within a TLS tunnel that provides authentication and potentially encryption)

336. Which one of the following is not a routing protocol?

a. OSPF

b. BGP

c. RPC

d. RIP

Ans. c. RPC

(There are numerous dynamic routing protocols, including RIP, OSPF, and BGP, but RPC is not a routing protocol)

337. Which of the following is not an example of LAN technologies?

a. Ethernet

b. ATM

c. Token Ring

d. FDDI

Ans. b.   ATM

(Ethernet, Token Ring, and FDDI are common LAN technologies. ATM is more common in a WAN environment)

338. Which of the following is the least resistant to EMI?

a. Thinnet

b. 10Base-T UTP

c. 10Base5

d. Coaxial cable

Ans. b. 10Base-T UTP

(10Base-T UTP is the least resistant to EMI because it is unshielded)

339. Which networking technology is based on the IEEE 802.3 standard?

a. Token Ring

b. Ethernet

c. FDDI

d. HDLC

Ans. b. Ethernet

(Ethernet networking technology is based on the IEEE 802.3 standard)

340. .... is a topology for a Local Area Network (LAN) in which all nodes are individually connected to a central connection point, like a hub or a switch.

a. Ring topology

b. Star topology

c. Bus topology

d. Mesh Topology

Ans. b. Star topology

(A switch in star topologies serves as the central meeting place for all cables from computers and devices)

341. Network that provides shared communication and resources in a relatively small area is known

a. LAN

b. WAN

c. WAE

d. SAN

Ans. a. LAN

(A local-area network (LAN) is a computer network that spans a relatively small area. Most often, a LAN is confined to a single room, building or group of buildings, however, one LAN can be connected to other LANs over any distance via telephone lines and radio waves)

342. When was WAP 2.0 released?

a. 2003

b. 2001

c. 2002

d. 2000

Ans. c. 2002

(A re-engineered WAP 2.0 version was released in 2002)

343. .... is the unauthorized access from a wireless device through a Bluetooth connection.

a. Piggybacking

b. Bluesnarfing

c. Masquerading

d. Emanations

Ans. b. Bluesnarfing

(Bluesnarfing allows hackers to connect with your Bluetooth devices without your knowledge and extract information from them)

344. …………….. is a high-speed token-passing technology that employs two rings with traffic flowing in opposite directions.

a. Fiber Distributed Data Interface (FDDI)

b. Internet Message Access Protocol (IMAP)

c. Ethernet

d. Token Ring

Ans. a. Fiber Distributed Data Interface (FDDI)

(Fiber Distributed Data Interface (FDDI) is a high-speed network technology, usually implemented as a dual token-passing ring within a ring topology (for campus networks) or star topology (within a building))

345. Which one of the following IP addresses is not a private IP address as defined by RFC 1918?

a. 10.0.0.18

b. 169.254.1.119

c. 172.31.8.204

d. 192.168.6.43

Ans. b. 169.254.1.119

(The 169.254.x.x subnet is in the APIPA range, which is not part of RFC 1918. The addresses in RFC 1918 are 10.0.0.0-10.255.255.255, 172.16.0.0-172.31.255.255, and 192.168.0.0-192.168.255.255)

346. .... is a logical pathway or circuit created over a packet-switched network between two specific endpoints.

a. Circuit Switching

b. Virtual Circuits

c. Packet Switching

d. Datagram Networks

Ans. b. Virtual Circuits

(A virtual circuit (VC) is a means of transporting data over a packet switched computer network in such a way that it appears as though there is a dedicated physical layer link between the source and destination end systems of this data)

347. What was developed to manage telephone calls over the public switched telephone network?

a. Circuit switching

b. Permanent virtual circuits (PVCs)

c. Switched virtual circuits (SVCs)

d. Packet Switching

Ans. a. Circuit switching

(Circuit switching was originally developed to manage telephone calls over the public switched telephone network. In circuit switching, a dedicated physical pathway is created between the two communicating parties)

348. …………….. is an Internet mail server protocol that supports incoming and outgoing messages.

a. Internet Message Access Protocol (IMAP)

b. Post Office Protocol (POP)

c. Interior Gateway Protocol (IGP)

d. Distance-Vector Routing Protocol

Ans. b. Post Office Protocol (POP)

(Post Office Protocol (POP) is an application-layer Internet standard protocol used by local e-mail clients to retrieve e-mail from a remote server over a TCP/IP connection)

349. A technique used by malicious users to forge an e-mail to make it appear to be from a legitimate source is known as ………

a. E-mail Relaying

b.   E-mail Authorization

c.   Electronic spamming

d.   E-mail spoofing

Ans. d.   E-mail spoofing

(Email spoofing is a tactic used in phishing and spam campaigns because people are more likely to open an email when they think it has been sent by a legitimate source)

350. Simple Network Management Protocol (SNMP) was released to the networking world in the year ………..

a.   1978

b.   1988

c.   1968

d.   1958

Ans. b. 1988

(Simple Network Management Protocol (SNMP) was released to the networking world in 1988 to help with the growing demand of managing network IP devices)

351. ………………… is a layer 2 connection mechanism that uses packet-switching technology to establish virtual circuits between communication endpoints.

a.   X.25

b. Frame Relay

c. Multiprotocol Label Switching

d. ATM

Ans. b. Frame Relay

(Frame Relay is a standardized wide area network technology that specifies the physical and data link layers of digital telecommunications channels using a packet switching methodology)

352. A phenomenon that occurs when electrical signals of one wire spill over to the signals of another wire is known as ....

a. Crosstalk

b. Attenuation

c. Cabling Problems

d. Collision

Ans. a. Crosstalk

(In electronics, crosstalk is any phenomenon by which a signal transmitted on one circuit or channel of a transmission system creates an undesired effect in another circuit or channel)

353. Ethernet uses .... to provide media-sharing capabilities.

a. CSMA

b. SMTP authentication

c. CDDI

d. UDP

Ans. a. CSMA

(Ethernet protocols define how nodes are to communicate, recover from errors, and access the shared network cable. Ethernet uses CSMA to provide media-sharing capabilities)

354. A method of monitoring multiple devices and controlling network access transmission is known as ....

a. Ethernet

b. Polling

c. Attenuation

d. Token Ring

Ans. b. Polling

(Polling is the process where the computer or controlling device waits for an external device to check for its readiness or state, often with low-level hardware)

355. .... is implemented in a star topology, to provide easy network configuration.

a. 10GBase-T

b. 10Base-T

c. 100Base-TX

d. 1000Base-T

Ans. b. 10Base-T

(10Base-T is usually implemented in a star topology, which provides easy network configuration)

356. Who developed the Token Ring technology?

a. Microsoft

b. IBM

c. Swiss developers

d. Sun Microsystems

Ans. b. IBM

(Token Ring technology was developed by IBM during the 1980s as an alternative to Ethernet)

357. Fiber Distributed Data Interface (FDDI) technology was developed by ....

a. National Institute of Standards and Technology (NIST)

b. American National Standards Institute (ANSI)

c.	Federal Bureau of Investigation

d.	National Security Agency

Ans. b. American National Standards Institute (ANSI)

(Fiber Distributed Data Interface (FDDI) technology, was developed by the American National Standards Institute (ANSI) in the 1980s. It is a high-speed, token-passing, media access technology)

358. Concentrator that connects an SAS device to the primary ring is known as ……………

a.	Single-attachment station (SAS)

b.	Dual-attached concentrator (DAC)

c.	Single-attached concentrator (SAC)

d.	Dual-attachment station (DAS)

Ans. c. Single-attached concentrator (SAC)

(Single Attached Concentrators (SAC) are connected only to the primary ring through a tree. SAC are less reliable due to the single connection to the backbone)

359. Which one of the following detect DoS attacks?

a.	Host-based IDS

b.	Network-based IDS

c.	Vulnerability scanner

d.   Penetration testing

Ans. b. Network-based IDS

(Network-based IDSs are usually able to detect the initiation of an attack or the ongoing attempts to perpetrate an attack (including denial of service, or DoS). They are, however, unable to provide information about whether an attack was successful or which specific systems, user accounts, files, or applications were affected)

360. If a system wants all computers on its subnet to receive a message, it will use the .... method.

a.   Multicast method

b.   Unicast method

c.   Broadcast method

d.   Anycast method

Ans. c. Broadcast method

(Broadcasting is a method of transferring a message to all recipients simultaneously. If a system wants all computers on its subnet to receive a message, it will use the broadcast method.)

361. Which one of the following is not the characteristic of Ethernet?

a.   Uses broadcast and collision domains

b. Uses an active monitor and beaconing

c. Uses CSMA/CD access method

d. Uses coaxial, twisted-pair, or fiber-optic media

Ans. b. Uses an active monitor and beaconing

(Ethernet uses broadcast and collision domains, CSMA/CD access method as well as coaxial, twisted-pair, or fiber-optic media. While option b is the characteristic of Token Ring)

362. What is used to report multicast group memberships to routers?

a. Classless Inter-Domain Routing (CIDR)

b. Internet Group Management Protocol (IGMP)

c. Address Resolution Protocol (ARP)

d. Internet Control Message Protocol (ICMP)

Ans. b. Internet Group Management Protocol (IGMP)

(The Internet Group Management Protocol (IGMP) is a communications protocol used by hosts and adjacent routers on IPv4 networks to establish multicast group memberships)

363. .... is a UDP-based protocol that allows servers to assign IP addresses to network clients in real time.

a. Simple Mail Transfer Protocol (SMTP)

b. Post Office Protocol (POP3)

c. Dynamic Host Configuration Protocol (DHCP)

d. Hypertext Transport Protocol (HTTP)

Ans. c. Dynamic Host Configuration Protocol (DHCP)

(The Dynamic Host Configuration Protocol (DHCP) is a standardized network protocol used on Internet Protocol (IP) networks. The DHCP is controlled by a DHCP server that dynamically distributes network configuration parameters, such as IP addresses, for interfaces and services.)

364. Which of the following is an effective method to shield networks from unauthenticated DHCP?

a. Use of SYN caches

b. Use of DHCP snooping

c. Use of cookies

d. Use of CSMA/CD access method

Ans. b. Use of DHCP snooping

(An effective method to shield networks from unauthenticated DHCP clients is through the use of DHCP snooping on network switches. DHCP snooping ensures that DHCP servers can assign IP addresses to only selected systems, identified by their MAC addresses)

365. Which of the following protocol is basically IP's "messenger boy."?

a. ICMP

b. DHCP

c. TCP

d. HTTP

Ans. a. ICMP

(The Internet Control Message Protocol (ICMP) is basically IP's "messenger boy." ICMP delivers status messages, reports errors, replies to certain requests, and reports routing information and is used to test connectivity and troubleshoot problems on IP networks)

366. The two main components within the SNMP architecture are

a. Security professionals and users

b. Managers and agents

c. Data owners and company attorneys

d. Routing and switching

Ans. b. Managers and agents

(The two main components within SNMP are managers and agents. The manager is the server portion, which polls different devices to check status information. The agent is a piece of software that runs on a network device, which is commonly integrated into the operating system)

367. A method of resolving hostnames to IP addresses is known as ....

a. FTP

b. DNS

c. URL

d. DHCP

Ans. b. DNS

(The Domain Name Service (DNS) is a method of resolving hostnames to IP addresses so names can be used instead of IP addresses within networked environments)

368. Which of the following is known as third-generation firewalls?

a. Application-level gateway

b. Stateful inspection

c. Circuit-level gateway

d. Static packet-filtering

Ans. b. Stateful inspection

(The stateful inspection technology, also called stateful filtering, is considered as the third generation of firewalls.

This type of firewall performs two operations: first classifies traffic based on the target port. Secondly, it traces traffic status by monitoring each interaction of each specific connection until its closing)

369. A gateway that lies between a network and the Internet and performs transparent routing and address translation is known as ....

a. SMTP-AUTH

b. IGP

c. NAT

d. VRRP

Ans. c. NAT

(Network address translation (NAT) is a method of remapping one IP address space into another by modifying network address information in Internet Protocol (IP) datagram packet headers while they are in transit across a traffic routing device)

370. Which one of the following cannot be considered as the basic types of Network address translation (NAT)?

a. Static mapping

b. Dynamic mapping

c. Port address translation (PAT)

d.   Data mapping

Ans. a. Data mapping

(The three basic types of NAT implementations are static mapping, dynamic mapping and Port address translation (PAT). While Data mapping is not a type of NAT)

371. …………….. refers to the constant changes in the availability of routes.

a.   Route Dampening

b.   Route flapping

c.   Black hole

d.   Routing policy

Ans. b. Route flapping

(Route flapping is a situation where a route fluctuates repeatedly between being announced, then withdrawn, then announced, then withdrawn, and so on)

372. Interior Gateway Routing Protocol (IGRP) was developed by ………………

a.   Cisco Systems

b.   IBM

c.   Sun Microsystems

d.   Netscape

Ans. a. Cisco Systems

(Interior Gateway Routing Protocol (IGRP) is a distance vector interior gateway protocol (IGP) developed by Cisco)

373. .... is a link-state protocol that allows each router to independently build a database of a network's topology.

a.   VRRP

b.   IS-IS

c.   EIGRP

d.   IGRP

Ans. b. IS-IS

(Intermediate System to Intermediate System (IS-IS) is a routing protocol designed to move information efficiently within a computer network, a group of physically connected computers or similar devices)

374. A LAN device that is used to connect LAN segments is known as a ....

a.   Bridge

b.   Repeater

c.   Hub

d.   Router

Ans. a. Bridge

(A bridge is a product that connects a local area network (LAN) to another local area network that uses the same protocol, for example, Ethernet or token ring.)

375. Which of the following can connect two or more LAN segments over a MAN by using telecommunications links?

a. Local bridge

b. Translation bridge

c. Remote bridge

d. Network bridge

Ans. c. Remote bridge

(Remote bridge is a device that connects two LAN segments together that are in geographically dispersed locations. It connects LANs via a WAN)

376. Which of the following combines the functionality of a repeater and the functionality of a bridge?

a. Hubs

b. Routers

c. Switches

d. Packets

Ans. c.   Switches

(Switches combine the functionality of a repeater and the functionality of a bridge. A switch amplifies the electrical signal, like a repeater, and has the built-in circuitry and intelligence of a bridge)

377. .... allow an attacker to gain access to traffic in various VLAN segments?

a.   Double tagging attack

b.   VLAN hopping attacks

c.   Switch spoofing attacks

d.   Spear phishing attacks

Ans. b. VLAN hopping attacks

(VLAN hopping is a computer security exploit, a method of attacking networked resources on a virtual LAN (VLAN). The basic concept behind all VLAN hopping attacks is, for an attacking host on a VLAN to gain access to traffic on other VLANs that would normally not be accessible)

378. What is used to restrict access to one network from another network?

a.   Firewalls

b.   Gateways

c.   Proxy servers

d. Honeypot

Ans. a. Firewalls

(Firewalls are used to restrict access to one network from another network. Most companies use firewalls to restrict access to their networks from the Internet)

379. A firewall technology that makes access decisions based upon network level protocol header values is known as ....

a. Proxy Firewalls

b. Kernel proxy

c. Packet filtering

d. Dynamic Packet filtering

Ans. c. Packet filtering

(Packet filtering is a firewall technique used to control network access by monitoring outgoing and incoming packets and allowing them to pass or halt based on the source and destination Internet Protocol (IP) addresses, protocols and ports)

380. .... works at the session layer of the OSI model and monitors traffic from a network-based view.

a. Circuit-level proxy

b. Application-level proxy

c. Kernel Proxy

d. Next-generation Firewall

Ans. a. Circuit-level proxy

(Circuit-level gateways work at the session layer of the OSI model, or as a "shim-layer" between the application layer and the transport layer of the TCP/IP stack. They monitor TCP handshaking between packets to determine whether a requested session is legitimate)

381. Which of the following is considered as a fifth-generation firewall?

a. Kernel proxy firewall

b. Stateful filtering

c. Packet filtering

d. Application-level proxy

Ans. a. Kernel proxy firewall

(The fifth generation firewall is the kernel proxy, a specialized form that works under the Windows NT Executive, which is the kernel of Windows NT)

382. A firewall that communicates directly with a perimeter router and the internal network is known as a ....

a. Dual-Homed Firewall

b.   Screened host

c.   Screened Subnet

d.   Bastion Host

Ans. b.   Screened host

(Screened host is a firewall that communicates directly with a perimeter router and the internal network)

383. Which of the following is not a firewall rules?

a.   Stealth rule

b.   Silent rule

c.   Noisy rule

d.   Negate rule

Ans. c. Noisy rule

(Some of the common firewall rules include silent rule, stealth rule, cleanup rule, and negate rule)

384. .... is a computer that is intended to be exploited by attackers, with the administrator's goal being to gain information on the attack tactics, techniques, and procedures.

a.   Privilege escalation

b.   Honeypot

c.   Honeynet

d. Honey collection

Ans. b. Honeypot

(A honeypot is a computer system that is set up to act as a decoy to lure cyberattackers, and to detect, deflect or study attempts to gain unauthorized access to information systems)

385. In an SDN architecture, ………….. is a standardized, open-source communication interface between controllers and networking devices.

a. OpenFlow

b. ClosedFlow

c. API

d. Overlays

Ans. a. OpenFlow

(OpenFlow is a standardized, open-source communications interface between controllers and networking devices in an SDN architecture)

386. ………………….. is an EDI infrastructure developed and maintained by a service bureau.

a. Local-Area Network (LAN)

b. Value-Added Network (VAN)

c. Wide-Area Network (WAN)

d.   Storage Area network (SAN)

Ans. b. Value-Added Network (VAN)

(A Value-Added Network (VAN) is a hosted service used for sharing received, stored and forwarded messages. It is an EDI infrastructure developed and maintained by a service bureau)

387. ………………….. is a multipoint, layer 2 VPN that connects two or more customer devices using Ethernet bridging techniques.

a.   Virtual Private LAN Service (VPLS)

b.   Synchronous Optical Networks (SONETs)

c.   Metropolitan Area Network (MAN)

d.   Metro Ethernet

Ans. a. Virtual Private LAN Service (VPLS)

(Virtual Private LAN Services (VPLS) is a class of VPN that supports the connection of multiple sites in a single bridged domain over a managed IP/MPLS network)

388. A method of combining multiple channels of data over a single transmission path is known as …………….

a.   Masquerading

b.   Multicasting

c. Demultiplexing

d. Multiplexing

Ans. d. Multiplexing

(Multiplexing is a popular networking technique that integrates multiple analog and digital signals into a signal transmitted over a shared medium)

389. A connection-oriented channel that provides a consistent data throughput for time-sensitive applications is termed as …………..

a. Available bit rate (ABR)

b. Constant bit rate (CBR)

c. Variable bit rate (VBR)

d. Unspecified bit rate (UBR)

Ans. b. Constant bit rate (CBR)

(Constant bit rate (CBR) is a term used in telecommunications, relating to the quality of service. When referring to codecs, constant bit rate encoding means that the rate at which a codec's output data should be consumed is constant)

390. …………… is a protocol used in networks that use dedicated, leased lines with permanent physical connections.

a. Synchronous Data Link Control (SDLC)

b. High-Level Data Link Control (HDLC)

c. Point-to-Point Protocol (PPP)

d. High-Speed Serial Interface (HSSI)

Ans. a. Synchronous Data Link Control (SDLC)

(Synchronous Data Link Control (SDLC) is a protocol that is used for transferring synchronous, code-transparent, serial-by-bit information over a communications line. Transmission exchanges can be duplex or half-duplex over switched or non-switched lines)

391. An interface that is used to connect multiplexers and routers to high-speed communications services such as ATM and frame relay is known as ....

a. Fiber Distributed Data Interface (FDDI)

b. Small Computer System Interface (SCSI)

c. High-Speed Serial Interface (HSSI)

d. Operating System Interface (OSI)

Ans. c. High-Speed Serial Interface (HSSI)

(High-Speed Serial Interface (HSSI) is a short-distance communications interface that is commonly used to interconnect routing and switching devices on local area networks (LANs) with the higher-speed lines of a WAN)

392. An application that creates the SIP requests for initiating a communication session is known as

....

a. UAS

b. UAA

c. UAC

d. HDLC

Ans. c. UAC

(The UAC is the application that creates the SIP requests for initiating a communication session. UACs are generally messaging tools and soft-phone applications that are used to place VoIP calls)

393. .... is a secure, private connection through an untrusted network.

a. Intranet

b. DMZ

c. Virtual Private Network (VPN)

d. Extranet

Ans. c. Virtual Private Network (VPN)

(A virtual private network (VPN) provides a secure, encrypted tunnel to transmit data between a remote user via the Internet and the company network)

394. .... is used when a specific application

layer traffic type needs protection.

a. L2TP

b. TLS VPN

c. IPSec

d. PPTP

Ans. b. TLS VPN

(TLS VPN is used when a specific application layer traffic type needs protection)

395. Which one of the following is the least secure authentication method?

a. PAP

b. EAP

c. CHAP

d. MS-CHAP

Ans. a. PAP

(PAP is one of the least secure authentication methods because the credentials are sent in cleartext, which renders them easy to capture by network sniffers)

396. Lightweight EAP was developed by ……………..

a. Cisco

b. DELL

c. IBM

d. Swiss Developers

Ans. a. Cisco

(Lightweight EAP was developed by Cisco and was the first implementation of EAP and 802.1X for wireless networks. It uses preshared keys and MS-CHAP to authenticate client and server to each other.)

397. Which of the following is the good example of a link encryption technology?

a. Point-to-Point Tunneling Protocol

b. Transport Layer Security

c. Secure Sockets Layer

d. Routing Information Protocol

Ans. a. Point-to-Point Tunneling Protocol

(The Point-to-Point Tunneling Protocol is an example of a link encryption technology)

398. Which of the following cannot be linked over a VPN?

a. Two distant Internet-connected LANs

b. Two systems without an intermediary network

connection

c. Two systems on the same LAN

d. A system connected to the Internet and a LAN connected to the Internet

Ans. b. Two systems without an intermediary network connection

(An intermediary network connection is required for a VPN link to be established.)

399. Which of the following types of firewall automatically adjusts its filtering rules based on the content of the traffic of existing sessions?

a. Static packet filtering

b. Application-level gateway

c. Stateful inspection

d. Dynamic packet filtering

Ans. d. Dynamic packet filtering

(Dynamic packet-filtering firewalls enable the real-time modification of the filtering rules based on traffic content)

400. Which of the following technology is not specifically associated with 802.11 wireless networking?

a. WAP

b.   WPA

c.   WEP

d.   802.11i

Ans. a. WAP

(Wireless Application Protocol (WAP) is a technology associated with cell phones accessing the Internet rather than 802.11 wireless networking)

401. Which one of the following cannot be considered as a benefit of NAT?

a.   Hiding the internal IP addressing scheme

b.   Sharing a few public Internet addresses with a large number of internal clients

c.   Using the private IP addresses from RFC 1918 on an internal network

d.   filtering network traffic to prevent brute-force attacks

Ans. d.   filtering network traffic to prevent brute-force attacks

(NAT does not protect against or prevent brute-force attacks)

402. The first WLAN standard, 802.11, was developed in the year ....

a. 1997

b. 1994

c. 1998

d. 1996

Ans. a. 1997

(In 1997, the Institute of Electrical and Electronics Engineers (IEEE) created the first WLAN standard. They called it 802.11 after the name of the group formed to oversee its development)

403. Which of the following standard was the first extension to the 802.11 WLAN standard?

a. 802.11a

b. 802.11b

c. 802.11e

d. 802.11f

Ans. b. 802.11b

(802.11b was the first extension to the 802.11 WLAN standard. Although 802.11a was conceived and approved first, it was not released first because of the technical complexity involved with this proposal.)

404. .... is a MAN wireless standard, which allows for wireless traffic to cover a much wider

geographical area.

a. 802.16

b. 802.11ac

c. 802.15.4

d. 802.11e

Ans. a. 802.16

(802.16 is a MAN wireless standard, which allows for wireless traffic to cover a much wider geographical area. This technology is also referred to as broadband wireless access)

405. .... is the most popular protocols based on the IEEE 802.15.4 standard.

a. WiMAX

b. ZigBee

c. Bluejacking

d. ZWave

Ans. b. ZigBee

(ZigBee is one of the most popular protocols based on the IEEE 802.15.4 standard. It is intended to be simpler and cheaper than most WPAN protocols and is very popular in the embedded device market)

406. Why was ICMP developed?

a. To send status messages

b. To hold user data

c. To transmit user data

d. To prevent attack

Ans. a. To send status messages

(ICMP was developed to send status messages, not to hold or transmit user data)

407. ………………. is a technical specification indicating how multimedia data and e-mail binary attachments are to be transferred.

a. E-mail Encryption Standards

b. Multipurpose Internet Mail Extensions (MIME)

c. Pretty Good Privacy

d. Software Cryptography Systems

Ans. b. Multipurpose Internet Mail Extensions (MIME)

(MIME (Multipurpose Internet Mail Extensions) is a standard which was proposed by Bell Communications in 1991 in order to expand upon the limited capabilities of email, and in particular to allow documents (such as images, sound, and text) to be inserted in a message)

408. ICMP is used as the core protocol for a network tool called ....

a. URL encode

b. DNS check

c. Traceroute

d. Spam blacklist check

Ans. c. Traceroute

(Internet Control Message Protocol (ICMP) is used as the core protocol for a network tool called Traceroute)

409. .... is a complete cryptosystem that uses cryptographic protection to protect e-mail and files.

a. Multipurpose Internet Mail Extensions

b. Gnu Privacy Guard

c. Threshold cryptosystem

d. Pretty Good Privacy

Ans. d. Pretty Good Privacy

(Pretty Good Privacy (PGP) is an encryption program that provides cryptographic privacy and authentication for data communication. PGP is used for signing, encrypting, and decrypting texts, e-mails, files, directories, and whole disk partitions and to increase the security of e-mail communications)

410. Who created the first version of Pretty Good Privacy (PGP) encryption?

a.   Phil Zimmermann

b.   Hal Finney

c.   Nosaj Thing

d.   Andreas Buhl

Ans. a. Phil Zimmermann

(Pretty Good Privacy (PGP) was designed by Phil Zimmerman as a freeware e-mail security program and was released in 1991)

411. What is the name of the text file that a browser maintains on the user's hard drive or memory segment?

a.   Honeypot

b.   Cookies

c.   Cache

d.   Footprints

Ans. b.   Cookies

(Cookies are text files that a browser maintains on a user's hard drive or memory segment in order to provide a persistent, customized web experience for each visit)

412. .... is a collection of compromised PCs (often called zombies) organized in a network controlled by a third party.

a. Botnet

b. Bot herder

c. Honeypot

d. Bots

Ans. a. Botnet

(A botnet is a collection of Internet-connected devices, each of which is running one or more bots. Botnets can be used to perform distributed denial-of-service attack (DDoS attack), steal data, send spam, and allow the attacker access to the device and its connection)

413. An attack that forces the victim to use a malicious DNS server instead of the legitimate one is known as.........

a. Network eavesdropping

b. DNS hijacking

c. Ping of Death

d. Sniffing Attack

Ans. b. DNS hijacking

(DNS hijacking (sometimes referred to as DNS redirection) is a type of malicious attack that overrides a computer's TCP/IP settings to point it at a rogue DNS server, thereby invalidating the default DNS settings)

414. Which one of the following does not fit into the category of a DNS Hijacking?

a. Host based

b. Network based

c. Server based

d. Model based

Ans. d. Model based

(The three categories of a DNS Hijacking include host based, network based, and server based)

415. For which of the following, tunnel connections need not to be established?

a. WAN links

b. LAN pathways

c. Dial-up connections

d. Stand-alone systems

Ans. d. Stand-alone systems

(A stand-alone system has no need for tunneling because

no communications between systems are occurring and no intermediary network is present)

416. ………………….. is needed to allow an outside entity to initiate communications with an internal system behind a NAT proxy.

a. IPSec tunnel

b. Static mode NAT

c. Static private IP address

d. Reverse DNS

Ans. b. Static mode NAT

(Static mode NAT is needed to allow an outside entity to initiate communications with an internal system behind a NAT proxy)

417. Why it is so difficult to stop spam?

a. Filters are ineffective at blocking inbound messages.

b. The source address is usually spoofed.

c. It is an attack requiring little expertise.

d. Spam can cause denial-of-service attacks.

Ans. b. The source address is usually spoofed.

(It is often difficult to stop spam because the source of

the messages is usually spoofed)

418. What do most Virtual Private Networks (VPNs) use to protect transmitted data?

a. Obscurity

b. Encryption

c. Encapsulation

d. Transmission logging

Ans. b. Encryption

(Most VPNs use encryption to protect transmitted data. Obscurity, encapsulation, and transmission logging do not protect data as it is transmitted)

419. Which one of the following is not a VPN protocol?

a. PPTP

b. L2F

c. SLIP

d. IPSec

Ans. c. SLIP

(SLIP is a dial-up connection protocol, a forerunner of PPP. It is not a VPN protocol.)

420. What can be bypassed if the operating system does not have packet forwarding or routing disabled?

a. Dual-homed firewalls

b. Multihomed Firewalls

c. Stateful inspection firewalls

d. standalone firewalls

Ans. a. Dual-homed firewalls

(Dual-homed firewalls can be bypassed if the operating system does not have packet forwarding or routing disabled)

421. …………….. is a signaling protocol widely used for VoIP communications sessions.

a. RIP

b. IP

c. SLIP

d. SIP

Ans. a. SIP

(The Session Initiation Protocol (SIP) is a communications protocol for signaling and controlling multimedia communication sessions in applications of Internet telephony for voice and video calls, in private IP telephone systems, as well as in instant messaging over Internet Protocol (IP) networks)

422. The loss of signal strength when a cable exceeds its maximum length is known as …………..

a.   Crosstalk

b.   Attenuation

c.   Cabling Problems

d.   Collision

Ans. b. Attenuation

(Attenuation is a general term that refers to a reduction in signal strength, commonly occurring while transmitting analog or digital signals over long distances)

423. …………….. is an encapsulation protocol used for telecommunication connections.

a.   Synchronous Data Link Control (SDLC)

b.   High-Level Data Link Control (HDLC)

c.   Point-to-Point Protocol (PPP)

d.   High-Speed Serial Interface (HSSI)

Ans. c. Point-to-Point Protocol (PPP)

(In computer networking, Point-to-Point Protocol (PPP)

is a data link layer (layer 2) communications protocol used to establish a direct connection between two nodes)

424. The act of combining the server, storage, and network capabilities into a single framework is known as ....

a. Network convergence

b. Network Topology

c. Network eavesdropping

d. Network layer

Ans. a. Network convergence

(Network convergence is the efficient coexistence of telephone, video and data communication within a single network. The use of multiple communication modes on a single network offers convenience and flexibility that are not possible with separate infrastructures)

425. What authentication protocol offers no encryption or protection for logon credentials?

a. PAP

b. CHAP

c. SSL

d. RADIUS

Ans. a. PAP

(PAP, or Password Authentication Protocol, is a standardized authentication protocol for PPP. PAP transmits usernames and passwords in the clear. It offers no form of encryption. It simply provides a means to transport the logon credentials from the client to the authentication server)

426. ……….. is a type of denial of service attack in which a system is flooded with spoofed ping message.

a. Smurf Attack

b. Phishing

c. E-mail spoofing

d. Scam

Ans. a. Smurf Attack

(The Smurf attack is a distributed denial-of-service attack in which large numbers of Internet Control Message Protocol (ICMP) packets with the intended victim's spoofed source IP are broadcast to a computer network using an IP broadcast address.)

427. A private telephone switch that is located on a company's property is known as ……………

a. Sequenced Packet Exchange (SPX)

b. Private Branch Exchange (PBX)

c. Multipurpose Internet Mail Extensions

d. Gnu Privacy Guard

Ans. b. Private Branch Exchange (PBX)

(A PBX (private branch exchange) is a telephone system within an enterprise that switches calls between enterprise users on local lines while allowing all users to share a certain number of external phone lines)

428. Which one of the following is not true with regard to firewalls?

a. They are able to log traffic information.

b. They are able to block viruses.

c. They are able to issue alarms based on suspected attacks.

d. They are unable to prevent internal attacks.

Ans. b. They are able to block viruses.

(Most firewalls offer extensive logging, auditing, and monitoring capabilities as well as alarms and even basic IDS functions. Firewalls are unable to block viruses or malicious code transmitted through otherwise authorized communication channels)

429. The process of finding netBIOS user names, computer names, workgroup names and domain names is known as ……..

a. Enumeration

b. Remuneration

c. Polling

d. Masquerading

Ans. a. Enumeration

(Enumeration is a process that involves gathering information about a network such as the hosts, connected devices, along with usernames, group information and related data. Using protocols like ICMP and SNMP, network enumeration offers a better view of the network for either protection or hacking purposes)

430. A criminal who controls all the computers in the botnet via one or more command and control servers is called as ……………..

a. Bot herder

b. Zombie

c. Botnet

d. Attacker

Ans. a. Bot herder

(Bot herders are hackers who use automated techniques to scan specific network ranges and find vulnerable systems, such as machines without current security patches, on which to install their bot program)

Chapter 12
Identity and Access Management

431. The flow of information between a subject and an object is known as

a.   Subject

b.   Access

c.   Entity

d.   Dataflow

Ans. b. Access

(Access is the flow of information between a subject and an object)

432. .... is an active entity that requests access to an object or the data within an object.

a.   Subject

b.   Directory

c.   Database

d.   Field

Ans. a. Subject

(A subject is an active entity that requests access to an object, resource or the data within an object)

433. Which of the following is the primary objective of access control?

a. Preserve confidentiality, integrity, and availability of systems.

b. Ensure that only valid objects can authenticate on a system.

c. Prevent unauthorized access to subjects.

d. Ensure that all subjects are authenticated.

Ans. a. Preserve confidentiality, integrity, and availability of systems

(Access control mechanisms help to prevent losses, including any loss of confidentiality, loss of availability, or loss of integrity. Subjects authenticate on a system and objects are accessed. A first step in access control is the identification and authentication of subjects, but access control also includes authorization and accountability)

434. Which one of the following is not needed for system accountability?

a. Identification

b. Authentication

c. Auditing

d. Authorization

Ans. d. Authorization

(Authorization is not needed for accountability. However, users must be identified and authenticated and their actions logged using some type of auditing to provide accountability)

435. Which of the following types of access control attempts to direct, confine, or control the actions of subjects to force or encourage compliance with security policies?

a. Preventive Access Control

b. Directive Access Control

c. Corrective Access Control

d. Recovery Access Control

Ans. b. Directive Access Control

(A directive access control is deployed to direct, confine, or control the actions of subject to force or encourage compliance with security policies)

436. What gathers the necessary information from multiple sources and stores it in one central directory?

a. Meta-directory

b. Active Directory

c. Multiple directory

d. Open directory

Ans. a. Meta-directory

(Meta-Directory is a set of software components that synchronize data from one or more external data sources into a single repository. It is a directory that acts as a superset of all other directories)

437. ……………. is the main gateway between users and the corporate web-based resources and information.

a. SSO software

b. WAM software

c. Meta-directory

d. Access control software

Ans. b. WAM software

(The WAM software is the main gateway between users and the corporate web-based resources. It is commonly a plug-in for a web server, so it works as a front-end process)

438. A hierarchical tree-like structure system that tracks subjects and their authorization chains is known as ……………

a. Authoritative system of record (ASOR)

b. Record Retention

c. Records Series Management Tool (RSMT)

d. Records Classification System

Ans. a. Authoritative system of record (ASOR)

(The Authoritative system of record (ASOR) is the hierarchical parent system that track users, their accounts, and their authorization chains)

439. A system that scans a person's physiological attribute or behavioral trait and compares it to a record created in an earlier enrollment process is ....

a. Records Classification System

b. Scanner

c. Biometric system

d. Authoritative system of record

Ans. c. Biometric system

(A biometric system is a technological system that uses information about a person to identify that person. Biometric systems rely on specific data about unique biological traits in order to work effectively)

440. The process of tracking and recording subject activities within logs is known as ....

a. Auditing

b. Authorization

c. Authenticating

d. Accounting

Ans. a. Auditing

(Auditing is the process of tracking and recording subject activities within logs. Logs typically record who took an action, when and where the action was taken, and what the action was.)

441. Which one of the following is the most accurate Biometric system?

a. Palm Scan

b. Hand Geometry

c. Iris Scan

d. Fingerprint

Ans. c. Iris Scan

(Focusing on the colored area around the pupil, iris scans are one of the most accurate forms of biometric authentication)

442. Typically, an access control list (ACL) is based on?

a. An object

b. A subject

c. A role

d.   An account

Ans. a. An object

(ACL is based on an object and includes a list of subjects that are granted access. A capability table is focused on a subject and includes a list of objects the subject can access. Roles and accounts are examples of subjects and may be included in an ACL, but they aren't the focus)

443. What type of access controls rely upon the use of labels?

a.   Discretionary

b.   Nondiscretionary

c.   Mandatory

d.   Role based

Ans. c. Mandatory

(Mandatory access controls rely on use of labels for subjects and objects. Discretionary access control systems allow an owner of an object to control access to the object. Nondiscretionary access controls have centralized management such as a rule-based access control deployed on a firewall. Role-based access controls define a subject's access based on job-related roles)

444. In …………….. attack, the password is copied and reused by the attacker at another time.

a. Replay attack

b. Dictionary attacks

c. Brute-force attack

d. Rainbow table

Ans. a. Replay attack

A replay attack (also known as playback attack) is a form of network attack in which a valid data transmission is maliciously or fraudulently repeated or delayed.

445. Fact- or opinion-based information that is used to verify an individual's identity is known as ....

a. Cognitive passwords

b. Biometric systems

c. Hand Geometry

d. Dynamic passwords

Ans. a. Cognitive passwords

(A cognitive password is a form of knowledge-based authentication that requires a user to answer a question, presumably something they intrinsically know, to verify their identity)

446. Which one of the following does not fit in the category of access control models?

a. Discretionary

b. Mandatory

c. Role-based

d. Operation-based

Ans. d. Operation-based

(There are three main access control models which includes discretionary access control, mandatory access control, and role-based access control)

447. .... is a centralized access control technique that allows a subject to be authenticated only once on a system and to access multiple resources without authenticating again.

a. Kerberos

b. Single sign-on

c. Double sign-on

d. Decentralized access control

Ans. b. Single sign-on

(Single sign-on (SSO) is a property of access control of multiple related, yet independent, software systems. With this property, a user logs in with a single ID and password to gain access to a connected system or systems without using different usernames or passwords, or in some configurations seamlessly sign on at each system)

448. What tool is used by a security professional to test the strength of a password?

a. Password checker

b. Token device

c. Password generator

d. Password detector

Ans. a. Password checker

(Password checker is a tool used by a security professional to test the strength of a password)

449. Random values that are added to the encryption process to add more complexity and randomness are known as ....

a. Peppers

b. Salts

c. Pseudo-Random Number

d. Python code

Ans. b. Salts

(In password protection, Salt is a random string of data used to modify a password hash)

450. What generates and displays one-time passwords that are synchronized with an

authentication server?

a. Asynchronous token

b. Synchronous token

c. Smartcards

d. Memory cards

Ans. b. Synchronous token

(A synchronous token device synchronizes with the authentication service by using time or counter as the core part of the authentication process. Synchronous tokens use a secret key and time to create a one-time password)

451. ………………….. are nonintrusive attacks that are used to uncover sensitive information about how a component works, without trying to compromise any type of flaw or weakness.

a. Fault generation

b. Side-channel attacks

c. Mathematical attack

d. Birthday attack

Ans. b. Side-channel attacks

(Side-channel attacks aim to retrieve secret data from a crypto-graphic system by observing factors outside the normal computation. These types of attacks are designed to be non-intrusive and to find out sensitive information about how component works)

452. .... uses needleless and ultrasonic vibration to remove the outer protective material on the card's circuits.

a. Software attacks

b. Microprobing

c. Fault generation

d. Side-channel attacks

Ans. b. Microprobing

(Microprobing is one of the well-known invasive attacks. Microprobing means attaching microscopic needles onto the internal wiring of a chip; this can be used to either read out internal secrets that are not intended to leave the chip, or it can be used for fault attacks)

453. A technology that provides data communication through the use of radio waves is known as ....

a. Service-oriented architecture (SOA)

b. Radio frequency interference (RFI)

c. Radio-frequency identification (RFID)

d. Radio-frequency spectrum channels

Ans. c. Radio-frequency identification (RFID)

(RFID (radio frequency identification) is a technology that incorporates the use of electromagnetic or electrostatic coupling in the radio frequency (RF) portion of the electromagnetic spectrum to uniquely identify an object, animal, or person)

454. .... is an example of an SSO system for distributed environments, and is a de facto standard for heterogeneous networks.

a. MS-CHAP

b. Password Authentication Protocol

c. RADIUS

d. Kerberos

Ans. d. Kerberos

(Kerberos is an authentication protocol that was designed in the mid-1980s as part of MIT's Project Athena. It is an example of an SSO system for distributed environments, and is a de facto standard for heterogeneous networks)

455. Kerberos uses .... to provide end-to-end security and to authenticate clients to servers.

a. Symmetric key cryptography

b. Asymmetric key cryptography

c. Public-key encryption

d. Pre-shared key encryption

Ans. a. Symmetric key cryptography

(Kerberos uses symmetric key cryptography to authenticate clients to servers and provides end-to-end security. Although it allows the use of passwords for authentication, it was designed specifically to eliminate the need to transmit passwords over the network)

456. Which is the most important component in a Kerberos environment?

a. Kerberos Authentication Server

b. Network programs

c. Key Distribution Center (KDC)

d. Ticket Granting Ticket (TGT)

Ans. c. Key Distribution Center (KDC)

(The Key Distribution Center (KDC) is the most important component in a Kerberos environment. It is responsible for managing all the secret keys, authenticating all users, and issuing tickets to valid users)

457. .... access control uses fences, security policies, security awareness training, and antivirus software to stop an unwanted or unauthorized activity from occurring.

a. Preventive

b. Detective

c. Corrective

d. Authoritative

Ans. a. Preventive

(A preventive access control is deployed to stop an unwanted or unauthorized activity from occurring. While detective controls discover the activity after it has occurred, and corrective controls attempt to reverse any problems caused by the activity. Access controls are not categorized as authoritative)

458. Which one of the following is not used to support single sign-on (SSO)?

a. Kerberos

b. Federated identity management system

c. TACACS+

d. SPML

Ans. c. TACACS+

(TACACS+ is a centralized authentication service used for remote access clients but not for single sign-on. Kerberos and federated identity management systems are used to support single sign-on. Service Provisioning Markup Language (SPML) is a language used with some federated identity systems)

459. While attempting to identify risks, what should an organization identify first?

a. Assets

b. Threats

c. Vulnerabilities

d. Public attacks

Ans. a. Assets

(An organization must first identify the value of assets so that they can focus on risks on their most valuable assets. They can then identify threats and vulnerabilities. Public attacks can be evaluated to determine risk to the organization, but this should not be the first step)

460. What should an organization do to identify weaknesses?

a. Asset valuation

b. Vulnerability analysis

c. Threat modeling

d. Access review

Ans. b. Vulnerability analysis

(A vulnerability analysis identifies weaknesses and can include periodic vulnerability scans and penetration tests. Asset valuation determines the value of assets, not weaknesses. Threat modeling attempts to identify threats, but doesn't identify weaknesses. An access review audits account management and object access practices)

461. Which of the following types of attack attempts to detect flaws in smart cards?

a.   Whaling

b.   Side-channel attack

c.   Brute-force

d.   Rainbow table attack

Ans. b. Side-channel attack

(A side-channel attack is a passive, noninvasive attack to observe the operation of a device. Methods include power monitoring, timing, and fault analysis attacks. Whaling is a type of phishing attack that targets high-level executives. A brute-force attack attempts to discover passwords by using all possible character combinations. A rainbow table attack is used to crack passwords)

462. An interactive application that provides a specific type of web service functionality is known as ....

a.   Web portal

b.   Federated identity

c.   Portlet

d.   Portability

Ans. c. Portlet

(Portlet is a component of a portal website that provides access to some specific information source or application, such as news updates, technical support, or an e-mail program among many other possibilities)

463. .... is a universal and foundational standard that provides a structure for other independent markup languages to be built from and still allow for interoperability.

a.   XML

b.   SGML

c.   SPML

d.   GML

Ans. a. XML

(XML is a universal and foundational standard that provides a structure for other independent markup languages to be built from and still allow for interoperability)

464. Which of the following markup language is used to display static web pages?

a.   SAML

b.   HTML

c. XML

d. SPML

Ans. b. HTML

(Hypertext Markup Language (HTML) is commonly used to display static web pages. HTML describes how data is displayed using tags to manipulate the size and color of the text)

465. An XML-based language that is commonly used to exchange authentication and authorization (AA) information between federated organizations is called as ....

a. Hypertext Markup Language (HTML)

b. Security Assertion Markup Language (SAML)

c. Service Provisioning Markup Language (SPML)

d. Directory Service Markup Language (DSML)

Ans. b. Security Assertion Markup Language (SAML)

(Security Assertion Markup Language (SAML) is an XML standard that allows the exchange of authentication and authorization data to be shared between security domains)

466. The Extensible Access Control Markup Language (XACML) is used to ....

a. Define access control policies

b. Exchange user information

c. Exchange authentication and authorization (AA) information

d. Display static web pages

Ans. a. Define access control policies

(Extensible Access Control Markup Language (XACML) is used to define access control policies within an XML format, and it commonly implements role-based access controls)

467. IBM developed a ticket-based authentication system known as …………..

a. NetSP

b. SESAME

c. KryptoKnight

d. Kerberos

Ans. c. KryptoKnight

(KryptoKnight is a ticket-based authentication system developed by IBM)

468. Why was SESAME developed?

a. To address weaknesses in Kerberos

b. To prevent unauthorized access

c. To protect credentials

d. To exchange user information

Ans. a. To address weaknesses in Kerberos

(The Secure European System for Applications in a Multivendor Environment (SESAME) is a ticket-based authentication system developed to address weaknesses in Kerberos)

469. .... is an open standard designed to work with HTTP and it allows users to log on with one account.

a. IDaaS

b. OpenID

c. Public systems

d. OAuth

Ans. d. OAuth

(OAuth (Open Authorization) is an open standard for token-based authentication and authorization on the Internet)

470. A framework that dictates how subjects access object is known as ....

a. Access Control Model

b. OSI Model

c. TCP model

d. Business model

Ans. a. Access Control Model

(An Access Control Model is an abstract, formal security model of protection state in computer systems that characterizes the rights of each subject with respect to every object in the system)

471. In the electronic authentication process, who executes the identity proofing?

a. Subscriber

b. Registration authority

c. Applicant

d. Credential service provider

Ans. b. Registration authority

(The Registration authority performs the identity proofing after registering the applicant with the CSP. An applicant becomes a subscriber of the CSP)

472. Which of the following access control model use a centrally administrated set of controls to determine how subjects and objects interact?

a. Role-based access control (RBAC)

b. Mandatory access control

c. Discretionary Access Control

d. Rule-Based Access Control (RAC)

Ans. a. Role-based access control (RBAC)

(Non-discretionary or role based access control (RBAC), uses a centrally administrated set of controls to determine how subjects and objects interact)

473. Which of the following focuses more on the trends and patterns of data than on the actual content?

a. Traffic analysis

b. Event logging

c. Keystroke monitoring

d. Security auditing

Ans. a. Traffic analysis

(Traffic analysis focuses more on the patterns and trends of data rather than the actual content. Keystroke monitoring records specific keystrokes to capture data. Event logging logs specific events to record data. Security auditing records security events and/or reviews logs to detect security incidents)

474. A network protocol that provides client/server authentication and authorization, and audits remote users is termed as ....

a. RADIUS

b. PPP

c. CHAP

d. TACACS

Ans. a. RADIUS

(Remote Authentication Dial-In User Service (RADIUS) is a networking protocol that provides centralized Authentication, Authorization, and Accounting (AAA or Triple A) management for users who connect and use a network service)

475. TACACS+ was developed by …………..

a. IBM

b. Cisco

c. Netscape

d. Phil Zimmermann

Ans. b. Cisco

(Terminal Access Controller Access-Control System Plus (TACACS+) is a protocol developed by Cisco and released as an open standard beginning in 1993. Although derived from TACACS, TACACS+ is a separate protocol that handles authentication, authorization, and accounting (AAA) services)

476. Which of the following is not the function of the Diameter?

a. Authentication

b. Authorization

c. Accounting

d. Analysis

Ans. d. Analysis

(Diameter provides the AAA functionality which includes Authentication, Authorization and Accounting)

477. Which of the following process does not belong to the identity and access provisioning life cycle?

a. Creation of account

b. Management of account

c. Altering of account

d. Deletion of account

Ans. c. Altering of account

(The identity and access provisioning life cycle refers to the creation, management, and deletion of accounts. Although these activities may seem mundane, they are essential to a system's access control capabilities)

478. The act of deleting specific incriminating data within audit logs is called as ....

a.   Scrubbing

b.   Sniffing

c.   Enumeration

d.   Obliterating

Ans. a. Scrubbing

(Scrubbing is the process of amending or removing data in a database that is incorrect, incomplete, improperly formatted, or duplicated)

479. Which one of the following is an example of technical access controls?

a.   Network architecture

b.   Network segregation

c.   Perimeter security

d.   Computer controls

Ans. a. network architecture

(Network architecture is an example of technical access controls while network segregation, perimeter security, and computer controls are examples of physical access controls)

480. What type of auditing is used to track each keystroke made by a user?

a.   Audit trails

b.   Dynamic Monitoring

c.   Keystroke Monitoring

d.   Basic Monitoring

Ans. c. Keystroke Monitoring

(Keystroke monitoring is a type of monitoring that can review and record keystrokes entered by a user during an active session)

481. A set of precomputed hash values that represents password combinations is called as ....

a.   Rainbow table

b.   Replay attack

c.   Authorization creep

d.   Brute-force

Ans. a. Rainbow table

(A rainbow table is a set of precomputed hash values that represents password combinations. Rainbow tables are used in password attack processes and usually produce results more quickly than dictionary or brute-force attacks)

482. ……….. is a variant of phishing that targets senior or high-level executives such as CEOs and presidents within a company.

a. Rainbow table

b. Spear phishing

c. Whaling

d. Vishing

Ans. c. Whaling

(Whaling is a form of phishing that targets high-level executives. Spear phishing targets a specific group of people but not necessarily high-level executives. Vishing is a form of phishing that commonly uses Voice over IP (VoIP). Rainbow table attacks are a type of attack that attempts to discover the password from the hash)

483. Which of the following is the best choice to support federated identity management systems?

a. Kerberos

b. Hypertext Markup Language (HTML)

c. Extensible Markup Language (XML)

d. Service Provisioning Markup Language (SPML)

Ans. d. Service Provisioning Markup Language (SPML)

(SPML is an XML-based framework used to exchange

user information for single sign-on (SSO) between organizations within a federated identity management system. Kerberos supports SSO in a single organization, not a federation. HTML only describes how data is displayed. XML could be used, but it would require redefining tags already defined in SPML)

484. Which of the following access control method is considered user-directed?

a. Nondiscretionary

b. Mandatory

c. Identity-based

d. Discretionary

Ans. d. Discretionary

(The Discretionary access control model allows users, or data owners, the discretion of letting other users access their resources. DAC is implemented by ACLs, which the data owner can configure)

485. .... is not a part of Kerberos authentication implementation?

a. Message authentication code

b. Ticket granting service

c. Authentication service

d. Users, programs, and services

Ans. a. Message authentication code

(Message authentication code (MAC) is a cryptographic function and is not a key component of Kerberos. Kerberos is made up of a KDC, a realm of principals (users, services, applications, and devices), an authentication service, tickets, and a ticket granting service.)

486. What role does biometrics play in access control?

a. Authorization

b. Availability

c. Authentication

d. Accountability

Ans. c. Authentication

(Biometrics is a technology that validates an individual's identity by reading a physical attribute. In some cases, biometrics can be used for identification, but that was not listed as an answer choice)

487. Which of the following is derived from a passphrase?

a. Personal password

b. Virtual password

c. User ID

d. Valid password

Ans. b. Virtual password

(Passphrase is a plain-language phrase, typically longer than a password, from which a virtual password is derived)

488. The process of detecting an unauthorized use of, or attack upon, a computer, network, or telecommunications infrastructure is known as ....

a. Intrusion detection

b. Authentication

c. Authorization

d. Discretion

Ans. a. Intrusion detection

(Intrusion detection is the process of monitoring the events occurring in a computer system or network and analyzing them for signs of possible incidents, which are violations or imminent threats of violation of computer security policies, acceptable use policies, or standard security practices)

489. Which of the following is the function of network-based IDSs?

a. Provides end-to-end transmission

b. Monitor network communications

c. Establishes connection between two applications

d. Transforms bits to electrical signals

Ans. b. Monitor network communications

(Network-based intrusion system (NBIS) tries to detect malicious activity such as denial-of-service attacks, port scans and attacks by monitoring the network traffic)

490. Which of the following is not a common component of IDS?

a. Sensors interfaces

b. Analyzers interfaces

c. Administrator interfaces

d. Active interfaces

Ans. d. Active interfaces

(Although different types of intrusion detection system (IDS) products are available, they all have three common components which include sensors, analyzers, and administrator interfaces)

491. In discretionary access control security, who has delegation authority to grant access to data?

a. User

b. Security officer

c. Security policy

d. Owner

Ans. d. Owner

(Only the data owner can decide who can access the resources he owns)

492. What can be installed on individual workstations and/or servers to watch for inappropriate or anomalous activity?

a. Network-based IDS (NIDS)

b. Host-based IDS (HIDS)

c. Network Node Intrusion Detection System (NNIDS)

d. Knowledge-based (Signature-based) IDS

Ans. b. Host-based IDS (HIDS)

(A host-based intrusion detection system (HIDS) is an intrusion detection system that monitors and analyzes the internals of a computing system as well as (in some cases) the network packets on its network interfaces)

493. Which one of the following does not fit into the category of Anomaly-based IDS?

a. Statistical anomaly–based

b. Protocol anomaly–based

c. Traffic anomaly–based

d. Temporal anomaly–based

Ans. d. Temporal anomaly–based

(The three types of Anomaly-based IDS are statistical anomaly–based, protocol anomaly–based, and traffic anomaly–based while Temporal anomaly–based do not exist)

494. Which one of the following is the function of Traffic Anomaly–Based IDS?

a. Reconfigure important settings

b. Detect an attack in progress

c. Detect changes in traffic patterns

d. Provide end-to-end transmission

Ans. c. Detect changes in traffic patterns

(Most behavioral-based IDSs have traffic anomaly–based filters, which detect changes in traffic patterns, as in DoS attacks or a new service that appears on the network)

495. ………….. is made up of a knowledge base, inference engine, and rule-based programming.

a. An Expert system

b. A stand-alone system

c. Operating System

d. Knowledge system

Ans. a. An Expert system

(An expert system is made up of a knowledge base, inference engine, and rule-based programming)

496. What does Network-based IDSs use for monitoring purposes?

a. Sensors

b. Analyzer

c. Traffic

d. Networks

Ans. a. Sensors

(Network-based IDSs use sensors for monitoring purposes. A sensor, which works as an analysis engine, is placed on the network segment the IDS is responsible for monitoring.)

497. .... can help mitigate the success of an online brute-force attack?

a. Rainbow table

b. Account lockout

c. Salting passwords

d. Encryption of password

Ans. b. Account lockout

(An account lockout policy will prevent someone from logging into an account after they have entered an incorrect password too many times. A rainbow table is used by an attacker in offline password attacks, and password salts reduce the effectiveness of rainbow tables. Encrypting the password protects the password, but not against a brute-force attack)

498. Which of the following indicates the primary purpose of an intrusion detection system (IDS)?

a. Detect abnormal activity

b. Diagnose system failures

c. Rate system performance

d. Test a system for vulnerabilities

Ans. a. Detect abnormal activity

(An IDS automates the inspection of audit logs and real-time system events to detect abnormal activity indicating unauthorized system access. Although IDSs can detect system failures and monitor system performance, they don't include the ability to diagnose system failures or rate system performance. Vulnerability scanners are used to test systems for vulnerabilities)

499. Which of the following is true with regard to

host-based intrusion detection system (HIDS)?

a. It monitors an entire network.

b. It monitors a single system.

c. It's invisible to attackers and authorized users.

d. It cannot detect malicious code.

Ans. b. It monitors a single system.

(An HIDS monitors a single system looking for abnormal activity. A network-based IDS (NIDS) watches for abnormal activity on a network. An HIDS is normally visible as a running process on a system and provides alerts to authorized users.)

500. ………….. can be used to reduce the amount of logged or audited data using non-statistical methods?

a. Clipping levels

b. Sampling

c. Log analysis

d. Alarm triggers

Ans. a. Clipping levels

(Clipping is a form of non-statistical sampling that reduces the amount of logged data based on a clipping-level threshold. Sampling is a statistical method that extracts meaningful data from audit logs. Log analysis reviews log information looking for trends, patterns, and abnormal or unauthorized events. An alarm trigger is a notification sent to administrators when specific events or thresholds occur)

501. The company with high turnover rate should opt for which access control structure?

a. Role-based

b. Decentralized

c. Rule-based

d. Discretionary

Ans. a. Role-based

(A role-based structure is easier on the administrator because he only has to create one role, assign all of the necessary rights and permissions to that role, and plug a user into that role when needed. Otherwise, he would need to assign and extract permissions and rights on all systems as each individual came and left the company)

502. The technology that allows a user to remember just one password is ……………..

a. Password generation

b. Password dictionaries

c. Password rainbow tables

d. Password synchronization

Ans. d. Password synchronization

(Password synchronization technologies can allow a user to maintain just one password across multiple systems. The product will synchronize the password to other systems and applications, which happens transparently to the user)

503. The XACML does not define or support which of the following?

a. Trust management

b. Privilege management

c. Policy language

d. Query language

Ans. a. Trust management

(The extensible access control markup language (XACML) is a standard for managing access control policy and supports the enterprise-level privilege management. It includes a policy language and a query language. However, XACML does not define authority delegation and trust management)

504. Which of the following is an example of Corrective access control?

a. Restore backups

b. Patch systems

c. Signs

d. Hardware

Ans. b. Patch systems

(Examples of corrective access controls include intrusion detection systems, patch systems, antivirus solutions, alarms, mantraps, business continuity planning, and security policies)

505. Which of the following biometric methods obtains the patterns and colors around a person's pupil?

a. Iris scan

b. Palm scan

c. Retina pattern

d. Fingerprint

Ans. a. Iris scan

(Iris scan focuses on the colored area around the pupil. Iris scans are considered more acceptable by general users than retina scans because they don't reveal personal medical information)

506. Safes that are large enough to provide walk-in access are known as ……………..

a. Wall safe

b. Chests

c. Depositories

d. Vaults

Ans. d. Vaults

(Vaults are types of safes that are large enough to provide walk-in access)

507. Which of the following is the first step in protecting data's confidentiality?

a. Identify sensitive information

b. Craft a job description

c. Execute a risk ranking

d. Protecting Privacy

Ans. a. Identify sensitive information

(The first step in protecting data's confidentiality is to identify which information is sensitive and to what degree, and then implement security mechanisms to protect it properly)

508. Which one of the following is not a key aspect in creating or issuing secure identities?

a. Uniqueness

b. Nondescriptive

c. Issuance

d. Cessation

Ans. d. Cessation

(Creating or issuing secure identities should include three key aspects: uniqueness, nondescriptive, and issuance)

509. Which of the following is an example of a vulnerability scanner?

a. Nmap

b. SATAN

c. OWASP ZAP

d. Acunetix

Ans. b. SATAN

(Security Administrator Tool for Analyzing Networks (SATAN) was a free software vulnerability scanner for analyzing networked computer)

510. The WAM console allows the .... to configure access levels, authentication requirements, and account setup workflow steps and to perform overall maintenance.

a. Administrators

b. Users

c. Security professional

d. Manager

Ans. a. Administrators

(The WAM console allows the administrator to configure access levels, authentication requirements, and account setup workflow steps and to perform overall maintenance)

511. Which of the following biometric system is extremely invasive and involve a number of privacy issues?

a. Palm Scan

b. Retina scans

c. Hand Geometry

d. Fingerprint

Ans. b. Retina scans

(Retina scans are extremely invasive and involve a number of privacy issues)

512. An SSO technology allows ……….. to authenticate one time and then access resources in the environment without needing to reauthenticate.

a. Administrators

b. Users

c. Security professional

d. Manager

Ans. b. Users

(SSO technology allows a user to authenticate one time and then access resources in the environment without needing to reauthenticate)

513. ……………. is a method that captures the electrical signals when a person signs a name.

a. Keystroke dynamics

b. Signature dynamics

c. Password generator

d. Hand topology

Ans. b. Signature dynamics

(Signature dynamics is a method that captures the electrical signals when a person signs a name while keystroke dynamics captures electrical signals when a person types a certain phrase)

514. ……………. is a skewed representation of characteristics a person must enter to prove that the subject is a human and not an automated tool as in a software robot.

a. Honeypot

b. CAPTCHA

c. Cognitive passwords

d. Token device

Ans. b. CAPTCHA

(CAPTCHA is a computer program or system intended to distinguish human from machine input, typically as a way of thwarting spam and automated extraction of data from websites)

515. ……………….. is a type of two-factor authentication security device that may be used to authorize the use of computer services.

a. Hard token

b. Soft token

c. Smart card

d. Time-based token

Ans. b. Soft token

(A soft token is a software-based security token that generates a single-use login PIN. Soft tokens are stored on a general-purpose electronic device such as a desktop computer, laptop, PDA, or mobile phone and can be duplicated)

516. The act of generating a number from a string of text is known as ………..

a. Hashing

b. Private Key

c. One-Way Function

d. Encryption

Ans. a. Hashing

(Hashing is generating a value or values from a string of text using a mathematical function)

517. Which of the following is not an example of side-channel attacks?

a. Differential power analysis

b. Electromagnetic analysis

c. Timing analysis

d. Comprehensive analysis

Ans. d. Comprehensive analysis

(Some examples of side-channel attacks that have been carried out on smart cards are differential power analysis (examining the power emissions released during processing), electromagnetic analysis (examining the frequencies emitted), and timing (how long a specific process takes to complete))

518. Who is developing a framework and conformance testing programs specifically for interoperability issues?

e. National Institute of Standards and Technology (NIST)

f. American National Standards Institute (ANSI)

g. Federal Bureau of Investigation

h. National Security Agency

Ans. a. National Institute of Standards and Technology (NIST)

(National Institute of Standards and Technology (NIST) is developing a framework and conformance testing programs specifically for interoperability issues)

519. HyperText Markup Language (HTML) was invented by ………….. to define the structure of web pages.

a. Tatu Ylönen

b. John Mauchly

c. Tim Berners-Lee

d. J. Presper Eckert

Ans. c. Tim Berners-Lee

(Tim Berners-Lee, a scientist at CERN, invented the

HyperText Markup Language (HTML) to define the structure of web pages)

520. Which of the following authentication supports TACACS+?

a. Single-factor authentication

b. Two-factor authentication

c. Three-factor authentication

d. Multi-factor authentication

Ans. b. Two-factor authentication

(Terminal Access Controller Access Control System (TACACS) is available in three variations: TACACS, XTACACS (Extended TACACS), and TACACS+, which features two-factor authentication. TACACS also allows the division of the authentication, authorization, and accounting function, which gives the administrator more control over its deployment)

521. Software faults can be uncovered using ....

a. Differential power analysis

b. Electromagnetic analysis

c. Watchdog timers

d. Timing analysis

Ans. c. Watchdog timers

(Watchdog timers can prevent timing problems, infinite loops, deadlocks, and other software issues)

522. Which one of the following is not the primary types of authentication?

a. Something you remember

b. Something you know

c. Something you are

d. Something you have

Ans. a. Something you remember

(Authentication can be based on one or more of the following three factors - something you know, something you have and something you are)

523. A bank teller most likely fall under .... method of access control system.

a. Discretionary

b. Mandatory

c. Role-based

d. Rule-based

Ans. c. Role-based

(Bank tellers would most likely fall under a role-based access control system. These systems work well for organizations in which employee roles are identical)

524. .... is the easiest and most common form of offline password hash attack used to pick off insecure passwords.

a. Hybrid

b. Dictionary

c. Brute-force

d. Man-in-the-middle

Ans. b. Dictionary

(Dictionary attacks are an easy way to pick off insecure passwords. Passwords based on dictionary words allow attackers to simply perform password guessing or to use more advanced automated methods employing software programs)

525. Which of the following protocols is suggested to be turned off because it transmits usernames and passwords in plaintext?

a. SSH

b. HTTPS

c. Telnet

d. TFTP

Ans. c. Telnet

(Telnet transmits username and password information in clear text and thus can be used by attackers to gain unauthorized access)

526. Which of the following is the best way to store passwords?

a.   In a one-way encrypted file

b.   Using symmetric encryption

c.   Using asymmetric encryption

d.   By means of a digital signature

Ans. a. In a one-way encrypted file

(A salted, one-way encrypted file is the best way to store passwords. Cryptographic solutions to accomplish this include MD5, SHA, and HAVAL. Symmetric, asymmetric, and digital signatures are not the preferred way of storing passwords)

527. Which of the following best describes the term trust?

a.   A one-way-only bridge established between two domains

b.   A two-way-only bridge established between two domains

c.   A security bridge that is established after a valid

authentication

d. A security bridge that is established between two domains

Ans. d. A security bridge that is established between two domains

(A trust can be defined as a security bridge that is established between two domains. The trust can be one-way, two-way, or transitive and is not restricted to any mode)

528. Which form of access control has a many-to-many relationship and makes use of mapping between a user and a subset of goals?

a. MAC

b. DAC

c. Rule-based access control

d. Core RBAC

Ans. a. Core RBAC

(Core RBAC makes use of a many-to-many relationship and is useful in organizations that have well-defined roles. MAC makes use of labels. DAC is a nondiscretionary model. Rule-based access control makes use of ACLs)

529. Which of the following provides an upgrade path from RADIUS?

a. Diameter

b. TACACS

c. Kerberos

d. NetSP

Ans. a. Diameter

(Diameter is the only option that provides an upgrade path from RADIUS)

530. Which of the following best describes a rainbow table?

a. A table used for digital signatures

b. An attack against a biometric system

c. An attack against a fingerprint scanner

d. A table of precomputed password hashes

Ans. d. A table of precomputed password hashes

(A rainbow table is a type of precomputed hash. It utilizes the time memory trade-off principle. It is not an attack against a biometric or fingerprint system and has nothing to do with digital signatures)

531. Investigation is a good example of ....

a. Preventive control

b. Detective control

c. Deterrent control

d. Proactive control

Ans. b. Detective control

(Investigations are a good example of a detective control)

532. What type of attack makes best use of a time-memory tradeoff?

a. Rule-based

b. Dictionary

c. Rainbow table

d. Brute-force

Ans. c. Rainbow table

(Rainbow table is a simpler technique that leverages a compute time-storage tradeoff in password recover - hash tables)

533. Which of the following element is not used by Extensible Access Control Markup Language (XACML)?

a. Subject element

b. Resource element

c. Action element

d. Procrastination element

Ans. d. Procrastination element

(XACML uses a Subject element (requesting entity), a Resource element (requested entity), and an Action element (types of access) while Procrastination element does not exist)

534. Who develops and keeps track of all standardized languages?

a. NIST

b. OASIS

c. ANSI

d. FBI

Ans. b. OASIS

(OASIS develops and maintains the standards for how various aspects of web-based communication are built and maintained)

535. Which of the following information is not included in an access token?

a. User security identifier

b. User account password

c. User rights

d. Group membership

Ans. b. User account password

(The access token does not contain the user account password. The password is only used during authentication. Following authentication, the access token is used to gain access to resource)

536. Which of the following is an example of Type II authentication credentials?

a. Photo ID

b. Token device

c. Keystroke analysis

d. Cognitive question

Ans. a. Photo ID

(Photo ID is an example of Type II authentication credentials. While option b, c, and d are examples of three-factor authentication)

537. Which of the following terms is used to describe an event in which a person is denied access to a system when they should be allowed to enter?

a. False Negative

b. True Positive

c. False Positive

d. True Negative

Ans. a. False Negative

(In a security context, False Negative is used to describe an event in which a person is denied access to a system when they should be allowed to enter)

538. What is used for identification?

a. Password

b. Username

c. Surname

d. Last name

Ans. b. Username

539. A strong password should include what elements?

a. Only upper-case letters

b. Only lower-case letters

c. Only numbers

d. Upper, lower-case letters, numbers and symbols

Ans. d. Upper, lower-case letters, numbers and symbols

(A strong password should include upper, lower-case

letters, numbers as well as symbols)

540. Which of the following is not an example of a physical barrier access control mechanism?

a. Fences

b. Mantrap

c. One time passwords

d. Biometric locks

Ans. c. One time passwords

(A onetime password is a logical or technical access control mechanism, not a physical barrier access control mechanism)

541. Which of the following is the best countermeasure against man-in-the middle attacks?

a. UDP

b. IPSec

c. PPP

d. HIDS

Ans. b. IPSec

(IPSec is the best countermeasure against man-in-the-middle attacks. Use IPSec to encrypt data in a VPN tunnel as it passes between two communication partners. Even if someone intercepts the traffic, they will be unable to extract the contents of the messages because they are encrypted)

542. What can be used to stop piggybacking that has been occurring at a front entrance where employees should swipe their smart cards to gain entry?

a. Install security cameras

b. Use weight scales

c. Use key locks rather than electronic locks

d. Deploy a mantrap

Ans. d. Deploy a mantrap

(Piggybacking is the activity where an authorized or unauthorized individual gains entry into a secured area by exploiting the credentials of a prior person. A mantrap is a single-person room with two doors. It often includes a scale to prevent piggybacking. It requires proper authentication before unlocking the inner door to allow authorized personnel into a secured area)

543. Separation of duties is an example of what type of access control?

a. Detective

b. Corrective

c. Compensative

d. Preventive

Ans. d. Preventive

(Preventive access controls deter intrusion or attacks, for example, separation of duties or dual-custody processes)

544. What is the main purpose of separation of duties?

a. Increase the difficulty in performing administration

b. Prevent conflicts of interest

c. Grant a greater range of control to senior management

d. Inform managers that they are not trusted

Ans. b. Prevent conflicts of interest

(The primary purpose of separation of duties is to prevent conflicts of interest by dividing up admin powers amongst several trusted administrators. This prevents a single person from having all the privileges over an environment, and thus making them a primary target of attack and a single point of failure)

545. Which of the following identifies an operating system or network service based upon its ICMP message quoting (response) characteristics?

a. Social engineering

b. Smurf attack

c. Fingerprinting

d. Port scanning

Ans. c. Fingerprinting

(Fingerprinting identifies an operating system or network service based upon its ICMP message quoting characteristics. With ICMP message quoting, portions of the original ICMP request are repealed (or quoted) within the response)

546. Which of the following protocols uses port 88?

a. LDAP

b. Kerberos

c. TACACS

d. L2TP

Ans. b. Kerberos

(Kerberos uses port 88 while TACACS uses port 49, LDAP uses TCP and UDP ports 389. Secure LDAP uses SSL/TLS over port 636. L2TP uses port 1701)

547. In which form of access control environment, is access controlled by rules rather than by identity?

a. Most client-server environments

b. DAC

c. ACL

d. MAC

Ans. d. MAC

(A MAC environment controls access based on rules rather than by identity. DAC environments use identity to control access. ACLs are a specific example of an identity-based access control mechanism used in DAC environments. Most client-server environments use ACLs and thus use DAC solutions)

548. MAC uses ………….. to control access.

a. Geographic location

b. Sensitivity label

c. User accounts

d. Job descriptions

Ans. b. Sensitivity label

(Mandatory Access Control (MAC) uses sensitive labels (i.e., classifications or clearance levels) to control access. A sensitivity label is descriptive tag that indicates how important, valuable, volatile, or classified a resource is)

549…………. allows attackers and administrators

to dial large blocks of phone numbers in search of available modems.

a. War dialing

b. Spear-phishing

c. War driving

d. Spoofing

Ans. a. War dialing

(War dialing is an attack in which a long list of phone numbers is inserted into a war-dialing program in the hope of finding a modem that can be exploited to gain unauthorized access)

550. Which one of the following is not a logical access control?

a. Encryption

b. Network architecture

c. ID badge

d. Access control matrix

Ans. c. ID badge

(A logical control is the same thing as a technical control. All of the answers were logical in nature except ID badge. Badges are used for physical security and are considered physical controls)

551. When designing an access control system, which of the following items is the least important?

a. Risk

b. Threat

c. Vulnerability

d. Annual loss expectancy

Ans. d. Annual loss expectancy

(Before implementing any type of access control system, the security professional needs to consider potential vulnerabilities because these give rise to threats. Threats must also be considered because they lead to risks. Risk is the potential that the vulnerability may be exploited. Answer D is incorrect because it relates to the formula used for risk analysis)

552. Which style of authentication is not vulnerable to a dictionary attack?

a. CHAP

b. LEAP

c. WPA-PSK

d. PAP

Ans. d. PAP

(Only Password Authentication protocol (PAP) is not susceptible to a dictionary attack; no attack is needed because the password is transmitted in plaintext. CHAP, LEAP, WPA-PSK are all susceptible to dictionary attacks)

553. What types of copper cabling is most secure against eavesdropping and unauthorized access?

a. Single-mode fiber

b. Multimode fiber

c. Category 6 cabling

d. 802.11ac wireless

Ans. c. Category 6 cabling

(The only choice for copper cabling would be Category 6. Single-mode and multimode fiber are not examples of copper cabling. However, fiber is considered a more secure transmission medium than copper cabling because it does not emit any Electromagnetic Interference)

554. Which of the following biometric authentication system is most closely related with law enforcement?

a. Fingerprint recognition

b. Iris recognition

c. Facial recognition

d. Retina pattern recognition

Ans. a. Fingerprint recognition

(Fingerprints are most closely associated with law enforcement. Close behind this is facial recognition. Facial recognition technology has made great strides since the terrorist attacks of September 11. Common methods include the Markov model, eigenface, and fisherface. Iris and retina recognition are not typically associated with law enforcement)

555. Which one of the following is a major issue with signature-based IDSs?

a. They cannot detect zero-day attacks.

b. They detect only attacks in which activity deviates from normal behavior.

c. They are available only as host-based systems.

d. They are cost-prohibitive.

Ans. a. They cannot detect zero-day attacks.

(Signature-based Intrusion Detection System (IDSs) can detect only attack signatures that have been previously stored in their databases. These systems rely on the vendor for updates. Until then they are vulnerable to new zero-day or polymorphic attacks)

556. TACACS+ uses .... as its communication protocol?

a. TCP

b. UDP

c. ICMP

d. TCP and UDP

Ans. a. TCP

(Terminal Access Controller Access-Control System+ (TACACS+) uses TCP port 49 for communication. The strength of TACACS+ is that it supports authentication, authorization, and accounting)

557. Which of the following features does not apply to Mandatory Access Control (MAC)?

a. Multilevel

b. Label-based

c. Universally applied

d. Discretionary

Ans. d. Discretionary

(Mandatory Access Control (MAC) is typically built in and is a component of most operating systems. MAC's attributes include the following: It's nondiscretionary because it is hard-coded and cannot easily be modified, it's capable of multilevel control, it's label-based because it can be used to control access to objects in a database, and it's universally applied because changes affect all object)

558. Which of the following does not fit in the

category of physical access control?

a. CCTV

b. Mantraps

c. Data classification and labeling

d. Biometrics

Ans. c. Data classification and labeling

(CCTV, mantraps, biometrics, and badges are just some of the items that are part of physical access control. Data classification and labeling are preventive access control mechanisms)

559. The term identification is defined as ....

a. The act of verifying your identity

b. The act of claiming a specific identity

c. The act of finding or testing the truth

d. The act of inspecting or reviewing a user's actions

Ans. b. The act of claiming a specific identity

(Identification is defined as the act of claiming a specific identity. While authentication is the act of verifying your identity, validation is the act of finding or testing the truth, and auditing is the act of inspecting or reviewing a user's actions)

560. Mention the type of cryptography that SESAME uses to distribute keys?

a. Public key

b. Secret key

c. SHA hashing algorithm

d. Plaintext

Ans. a. Public key

(SESAME uses public key cryptography to distribute secret keys. It also uses the MD5 algorithm to provide a one-way hashing function. It does not distribute keys in plaintext, use SHA, or use secret key encryption)

561. What does RADIUS use for its transport protocol?

a. UDP

b. TCP

c. TCP and UDP

d. ICMP

Ans. a. UDP

(RADIUS (Remote Authentication Dial-in User Service) uses UDP ports 1812 and 1813. RADIUS performs authentication, authorization, and accounting for remote users. RADIUS can also use UDP 1645 for authentication and UDP 1646 for accounting)

562. Nondiscretionary access control comprises which of the following?

a.	Role- and task-based

b.	Rule-based and mandatory

c.	Labeled and mandatory

d.	None of the above because there are no subcategories

Ans.	a.	Role- and task-based

(Nondiscretionary access control includes role- and task-based mechanisms. Mandatory access controls are an example of label-based security and are not considered nondiscretionary. Rule-based access control is most commonly seen in ACLs and is used with routers)

563. A swipe card, smart card, or USB dongle can be described as ....

a.	An active token

b.	A static token

c.	Type I authentication

d.	Type III authentication

Ans. b. A static token

(A static token can be a swipe card, smart card, or USB token. These tokens are not active and are not considered type I (something you know) or type III (something you are) authentication)

564. .... is the most expensive means of verifying a user's identity.

a. Single sign-on

b. Tokens

c. Biometrics

d. Passwords

Ans. c. Biometrics

(Biometric systems are the most expensive means of performing authentication. They cost more than tokens, single sign-on, or passwords)

565. The ticket-granting service is a component of ....

a. TACACS

b. Kerberos

c. RADIUS

d. SESAME

Ans. b. Kerberos

(The ticket-granting service is a component of Kerberos)

566. The Privilege Attribute Certificate (PAC) is a component of ....

a.   TACACS

b.   Kerberos

c.   RADIUS

d.   SESAME

Ans. d.   SESAME

(SESAME uses a PAC in much the same way that Kerberos uses a key distribution center. RADIUS and TACACS do not use PACs)

567. .... is the best example of capabilities tables?

a.   Memory cards

b.   Kerberos

c.   Constrained user interface

d.   Router ACL

Ans. b. Kerberos

(A good example of a capability table is Kerberos. When a ticket is issued, it is bound to the user and specifies what resources a user can access. Answers A, C, and D do not meet that specification)

568. Which of the following is not an example of centralized access controls?

a. TACACS

b. RADIUS

c. Diameter

d. Kerberos

Ans. d. Kerberos

(TACACS, RADIUS, and Diameter are all examples of centralized access controls. While Kerberos is a network authentication protocol)

569. Which of the following is an example of type III authentication?

a. Keyboard dynamics

b. PIN

c. Smart Card

d. Photo ID

Ans. b. Keyboard dynamics

(Keyboard dynamics is an example of type III authentication. Keyboard dynamics analyzes the speed and pattern of typing. Different biometric systems such as keyboard dynamics have varying levels of accuracy. Smart Card and Photo ID is an example of type II authentication)

570. Which form of access control is based on job descriptions?

a. Role-based access control (RBAC)

b. Mandatory access control

c. Discretionary Access Control

d. Rule-Based Access Control (RAC)

Ans. a. Role-based access control (RBAC)

(Role-based access control (RBAC) is a method of regulating access to computer or network resources based on the roles of individual users within an enterprise)

Chapter 13
Security Assessment and Testing

571. A systematic assessment of the security controls of an information system is known as a ....

a. Audit

b. Accounting

c. Analysis

d. Evaluation

Ans. a. Audit

(An audit is a systematic assessment of the security controls of an information system)

572. Which of the following tools is used primarily to perform network discovery scans?

a. Nmap

b. Nessus

c. Metasploit

d. lsof

Ans. a. Nmap

(Nmap is a network discovery scanning tool that reports the open ports on a remote system)

573. What type of network discovery scan opens a full connection to the remote system on the

specified port?

a. TCP connect scan

b. Xmas scan

c. TCP SYN scan

d. TCP ACK scan

Ans. a. TCP connect scan

(TCP Connect Scanning opens up a full connection to the remote system on the specified port. This scan type is used when the user running the scan does not have the necessary permissions to run a half-open scan)

574. Which of the following network discovery scanning is known as "half-open" scanning?

a. TCP connect scanning

b. Xmas scanning

c. TCP SYN scanning

d. TCP ACK scanning

Ans. c. TCP SYN scanning

(The TCP SYN scan sends a SYN packet and receives a SYN ACK packet in response, but it does not send the final ACK required to complete the three-way handshake. TCP SYN scanning is known as "half-open" scanning.)

575. Nmap, a popular network security tool was originally released in the year …………..

a. 1997

b. 1996

c. 1998

d. 1994

Ans. a. 1997

(Nmap (Network Mapper), a security scanner was first published in September 1997)

576. Which of the following audit report pertains to financial controls?

a. SOC 1

b. SOC 2

c. SOC 3

d. SOC 4

Ans. a. SOC 1

(SOC 1 pertains to financial controls while SOC 2 and 3 pertains to trust services. SOC 4 does not exist)

577. What type of penetration test provides the attackers with detailed information about the systems they target?

a. Black box penetration test

b. White box penetration test

c. Gray box penetration test

d. Red box penetration test

Ans. b. White box penetration test

(White Box Penetration Test provides the attackers with detailed information about the systems they target. This bypasses many of the reconnaissance steps that normally precede attacks, shortening the time of the attack and increasing the likelihood that it will find security flaws.)

578. .... is the process of simulating attacks on a network and its systems at the request of the owner, senior management.

a. Static Testing

b. Penetration testing

c. Dynamic Testing

d. Fuzz testing

Ans. b. Penetration testing

(A penetration test, colloquially known as a pen test, is an authorized simulated attack on a computer system that looks for security weaknesses, potentially gaining access to the system's features and data)

579. Which of the following functions is not performed by Vulnerability scanners?

a. Identification of operating systems

b. Identification of misconfigured settings

c. Identification of active hosts on the network

d. Identification of malware on all hosts

Ans. d. Identification of malware on all hosts

(The function of Vulnerability scanners include identification of operating systems, identification of misconfigured settings and identification of active hosts on the network)

580. If the penetration testing team has intimate knowledge of the target, then the team comes under which degree of knowledge?

a. Zero knowledge

b. Partial knowledge

c. Full knowledge

d. Intimate knowledge

Ans. c. Full knowledge

(The teams that do not have any knowledge of the target and must start from ground zero belong to zero knowledge. The teams that has some information about the target come under partial knowledge while team with intimate knowledge of the target come under full knowledge)

581. An examination of a system for the purpose of identifying, defining, and ranking its vulnerabilities is known as …………..

a. Vulnerability test

b. Penetration test

c. Blind test

d. Double-blind test

Ans. a. Vulnerability test

(Vulnerability analysis, also known as vulnerability assessment, is a process that defines, identifies, and classifies the security holes (vulnerabilities) in a computer, network, or communications infrastructure)

582. What type of interface testing would identify flaws in a program's command-line interface?

a. Application programming interface testing

b. User interface testing

c. Physical interface testing

d. Security interface testing

Ans. b. User interface testing

(User interface testing includes assessments of both graphical user interfaces (GUIs) and command-line interfaces (CLIs) for a software program)

583. What types of test provide the most accurate and detailed information about the security state of a server?

a. Unauthenticated scan

b. Port scan

c. Half-open scan

d. Authenticated scan

Ans. d. Authenticated scan

(Authenticated scans can read configuration information from the target system and reduce the instances of false positive and false negative reports)

584. Which of the following is the advantage of HIDS?

a. System resource usage

b. Monitors OS or a single App

c. False positives are frequent

d. Susceptible to protocol based attacks

Ans. b. Monitors OS or a single App

(A host-based intrusion detection system (HIDS) is an intrusion detection system that monitors and analyzes the internals of a computing system as well as (in some cases) the network packets on its network interfaces.)

585. The process of examining the system log files to detect security events or to verify the effectiveness of security controls is known as ....

a. Log review

b. Code review

c. Interface testing

d. Files review

Ans. a. Log review

(A log review is the examination of system log files to detect security events or to verify the effectiveness of security controls)

586. Security assessment does not include which of the following?

a. Vulnerability scan

b. Risk assessment

c. Mitigation of vulnerabilities

d. Threat assessment

Ans. c. Mitigation of vulnerabilities

(Security assessments include many types of tests designed to identify vulnerabilities, and the assessment report normally includes recommendations for mitigation. The assessment does not, however, include actual mitigation of those vulnerabilities)

587. Who is the intended audience for a security assessment report?

a. Management

b. Security auditor

c. Security professional

d. Customers

Ans. a. Management

(Security assessment reports should be addressed to the organization's management. For this reason, they should be written in plain English and avoid technical jargon)

588. Which of the following is a major advantage of using third-party auditors?

a. Third-party auditors have knowledge that an organization wouldn't otherwise be able to leverage.

b. Their cost

c. Their use of automated scanners and report

d. The requirement for NDAs and supervision

Ans. a. Third-party auditors have knowledge that an organization wouldn't otherwise be able to leverage.

(Third-party auditors perform audits in multiple other organizations, and since their knowledge is constantly refreshed, they almost always have knowledge and insights that would otherwise be unavailable to the organization)

589. Which of the following audit report covers the information security controls of a service organization and is intended for public release?

a. SOC 1

b. SOC 2

c. SOC 3

d. Both B and C.

Ans. c. SOC 3

(The SOC 2 and SOC 3 reports are similar in scope, but the SOC 3 report is more general and intended for wider distribution than the SOC 2, which is more detailed)

590. Which of the following is true with regard to vulnerability assessment?

a. The aim is to identify as many vulnerabilities as possible

b. It is not concerned with the effects of the

assessment on other systems

c. It is a predictive test aimed at assessing the future performance of a system

d. Ideally the assessment is fully automated with no human involvement

Ans. a. The aim is to identify as many vulnerabilities as possible

(One of the principal goals of a vulnerability assessment is to identify as many security flaws as possible within a given system, while being careful not to disrupt other systems)

591. Which of the following does not fit into the category of vulnerability scans?

a. Network discovery scans

b. Network vulnerability scans

c. Web application vulnerability scan

d. Web application discovery scans

Ans. d. Web application discovery scans

(There are three main categories of vulnerability scans - network discovery scans, network vulnerability scans, and web application vulnerability scan)

592. ……………….. is the final step of the Fagan inspection process

a. Inspection

b. Rework

c. Follow-up

d. Overview

Ans. c. Follow-up

(The stages in the Fagan inspections process are: planning, overview meeting, preparation, inspection meeting, rework and follow-up)

593. What port is typically used to accept administrative connections using the SSH utility?

a. 20

b. 22

c. 25

d. 80

Ans. b. 22

(The SSH protocol uses port 22 to accept administrative connections to a server)

594. When scrutinizing a potential data breach by unauthorized access, the best source of information related to the activity can be found in ....

a. Audit logs

b. Performance logs

c. Traffic logs

d. Utilization logs

Ans. a. Audit logs

(When scrutinizing a potential data breach by unauthorized access, the best source of information related to the activity can be found in Audit logs. Because audit log is a document that records an event in an information (IT) technology system)

595. What document is required before kick starting a Penetration Test?

a. Non-disclosure agreement

b. Rules of Engagement document

c. Contractual license agreements

d. Record retention agreement

Ans. b. Rules of Engagement document

(Rules Of Engagement (RoE) deals with the manner in which the penetration test is to be conducted. Some of the directives that should be clearly mentioned in the rules of engagement before you kick start the penetration test are black box testing or gray box testing, client contact details, client it team notifications, sensitive data handling and status meeting)

596. What interface mode is required for an Intrusion Detection System (IDS)?

a. Inline mode

b. Promiscuous mode

c. Passive mode

d. Active mode

Ans. b. Promiscuous mode

(Network Intrusion Detection Systems (NIDS) usually consists of a network appliance (or sensor) with a Network Interface Card (NIC) operating in promiscuous mode and a separate management interface. The IDS is placed along a network segment or boundary and monitors all traffic on that segment)

597. External technical attacks against systems often begin with ……….

a. Vulnerability Scans

b. Social Engineering

c. Monitoring of SSL traffic

d. Analysis of degaussed media

Ans. b. Social Engineering

(External technical attacks against systems often occurs due to Social Engineering)

598. Which of the following is the first step in the Information System Security Audit Process?

a. Determine the scope

b. Determine the goals

c. Plan the audit

d. Document the result

Ans. b. Determine the goals

(The first step in the information system security audit process is to determine the goals, because everything else hinges on this)

599. .... is carried out by a third party to assess the internal controls of a service organization?

a. Social Engineering

b. Vulnerability Scans

c. SAS 70 audit

d. Network discovery scans

Ans. c. SAS 70 audit

(SAS 70 audit is carried out by a third party to assess the

internal controls of a service organization. The original focus of SAS 70 was on financial issues, but the industry stretched the use of the SAS 70 beyond its original intended purpose)

600. …………….. measures the effectiveness of an organization in performing a given task at a given point in time.

a. Key risk indicators

b. Key performance indicators

c. business continuity plan

d. disaster recovery plan

Ans. b. Key performance indicators

(A key performance indicator (KPI) is a quantifiable activity used to measure how a key aspect of your business is operating or how much volume it's receiving at a given point in time)

601. A blind test in which the network security staff is not notified that testing will occur is called as ………..

a. Multiple-blind test

b. Double-blind test

c. Single-blind test

d. Gray box test

Ans. b. Double-blind test

(A double-blind test is an extension of the blind testing strategy. Double-blind testing is an important component of testing, as it can test the organization's security monitoring and incident identification, escalation and response procedures)

602. .... is a systematic examination of the instructions that comprise a piece of software, performed by someone other than the author of that code.

a. Log review

b. Code review

c. Interface testing

d. Files review

Ans. b. Code review

(Code review is systematic examination of computer source code. It is intended to find mistakes overlooked in software development, improving the overall quality of software. Reviews are done in various forms such as pair programming, informal walkthroughs, and formal inspections)

603. The process of slightly manipulating the input is known as ....

a. Bit flipping

b. Flip flopping

c. Whaling

d. Phishing

Ans. a. Bit flipping

(A bit-flipping attack is an attack on a cryptographic cipher in which the attacker can change the ciphertext in such a way as to result in a predictable change of the plaintext, although the attacker is not able to learn the plaintext itself)

604. ……………….. is a security control implemented through the use of an IT asset.

a. Physical control

b. Technical control

c. Network control

d. Detective control

Ans. b. Technical control

(Technical controls are security controls that the computer system executes. The controls can provide automated protection from unauthorized access or misuse, facilitate detection of security violations, and support security requirements for applications and data)

605. Who should obtain an authorization letter that includes the extent of the authorized

penetration testing?

a. User

b. Security professionals

c. Management

d. Data owner

Ans. b. Security professionals

(Security professionals should obtain an authorization letter that includes the extent of the testing authorized, and this letter or memo should be available to members of the team during the testing activity)

606. ………….. is a form of social engineering, typically practiced in person or over the phone, in which the attacker invents a believable scenario in an effort to persuade the target to violate a security policy.

a. Pretexting

b. Whaling

c. Blackmailing

d. Phishing

Ans. a. Pretexting

(Pretexting is a social engineering technique in which a fictional situation is created for the purpose of obtaining personal and sensitive information from an unsuspecting individual. It usually involves researching a target and making use of his/her data for impersonation or manipulation)

607. Which of the following act imposes stiff criminal penalties on anyone who uses pretexting to obtain confidential information?

e. Electronic Communications Privacy Act of 1986

f. Telephone Records and Privacy Protection Act of 2006

g. Communications Assistance for Law Enforcement Act (CALEA) of 1994

h. Economic and Protection of Proprietary Information Act of 1996

Ans. b. Telephone Records and Privacy Protection Act of 2006

(Congress passed the Telephone Records and Privacy Protection Act of 2006 to strengthen protections for law enforcement officers and the public by providing criminal penalties for the fraudulent acquisition or unauthorized disclosure of phone records)

608. Which of the following is not a key element of a good technical audit report?

a. Recommended actions

b. Probability of exploitation

c. Impact of exploitation

d. Recommended thoughts

Ans. d. Recommended thoughts

(The key elements of a good technical audit report includes threats, vulnerabilities, probability of exploitation, impact of exploitation and recommended actions)

609. Which of the following approach is based on determining the cost that other firms are paying for a similar asset in the marketplace?

a. Income approach

b. Cost approach

c. Market approach

d. Product approach

Ans. c. Market approach

(The market approach is based on determining how much other firms are paying for a similar asset in the marketplace. It requires a fair amount of transparency in terms of what other organizations are doing)

610. ……………….. is a formal meeting of senior organizational leaders to determine whether the management systems are effectively

accomplishing their goals.

a. Objective review

b. Log review

c. Code review

d. Management review

Ans. d. Management review

(Management review is a formal meeting of senior organizational leaders to determine whether the management systems are effectively accomplishing their goals)

611. Which of the following best describes the Synthetic transactions?

a. Transactions that fall outside the normal purpose of a system

b. Real user monitoring (RUM)

c. Transactions that are synthesized from multiple users' interactions with the system

d. A way to test the behavior and performance of critical services

Ans. d. A way to test the behavior and performance of critical services

(Synthetic transactions are those that simulate the behavior of real users, but are not the result of real user interactions with the system. They allow an organization to ensure that services are behaving properly without having to rely on user complaints to detect problems.)

612. The technique which is used for detecting flaws in the code by bombarding it with massive amounts of random data is known as ....

a. Static Testing

b. Penetration testing

c. Dynamic Testing

d. Fuzz testing

Ans. d. Fuzz testing

(Fuzzing is a technique for detecting flaws in the code by bombarding it with massive amounts of random data. This is not part of a code review, which focuses on analyzing the source code, not its response to random data)

613. Which of the following is not an element of user accounts management audits?

a. Password hashing

b. Signed AUPs

c. Privileged accounts

d. Suspended accounts

Ans. a. Password hashing

(Password hashing is a very common approach to protecting user account passwords, but varies from one platform to the next. It is almost always controlled by the system itself and would normally not be part of the user accounts management audit)

614. Which operating system allows users to temporarily elevate their privileges in order to launch an application at a higher privilege level?

a. All major desktop operating systems

b. Recent versions of Windows

c. Linux and Windows

d. Recent versions of Mac OS X

Ans. a. All major desktop operating systems

(All major operating systems allow for the temporary elevation of user privileges, but Mac OS X and some versions of Linux require the user to do so from a terminal window)

615. Which of the following is not a form of social engineering?

a. Pretexting

b. Fishing

c. Whaling

d.	Blackmailing

Ans. b. Fishing

(The correct term for social engineering conducted over digital communications means is phishing, not fishing)

616. Which of the following best describes key performance indicator (KPI)?

a.	Any attribute of the ISMS that can be described as a value

b.	The value of a factor at a particular point in time

c.	A derived value that is generated by comparing multiple measurements against each other or against a baseline

d.	An interpretation of one or more metrics that describes the effectiveness of the ISMS

Ans. d.	An interpretation of one or more metrics that describes the effectiveness of the ISMS

(Key performance indicators (KPIs) are used by managers to assess the effectiveness of any critical business function. In the context of security, KPIs are based on metrics that describes the effectiveness of the ISMS)

617. The problems that occur below the level of the user interface, deep inside the operating system is known as ....

a. Kernel flaws

b. Buffer overflows

c. Symbolic links

d. File descriptor attacks

Ans. a. Kernel flaws

(Kernel flaws are problems that occur below the level of the user interface, deep inside the operating system. Any flaw in the kernel that can be reached by an attacker, if exploitable, gives the attacker the most powerful level of control over the system)

618. Which of the following test detects unauthorized file modifications?

a. Virus detectors

b. Integrity checkers

c. War dialing

d. Network scanning

Ans. b. Integrity checkers

(Integrity checkers uses cryptographic checksums to detect unauthorized modifications to files and performs necessary actions as configured)

619. Which of the following is the benefit of War driving?

a. Detects and deletes viruses

b. Detects unauthorized wireless access points

c. Detects unauthorized modems

d. Detects unauthorized file modifications

Ans. b. Detects unauthorized wireless access points

(War driving detects unauthorized wireless access points and prevents unauthorized access to a protected network)

620. Which of the following is not the benefit of Network scanning?

a. Identifies unauthorized hosts connected to a network

b. Identifies open ports

c. Identifies unauthorized services

d. Identifies potential vulnerabilities

Ans. d. Identifies potential vulnerabilities

(Some of the benefits of Network scanning include identification of unauthorized hosts connected to a network, identification of open ports, and identification of unauthorized services. While Vulnerability scanning identifies potential vulnerabilities on the target set)

621. Which of the following type of test detects and deletes viruses before the successful installation

on the system?

a. Vulnerability scanning

b. Virus detectors

c. Integrity checker

d. War dialing

Ans. b. Virus detectors

(Virus detector detects and deletes viruses before successful installation on the system. Vulnerability scanning identifies potential vulnerabilities on the target set. Integrity checker detects unauthorized file modifications. War dialing detects unauthorized modems and prevents unauthorized access to a protected network)

622. ………………….. is a networking protocol for synchronizing computer clocks between networked device.

a. File Transfer Protocol (FTP)

b. Simple Mail Transfer Protocol (SMTP)

c. Trivial File Transfer Protocol (TFTP)

d. Network Time Protocol (NTP)

Ans. d. Network Time Protocol (NTP)

(The Network Time Protocol (NTP) version 4, described in RFC 5905, is the industry standard for synchronizing computer clocks between networked devices)

623. .... is a passive way to monitor the interactions of real users with a web application or system.

a. Synthetic Transactions

b. Real user monitoring (RUM)

c. Misuse Case Testing

d. Security Testing

Ans. b. Real user monitoring (RUM)

(Real user monitoring (RUM) is a passive monitoring technology that records all user interaction with a website or client interacting with a server or cloud-based application)

624. Which type of fuzz testing modifies known inputs to generate synthetic inputs that may trigger unexpected behavior?

a. Generational Fuzzing

b. Mutation fuzzing

c. Intelligent Fuzzing

d. File Fuzzing

Ans. b. Mutation fuzzing

(Mutation fuzzing modifies known inputs to generate synthetic inputs that may trigger unexpected behavior. It might alter the characters of the content, append strings to the end of the content, or perform other data manipulation technique)

625. .... is a use case that includes threat actors and the tasks they want to perform on the system.

a. Security use case

b. Misuse case

c. Mitigation use case

d. Narrative use case

Ans. b. Misuse case

(Misuse case is a use case that includes threat actors and the tasks they want to perform on the system. The threat actor's misuse cases are meant to threaten a specific portion or legitimate use case of our system.)

626. Which of the following type of test is most intrusive to regular operations and business productivity?

a. Parallel Test

b. Full-Interruption Test

c. Simulation Test

d. Checklist Test

Ans. b. Full-Interruption Test

(Full-Interruption Test is most intrusive to regular operations and business productivity. The original site is actually shut down, and processing takes place at the alternate site. The recovery team fulfills its obligations in preparing the systems and environment for the alternate site)

627. ………………….. is the process of exposing people to security issues so that they may be able to recognize them and better respond to them.

a. Security training

b. Security awareness training

c. Business Continuity Plan

d. Disaster Recovery Plan

Ans. b. Security awareness training

(Security Awareness Training specializes in making sure your employees understand the mechanisms of spam, phishing, spear-phishing, malware and social engineering and can apply this knowledge in their day-to-day job)

628. The process of manipulating individuals so that they perform actions that violate security protocols is known as ……………

a. Social engineering

b. Port Scanning

c. Social Networking

d. Network scanning

Ans. a. Social engineering

(Social engineering is a non-technical strategy cyber attacker's use that relies heavily on human interaction and often involves tricking people into breaking standard security practices. The success of social engineering techniques depends on attackers' ability to manipulate victims into performing certain actions or providing confidential information)

629. What is the most popular form of social engineering?

a. Spear Phishing

b. Phishing

c. Vishing

d. Pretexting

Ans. b. Phishing

(The most popular form of social engineering is phishing, which is a social engineering conducted through a digital communication)

630. An automatic attack that is triggered simply by visiting a malicious website is termed as ....

a. Drive-by download

b. Phishing

c. Whaling

d. Spear Phishing

Ans. a. Drive-by download

(A drive-by download refers to the unintentional download of a virus or malicious software (malware) onto your computer or mobile device. A drive-by download will usually take advantage of (or "exploit") a browser, app, or operating system that is out of date and has a security flaw)

Chapter 14
Security Operations

631. In the context of security operations, the ability to take actions is known as ....

a. Permissions

b. Rights

c. Access

d. Access control

Ans. b. Rights

(Rights refer to the ability to take actions. Access rights are synonymous with permissions, but rights can also refer to the ability to take action on a system, such as the right to change the system time. Privileges are the combination of both rights and permission)

632. An organization ensures that users are granted access to only the data they need to perform specific work tasks. What principle are they following?

a. Principle of least privilege

b. Separation of duties

c. Need to know

d. Role-based access control

Ans. c. Need to know

(Need to know is the requirement to have access to,

knowledge about, or possession of data to perform specific work tasks, but no more. The principle of least privilege includes both rights and permissions, but the term principle of least permission is not valid within IT security. Separation of duties ensures that a single person doesn't control all the elements of a process. Role-based access control grants access to resources based on a role)

633. What is the primary benefit of job rotation and separation of duties policies?

a. Preventing collusion

b. Preventing fraud

c. Encouraging collusion

d. Correcting incidents

Ans. b. Preventing fraud

(Job rotation and separation of duties policies help prevent fraud. Collusion is an agreement among multiple persons to perform some unauthorized or illegal actions, and implementing these policies helps prevent fraud)

634. Why it is necessary for an organization to enforce a mandatory vacation policy?

a. To rotate job responsibilities

b. To detect fraud

c. To increase employee productivity

d. To reduce employee stress levels

Ans. b. To detect fraud

(Mandatory vacation policies help detect fraud. They require employees to take an extended time away from their job, requiring someone else to perform their job responsibilities and this increases the likelihood of discovering fraud)

635. What is the primary purpose of operations security?

a. Protect the system hardware from environment damage

b. Monitor the actions of vendor service personnel

c. Safeguard information assets that are resident in the system

d. Establish thresholds for violation detection and logging.

Ans. c. Safeguard information assets that reside in a system

(The primary purpose for security operations practices is to safeguard information assets that reside in a system. These practices help identify threats and vulnerabilities, and implement controls to reduce the overall risk to organizational assets)

636. Which of the following is not a component of Operations Security "triples"?

a. Asset

b. Threat

c. Vulnerability

d. Risk

Ans. d. Risk

(The Operations Security domain is concerned with triples: threats, vulnerabilities and assets)

637. Who is responsible for implementing user clearances to computer-based information?

a. Security administrators

b. Operators

c. Data owners

d. Data custodians

Ans. a. Security administrators

(Security administrators is responsible for implementing user clearances in computer-based information systems at the B3 level of the TCSEC rating)

638. Which of the following perfectly describe "good" security practice?

a. Accounts should be monitored regularly

b. You should have a procedure in place to verify password strength

c. You should ensure that there are no accounts without passwords

d. All of the choices

Ans. d. All of the choices

(In many organizations accounts are created and then nobody ever touches those accounts again. This is a very poor security practice. Accounts should be monitored regularly, you should look at unused accounts and you should have a procedure in place to ensure that departing employees have their rights revoke prior to leaving the company. You should also have a procedure in place to verify password strength or to ensure that there are no accounts without passwords)

639. Root login should only be allowed via ....

a. Rsh

b. System console

c. Remote program

d. VNC

Ans. b. System console

(The root account must be the only account with a user ID of 0 (zero) that has open access to the UNIX shell. It must not be possible for root to sign on directly except at the system console. All other access to the root account must be via the 'su' command)

640. In order to avoid mishandling of media or information, one should consider using ……..

a. Labeling

b. Token

c. Ticket

d. SLL

Ans. a. Labeling

(In order to avoid mishandling of media or information, proper labeling must be used. All tape, floppy disks, and other computer storage media containing sensitive information must be externally marked with the appropriate sensitivity classification. All printed copies, printouts, etc., from a computer system must be clearly labeled with the proper classification)

641. Whose responsibility is to receive, record, release, and protect system and application files backed up on media such as tapes or disks?

a. Security Administrator

b. Tape Librarian

c. Network Administrator

d. Database Administrator

Ans. b. Tape Librarian

(Tape Librarians core responsibility is to receive, record, release, and protect system and application files backed up on media such as tapes or disks)

642. Which of the following activities is not considered a valid form of penetration testing?

a. Denial-of-service attacks

b. Port scanning

c. Distribution of malicious code

d. Packet sniffing

Ans. c. Distribution of malicious code

(Distribution of malicious code will almost always result in damage or loss of assets and is not used in a penetration test. However, denial-of-service attacks, port scanning, and packet sniffing may all be included in a penetration test)

643. ……………….. combines the concepts of separation of duties and two-person control into a single solution.

a. Partial knowledge

b. Zero knowledge

c. Split knowledge

d. Full Knowledge

Ans. c. Split knowledge

(Split knowledge combines the concepts of separation of duties and two-person control into a single solution)

644. ……………. is a set of known-good resources such as IP addresses, domain names, or applications.

a. Whitelist

b. Blacklist

c. Aggregation

d. Transitive Trust

Ans. a. Whitelist

(Whitelist is a set of known-good resources such as IP addresses, domain names, or applications)

645. Which of the following is the core responsibility of an Application Programmer?

a. Creates new database tables

b. Develops and maintains production software

c. Installs and maintains the LAN/WAN environment

d.   Obtains and validates information

Ans. b. Develops and maintains production software

(The application programmer is responsible for designing and testing program logic, coding programs, program documentation and preparation of programs for computer operations)

646. Which of the following tasks is not carried out by the security administrator?

a.   Manages password policies

b.   Carries out security assessment

c.   Reviews audit logs

d.   Creates new database tables

Ans. d. Creates new database tables

(Security administrator defines, configures, and maintains the security mechanisms protecting the organization. They carry out security assessment, manage password policies, and reviews audit logs. Whereas database administrator creates new database tables and manages the database)

647. .... should be implemented to establish a baseline of user activity and acceptable errors.

a.   Clipping level

b.   Assurance Level

c. Initial program load

d. Rebooting

Ans. a. Clipping level

(Clipping levels should be implemented to establish a baseline of user activity and acceptable errors)

648. The process for identifying, acquiring, installing, and verifying patches for products and systems is known as ....

a. Vulnerability management

b. Patch management

c. Configuration management

d. Remediation management

Ans. b. Patch management

(Patch management is an area of systems management that involves acquiring, testing, and installing multiple patches (code changes) to an administered computer system. Patch management tasks include: maintaining current knowledge of available patches, deciding what patches are appropriate for particular systems, ensuring that patches are installed properly, testing systems after installation, and documenting all associated procedures, such as specific configurations required)

649. TCB (Trusted Computing Base) does not

include which of the following?

a. Hardware

b. Software

c. Firmware

d. Malware

Ans. d. Malware

(The trusted computing base or TCB comprises the set of all hardware, software, and firmware components that are critical to establishing and maintaining its security)

650. The process of establishing and maintaining effective system controls, which is also part of operational security is known as ……………

a. Vulnerability management

b. Patch management

c. Configuration management

d. Remediation management

Ans. c. Configuration management

(Configuration management (CM) is a systems engineering process for establishing and maintaining consistency of a product's performance, functional, and physical attributes with its requirements, design, and operational information throughout its life)

651. What is used to ensure that transactions are properly entered into the system once?

a.   Media Viability Controls

b.   Hamming Code

c.   Input Controls

d.   Data Diddling

Ans. c. Input Controls

(Input Controls are used to ensure that transactions are properly entered into the system once. Input controls ensure that all data entered into the system is authorized, accurate, and complete.)

652. What takes place when a system failure happens in an uncontrolled manner?

a.   System reboot

b.   System cold start

c.   Emergency system restart

d.   System failure

Ans. c. Emergency system restart

(An emergency system restart takes place after a system failure happens in an uncontrolled manner. This could be a kernel or media failure caused by lower-privileged user processes attempting to access memory segments that are restricted)

653. Which of the following is not a part of a patch management process?

a. Evaluate patches

b. Test patches

c. Deploy all patches

d. Audit patches

Ans. c. Deploy all patches

(Only required patches should be deployed so an organization will not deploy all patches. Instead, an organization evaluates the patches to determine which patches are needed, tests them to ensure that they don't cause unintended problems, deploys the approved and tested patches, and audits systems to ensure that patches have been applied)

654. What would an administrator use to check systems for known issues that attackers may use to exploit the systems?

a. Versioning tracker

b. Vulnerability scanner

c. Security audit

d. Security review

Ans. b. Vulnerability scanner

(Vulnerability scanners are used to check systems for known issues and are part of an overall vulnerability management program. Versioning is used to track software versions and is unrelated to detecting vulnerabilities. Security audits and reviews help ensure that an organization is following its policies but wouldn't directly check systems for vulnerabilities)

655. Which of the following would not require updated documentation?

a. An antivirus signature update

b. Reconfiguration of a server

c. A change in security policy

d. The installation of a patch to a production server

Ans. a. An antivirus signature update

(Documentation is very important for data processing and networked environments. Continually documenting when virus signatures are updated would be overkill. The other answers contain events that certainly require documentation)

656. Which of the following is true with regard to transponder?

a. It is a card that can be read without sliding it through a card reader.

b. It is a biometric proximity device.

c. It is a card that a user swipes through a card reader to gain access to a facility.

d. It exchanges tokens with an authentication server

Ans. a. It is a card that can be read without sliding it through a card reader.

(A transponder is a type of physical access control device that does not require the user to slide a card through a reader. The reader and card communicate directly. The card and reader have a receiver, transmitter, and battery)

657. Which of the following is not considered a delaying mechanism?

a. Locks

b. Defense-in-depth measures

c. Warning signs

d. Access controls

And. c. Warning signs

(Every physical security program should have delaying mechanisms, which have the purpose of slowing down an intruder so security personnel can be alerted and arrive at the scene. A warning sign is a deterrence control, not a delaying control)

658. Which of the following are the two general

types of proximity identification devices?

a. Biometric devices and access control devices

b. Swipe card devices and passive devices

c. Preset code devices and wireless devices

d. User-activated devices and system sensing devices

Ans. d. User-activated devices and system sensing devices

(A user-activated device requires the user to do something: swipe the card through the reader and/or enter a code. A system sensing device recognizes the presence of the card and communicates with it without the user needing to carry out any activity)

659. Which of the following best describes a cipher lock?

a. A lock that uses cryptographic keys

b. A lock that uses a type of key that cannot be reproduced

c. A lock that uses a token and perimeter reader

d. A lock that uses a keypad

Ans. d. A lock that uses a keypad

(Cipher locks, also known as programmable locks, use keypads to control access into an area or facility. The lock can require a swipe card and a specific combination that's entered into the keypad)

660. Which of the following best describes a cold site?

a. Fully equipped and operational in a few hours

b. Partially equipped with data processing equipment

c. Expensive and fully configured

d. Provides environmental measures but no equipment

Ans. d. Provides environmental measures but no equipment

(A cold site only provides environmental measures—wiring, air conditioning, raised floors—basically a shell of a building and no more)

661. Patch management and vulnerability management tools use ……….. as a standard when scanning for specific vulnerabilities.

a. CPE dictionary

b. CVE dictionary

c. CPE feeds

d. Vulnerability assessment

Ans. b. CVE dictionary

(Patch management and vulnerability management tools commonly use the CVE dictionary as a standard when scanning for specific vulnerabilities)

662. Who designs data flow of systems based on operational and user requirements?

a. Application Programmer

b. Database Administrator

c. Systems Analyst

d. Network Administrator

Ans. c. Systems Analyst

(A systems analyst is a person who uses analysis and design techniques to solve business problems using information technology. He designs data flow of systems based on operational and user requirements)

663. Why should employers make sure employees take their vacations?

a. They have a legal obligation.

b. It is part of due diligence.

c. It is a way for fraud to be uncovered.

d. To ensure the employee does not get burnt out.

Ans. c. It is a way for fraud to be uncovered.

(Many times, employees who are carrying out fraudulent activities do not take the vacation they have earned because they do not want anyone to find out what they have been doing. Forcing employees to take vacations means that someone else has to do that person's job and can possibly uncover any misdeed)

664. Which of the following best describes due care and due diligence?

a. Due care is the continual effort to ensure that the right thing takes place, and due diligence is the continual effort to stay compliant with regulations.

b. Due care is based on the prudent person concept, whereas due diligence is not.

c. They mean the same thing.

d. Due diligence involves investigating the risks, whereas due care involves carrying out the necessary steps to mitigate these risks.

Ans. d. Due diligence involves investigating the risks, whereas due care involves carrying out the necessary steps to mitigate these risks.

(Due care and due diligence are legal terms that do not just pertain to security. Due diligence involves going through the necessary steps to know what a company's or individual's actual risks are, whereas due care involves carrying out responsible actions to reduce those risks)

665. Which of the following is not a true statement

with regard to CCTV lenses?

a. Lenses that have a manual iris should be used in outside monitoring

b. Zoom lenses will carry out focus functionality automatically

c. Depth of field increases as the size of the lens opening decreases

d. Depth of field increases as the focal length of the lens decreases

Ans. a. Lenses that have a manual iris should be used in outside monitoring

(Manual iris lenses have a ring around the CCTV lens that can be manually turned and controlled. A lens that has a manual iris would be used in an area that has fixed lighting, since the iris cannot self-adjust to changes of light)

666. Which is not a drawback to installing intrusion detection and monitoring systems?

a. It's expensive to install

b. It cannot be penetrated

c. It requires human response

d. It's subject to false alarms

Ans. b. It cannot be penetrated

(Monitoring and intrusion detection systems are expensive, require someone to respond when they set off an alarm, and, because of their level of sensitivity, can cause several false alarms. Like any other type of technology or device, they have their own vulnerabilities that can be exploited and penetrated.

667. What is remote journaling?

a. Backing up bulk data to an offsite facility

b. Backing up transaction logs to an offsite facility

c. Capturing and saving transactions to two mirrored servers in-house

d. Capturing and saving transactions to different media types

Ans. b. Backing up transaction logs to an offsite facility

(Remote journaling is a technology used to transmit data to an offsite facility, but this usually only includes moving the journal or transaction logs to the offsite facility, not the actual files)

668. Which of the following does not describe a reciprocal agreement?

a. The agreement is enforceable.

b. It is a cheap solution.

c. It may be able to be implemented right after a disaster.

d. It could overwhelm a current data processing site.

Ans. a. The agreement is enforceable.

(A reciprocal agreement is not enforceable, meaning that the company that agreed to let the damaged company work out of its facility can decide not to allow this to take place. A reciprocal agreement is a better secondary backup option if the original plan falls through)

669. ……………………….. is a mainframe term for loading the operating system's kernel into the computer's main memory.

a. Life-cycle assurance

b. Initial program load (IPL)

c. Separation of duties

d. Operational assurance

Ans. b. Initial program load (IPL)

(Initial program load (IPL) is a mainframe term for loading the operating system's kernel into the computer's main memory. On a personal computer, booting into the operating system is the equivalent to IPLing)

670. When does a system cold start takes place?

a. When the system shuts itself down in a controlled manner

b. When the system failure happens in an uncontrolled

manner

c. When an unexpected kernel or media failure happens

d. When the system finds inconsistent data

Ans. c. When an unexpected kernel or media failure happens

(A system cold start takes place when an unexpected kernel or media failure happens and the regular recovery procedure cannot recover the system to a more consistent state)

671. ………………….. are inexpensive access control mechanisms that are widely accepted and used.

a. Defense-in-depth measures

b. Locks

c. Warning signs

d. Access controls

Ans. b. Locks

(Locks are inexpensive access control mechanisms that are widely accepted and used. They are considered delaying devices to intruders)

672. Which of the following types of locks can be used on chained fence?

a. Padlocks

b. Preset locks

c. Programmable lock

d. Fixed locks

Ans. a. Padlocks

(Locks vary in functionality. Padlocks can be used on chained fences, preset locks are usually used on doors, and programmable locks (requiring a combination to unlock) are used on doors or vaults)

673. Which of the following is one of the two main types of mechanical locks?

a. Combination locks

b. Tumbler lock

c. Fixed locks

d. Non-Programmable lock

Ans. b. Tumbler lock

(Two main types of mechanical locks are the warded lock and the tumbler lock. The warded lock is the basic padlock that has a spring-loaded bolt with a notch cut in it. The tumbler lock has more pieces and parts than a ward lock)

674. Which of the following does not fit into the category of tumbler locks?

a. Pin tumbler

b. Wafer tumbler

c. Lever tumbler

d. Unpin tumbler

Ans. d. Unpin tumbler

(The three types of tumbler locks are the pin tumbler, wafer tumbler, and lever tumbler)

675. Which one of the following is the most commonly used tumbler lock?

a. Pin tumbler lock

b. Wafer tumbler lock

c. Disc tumbler lock

d. Lever tumbler lock

Ans. a. Pin tumbler lock

(The pin tumbler lock is the most commonly used tumbler lock. The key has to have just the right grooves to put all the spring-loaded pins in the right position so the lock can be locked or unlocked)

676. Which one of the following is not an attribute of cipher combination locks?

a. Hostage alarm

b. Door delay

c. Master keying

d. Biometric reader

Ans. d. Biometric reader

(Door delay, key override, master keying, hostage alarm are some functionalities commonly available on many cipher combination locks to improve the performance of access control and provide for increased security levels)

677. .... is designed to allow only authorized individuals access at certain doors at certain time

a. Smart lock

b. Hotel key card

c. Smart card

d. Cable lock

Ans. a. Smart lock

(Smart locks are designed to allow only authorized individuals access at certain doors at certain times)

678. .... is a tool shaped like an L and is used to apply tension to the internal cylinder of a lock.

a. Raking

b. Tension wrench

c. Cipher lock

d. Smart locks

Ans. b. Tension wrench

(A tension wrench is a tool shaped like an L and is used to apply tension to the internal cylinder of a lock. The lock picker uses a lock pick to manipulate the individual pins to their proper placement)

679. A tactic that intruders use to force the pins in a tumbler lock to their open position by using a special key is known as ....

a. Lock bumping

b. Piggybacking

c. Tension wrench

d. Bump key

Ans. a. Lock bumping

(Lock bumping is a tactic that intruders can use to force the pins in a tumbler lock to their open position by using a special key called a bump key)

680. In physical security, what are electronic access control (EAC) tokens used for?

a. To authenticate subjects

b. To control the amount of radiation that escapes from control rooms

c. To lock down a facility or system after an intrusion has been detected

d. To authenticate object

Ans. a. To authenticate subjects

(Electronic access control (EAC) tokens are used in physical security to authenticate subjects. They can be proximity readers, programmable locks, or biometric systems, which identify and authenticate users before allowing them entrance)

681. Which of the following services does proximity protection components provide?

a. Control pedestrian and vehicle traffic flows

b. Backing up bulk data to an offsite facility

c. Backing up transaction logs to an offsite facility

d. Capturing and saving transactions to different media types

Ans. a. Control pedestrian and vehicle traffic flows

(Proximity protection components are usually put into place to Control pedestrian and vehicle traffic flows)

682. A tool employed in the CPTED method is known as …………..

a. Landscaping

b. Fencing

c. Tension wrench

d. Raking

Ans. a. Landscaping

(Landscaping is a tool employed in the Crime Prevention Through Environmental Design (CPTED) method)

683. ………….. is a type of fencing that has sensors located on the wire mesh and at the base of the fence.

a. Vulnerability Assessment and Intrusion Detection

b. Perimeter Intrusion Detection and Assessment System (PIDAS)

c. Host-based intrusion detection systems (HIDS)

d. Network-based intrusion detection systems (NIDS)

Ans. b. Perimeter Intrusion Detection and Assessment System (PIDAS)

(Perimeter Intrusion Detection and Assessment System (PIDAS) is a type of fencing that has sensors located on the wire mesh and at the base of the fence. It is used to detect if someone attempts to cut or climb the fence)

684. An array of lights that provides an even amount of illumination across an area is usually referred to as ………..

a. Continuous lighting

b. Glare protection

c. Fixed lighting

d. standby lighting

Ans. a. Continuous lighting

(An array of lights that provides an even amount of illumination across an area is usually referred to as continuous lighting. Examples are the evenly spaced light poles in a parking lot, light fixtures that run across the outside of a building, or series of fluorescent lights used in parking garage)

685. …………………….. takes place when an IDS detects suspicious activities and turns on the lights within a specific area.

a. Standby lighting

b. Responsive area illumination

c. Continuous lighting

d. Reduced illumination

Ans. b. Responsive area illumination

(Responsive area illumination takes place when an IDS detects suspicious activities and turns on the lights within a specific area. When this type of technology is plugged into automated IDS products, there is a high likelihood of false alarms)

686. What is the main purpose of CCTV?

a. To identify threat/vulnerability

b. To detect, assess, and/or identify intruders

c. To identify data roles

d. To determine data security controls

Ans. b. To detect, assess, and/or identify intruders

(The purpose of CCTV is to detect, assess, and identify intruders)

687. .... is an electrical circuit that receives input light from the lens and converts it into an electronic signal, which is then displayed on the monitor.

a. DVD

b. CCD

c. LCD

d. CMOS

Ans. b. CCD

(Most of the CCTV cameras in use today employ light-sensitive chips called charged coupled devices (CCDs). A CCD is a device for the movement of electrical charge, usually from within the device to an area where the charge can be manipulated, for example conversion into a digital value)

688. What type of lenses is used in CCTV?

a. High-resolution lenses

b. Fixed focal length lenses

c. 'Fixed' lenses

d. Machine Vision Lenses

Ans. b. Fixed focal length lenses

(Two main types of lenses that are used in CCTV are fixed focal length and zoom (varifocal). The focal length of a lens defines its effectiveness in viewing objects from a horizontal and vertical view)

689. What lenses provide flexibility by allowing the viewer to change the field of view while maintaining the same number of pixels in the resulting image?

a. Digital zoom lenses

b. Optical zoom lenses

c. 'Fixed' lenses

d.   Machine Vision Lenses

Ans. b. Optical zoom lenses

(The optical zoom lenses provide flexibility by allowing the viewer to change the field of view while maintaining the same number of pixels in the resulting image, which makes it much more detailed)

690. What kind of lenses should be used in environments where the light changes, as in an outdoor setting?

a.   Auto iris lens

b.   Manual iris lenses

c.   'Fixed' lenses

d.   Optical zoom lenses

Ans. a. Auto iris lens

(An auto iris lens should be used in environments where the light changes, as in an outdoor setting. As the environment brightens, this is sensed by the iris, which automatically adjusts itself)

691. IDSs cannot be used to detect changes in which of the following?

a.   Beams of light

b.   Sounds and vibrations

c. Open ports

d. Electrical circuit

Ans. c. Open ports

(IDSs can be used to detect changes in beams of light, sounds and vibrations, motion as well as electrical circuit)

692. Which of the following systems detects the change in a light beam and thus can be used only in windowless rooms?

a. Electromechanical systems

b. Photoelectric system

c. Volumetric systems

d. Passive infrared (PIR) system

Ans. b. Photoelectric system

(A photoelectric system, or photometric system, detects the change in a light beam and thus can be used only in windowless rooms. These systems work like photoelectric smoke detectors, which emit a beam that hits the receiver)

693. Which of the following systems detect sounds made during a forced entry?

a. Acoustical detection system

b. Proximity detector

c. Vibration sensors

d. Electromechanical systems

Ans. a. Acoustical detection system

(An acoustical detection system uses microphones installed on floors, walls, or ceilings. The goal is to detect any sound made during a forced entry)

694. A standard image workstation or server that includes properly configured and authorized software is known as …………………..

a. Gold Masters

b. Whitelist

c. Blacklist

d. Silver Masters

Ans. a. Gold Masters

(A Gold Master is a standard image workstation or server that includes properly configured and authorized software. Organizations may have multiple images representing different sets of users)

695. The set of all activities required to provide one or more new cloud assets to a user or group of users is known as …………..

a. Whitelist

b. Fencing

c. Tension wrench

d. Cloud provisioning

Ans. d. Cloud provisioning

(Cloud provisioning is the set of all activities required to provide one or more new cloud assets to a user or group of users)

696. Which of the following does not fit in the category of cloud computing services?

a. Infrastructure as a Service (IaaS)

b. Platform as a Service (PaaS)

c. Software as a Service (SaaS)

d. People as a service (PaaS)

Ans. d. People as a service (PaaS)

(Cloud computing can be broken up into three main services: Software-as-a-Service (SaaS), Infrastructure-as-a-Service (IaaS) and Platform-as-a-Service (PaaS). These three services make up what Rackspace calls the Cloud Computing Stack, with SaaS on top, PaaS in the middle, and IaaS on the bottom)

697. The average length of time the hardware is functional without failure is termed as ....

a. Mean-Time-To-Repair (MTTR)

b. Mean-Time-To-Install (MTTI)

c. Mean-Time-Between Failure (MTBF)

d. Mean Time To Detect (MTTD)

Ans. b. Mean-Time-Between Failure (MTBF)

(Mean time between failures (MTBF) is the predicted elapsed time between inherent failures of a mechanical system, during normal system operation. MTBF can be calculated as the arithmetic mean (average) time between failures of a system)

698. The expected amount of time it takes to get a device fixed and back into production after its failure is termed as ……………..

a. Mean-Time-To-Repair (MTTR)

b. Mean-Time-To-Install (MTTI)

c. Mean-Time-Between Failure (MTBF)

d. Mean Time To Detect (MTTD)

Ans. a. Mean-Time-To-Repair (MTTR)

(Mean Time To Repair (MTTR) is a basic measure of the maintainability of repairable items. It represents the average time required to repair a failed component or device)

699. Which of the following devices does not represent single points of failure?

a. Firewalls

b. Routers

c. Network access servers

d. Tokens

Ans. d. Tokens

(Devices that could represent single points of failure are firewalls, routers, network access servers, T1 lines, switches, bridges, hubs, and authentication servers—to name a few)

700. .... is a technology used for redundancy and/ or performance improvement that combines several physical disks and aggregates them into logical arrays.

a. Massive array of inactive disks (MAID)

b. Redundant array of independent disks (RAID)

c. Direct access storage device (DASD)

d. Sequential access storage devices (SASD)

Ans. b. Redundant array of independent disks (RAID)

(RAID (redundant array of independent disks) is a data storage virtualization technology that combines multiple physical disk drive components into a single logical unit for the purposes of data redundancy, performance improvement, or both)

701. Which of the following plan focuses on malware, hackers, intrusions, attacks, and other security issues?

a. Business resumption plan

b. IT contingency plan

c. Cyber incident response plan

d. Disaster recovery plan

Ans. c. Cyber incident response plan

(Cyber incident response plan focuses on malware, hackers, intrusions, attacks, and other security issues. Also, it outlines procedures for incident response)

702. Which of the following plan focuses on establishing personnel safety and evacuation procedures?

a. Disaster recovery plan

b. Occupant emergency plan

c. Cyber incident response plan

d. Business resumption plan

Ans. b. Occupant emergency plan

(Occupant emergency plan establishes personnel safety and evacuation procedures)

703. .... is a U.S. government initiative, required by presidential directive, to ensure that agencies are able to continue operations after a disaster or disruption.

a. Crisis communications plan

b. Continuity of operations (COOP)

c. Cyber incident response plan

d. Disaster recovery plan

Ans. b. Continuity of operations (COOP)

(Continuity of operations (COOP) is a U.S. government initiative, required by presidential directive, to ensure that agencies are able to continue operations after a disaster or disruption)

704. .... is a science and an art that requires specialized techniques for the recovery, authentication, and analysis of electronic data for the purposes of a digital criminal investigation.

a. Digital evidence

b. Forensics

c. Dynamic monitoring

d. Digital monitoring

Ans. b. Forensics

(Forensics is a science and an art that requires specialized techniques for the recovery, authentication, and analysis of electronic data for the purposes of a digital criminal investigation)

705. Which of the following principle states that a criminal leaves something behind at the crime scene and takes something with them?

a. Principle of least privilege

b. Separation of duties

c. Need to know

d. Locard's principle of exchange

Ans. d. Locard's principle of exchange

(Locard's exchange principle applies to profiling. The principle states that a criminal leaves something behind at the crime scene and takes something with them)

706. Which of the following types of assessment is not performed by investigators?

a. Network analysis

b. Dynamic analysis

c. Media analysis

d. Software analysis

Ans. b. Dynamic analysis

(There are four general types of assessments performed by investigators which includes network analysis, media analysis, software analysis, and hardware/embedded device analysis)

707. Which one of the following is an example of Media analysis?

a. Disk imaging

b. Traffic analysis

c. Log analysis

d. Path tracing

Ans. a. Disk imaging

(Disk imaging is an example of Media analysis while traffic analysis, log analysis, and path tracing are examples of network analysis)

708. Which of the following pertains to auditing events that passively monitors events by using network sniffers, keyboard monitors, wiretaps, and line monitoring?

a. Physical surveillance

b. Computer surveillance

c. Active surveillance

d. Passive surveillance

Ans. b. Computer surveillance

(Computer surveillance pertains to auditing events, which passively monitors events by using network sniffers, keyboard monitors, wiretaps, and line monitoring)

709. .... is the act of gathering the necessary information so that the best decision making activities can take place.

a. Due Care

b. Due diligence

c. Due negligence

d. Enticement

Ans. b. Due diligence

(Due diligence is the act of gathering the necessary information so the best decision making activities can take place)

710. An act or omission that naturally and directly produces a consequence is known as ....

a. Direct cause

b. Proximate cause

c. Actual cause

d. Legal cause

Ans. b. Proximate cause

(Proximate cause is an act or omission that naturally and directly produces a consequence. It is the superficial or obvious cause for an occurrence. It refers to a cause that leads directly, or in an unbroken sequence, to a particular result)

711. An activity that involves developing and monitoring vendor relationships after the contracts are in place is known as ……………

a. Vulnerability management

b. Vendor management

c. Configuration management

d. Remediation management

Ans. b. Vendor management

(Vendor management is a discipline that enables organizations to control costs, drive service excellence and mitigate risks to gain increased value from their vendors throughout the deal life cycle)

712. ……………….. is a group of servers that are viewed logically as one server to users and can be managed as a single logical system.

a. Server cluster

b. Fault-tolerant server

c. Clustering

d. Cloud computing

Ans. a. Server cluster

(A server cluster is a collection of servers, called nodes that communicate with each other to make a set of services highly available to clients. Server clusters are based on one of the two clustering technologies in the Microsoft Windows Server 2003 operating systems)

713. The process of establishing the normal patterns of behavior for a given network or system is known as ....

a. Scrubbing

b. Intrusion detection

c. Bit flipping

d. Baselining

Ans. d. Baselining

(Baselining is the process of establishing the normal patterns of behavior for a given network or system)

714. What software is designed to detect and neutralize malicious software, including viruses,

worms, and Trojan horses?

a. Software token

b. Honeypot

c. Antimalware

d. SATAN

Ans. c. Antimalware

(Antimalware (commonly called antivirus) software is designed to detect and neutralize malicious software, including viruses, worms, and Trojan horses. The way this software works is by identifying a distinctive attribute of the malware, extracting that as its signature, and then updating all software systems with it)

715. ……….. are software updates intended to remove a vulnerability or defect in the software, or to provide new features or functionality for it.

a. Hashes

b. Switches

c. Patches

d. Hubs

Ans. c. Patches

(Patches are software updates intended to remove a vulnerability or defect in the software, or to provide new features or functionality for it. Patch management is, at least in a basic way, an established part of organizations' IT or security operations already)

716. …………….. is an application execution environment that isolates the executing code from the operating system to prevent security violations.

a.   Sandbox

b.   White box

c.   Staging

d.   Manual malware analysis

Ans. a. Sandbox

(In computer security, a sandbox is a security mechanism for separating running programs, usually in an effort to mitigate system failures or software vulnerabilities from spreading. It is often used to execute untested or untrusted programs or code, possibly from unverified or untrusted third parties, suppliers, users or websites, without risking harm to the host machine or operating system)

717. An entire network that is meant to be compromised is known as ……………..

a.   Honeynet

b.   Compromised network

c. Telnet

d. Subset

Ans. a. Honeynet

(A honeynet is an entire network that is meant to be compromised. Some honeynets are simply two or more honeypots used together)

718. An organization that is responsible for monitoring and advising users and companies about security preparation and security breaches is ....

a. ANSI

b. CERT

c. NIST

d. FEMA

Ans. b. CERT

(Computer Emergency Response Team (CERT) is an organization that is responsible for monitoring and advising users and companies about security preparation and security breaches)

719. .... is the acceptable amount of data loss measured in time.

a. Work recovery time (WRT)

b. Recovery point objective (RPO)

c. Recovery time objective (RTO)

d. Maximum tolerable downtime (MTD)

Ans. b. Recovery point objective (RPO)

(The recovery point objective (RPO) is the acceptable amount of data loss measured in time. This value represents the earliest point in time at which data must be recovered)

720. An event that causes the entire facility to be unusable for a day or longer is known as ……….

a. Disaster

b. Accident

c. Alerts

d. Problem

Ans. a. Disaster

(A disaster is an event that causes the entire facility to be unusable for a day or longer. This usually requires the use of an alternate processing facility and restoration of software and data from offsite copies)

721. Which of the following best describes the warm site?

a. Provides environmental measures but no

equipment

b. Expensive and fully configured

c. Partially configured with some equipment

d. Fully configured and operational in a few hours

Ans. c. partially configured with some equipment

(Warm site is a leased or rented facility that is usually partially configured with some equipment, such as HVAC, and foundational infrastructure components, but not the actual computers)

722. Which of the following is an empty data center?

a. Warm site

b. Cold site

c. Hot site

d. Scorching site

Ans. b. Cold site

(A cold site is essentially an empty data center. It may take weeks to get the site activated and ready for work. The cold site could have equipment racks and dark fiber (fiber that does not have the circuit engaged) and maybe even desks)

723. A company that has additional space and

capacity to provide applications and services such as call centers is known as ....

a. Service bureau

b. CERT

c. Contingency company

d. Customer Service Agents

Ans. a. Service bureau

(A service bureau is a company that has additional space and capacity to provide applications and services such as call centers. A company pays a monthly subscription fee to a service bureau for this space and service)

724. Which of the following is an advantage of Warm and Cold Site?

a. Highly available

b. Practical for proprietary hardware or software use

c. Annual testing available

d. Usually used for short-term solutions, but available for longer stays

Ans. b. Practical for proprietary hardware or software use

(Warm and Cold Site are usually practical for proprietary hardware or software use. While option a, c, and d, are the advantages of hot site)

725. What is used to ensure the availability of data and to provide a fault tolerant solution by duplicating hardware and maintaining more than one copy of the information?

a. Disk mirroring

b. Disk shadowing

c. Electronic vaulting

d. Remote journaling

Ans. b. Disk shadowing

(Disk shadowing is a technique for maintaining a set of two or more identical disk images on separate disk devices. Its primary purpose is to enhance reliability and availability of secondary storage by providing multiple paths to redundant data)

726. System architecture, system integrity, covert channel analysis, trusted facility management, and trusted recovery are elements of what security criteria?

a. Quality assurance

b. Operational assurance

c. Life cycle assurance

d. Quantity assurance

Ans. b. Operational assurance

(Operational assurance focuses on the basic features and architecture of a system that lend themselves to supporting security. There are five requirements or elements of operation assurance which include system architecture, system integrity, covert channel analysis, trusted facility management and trusted recovery)

727. .... is a combination of technologies and processes that work together to ensure that some specific thing is always up and running.

a. Disaster recovery (DR)

b. High availability (HA)

c. Business impact analysis (BIA)

d. Business continuity Plan (BCP)

Ans. b. High availability (HA)

(High availability (HA) is a combination of technologies and processes that work together to ensure that some specific thing is always up and running. The specific thing can be a database, a network, an application, a power supply, etc)

728. The capability of a technology to continue to operate as expected even if something unexpected takes place is known as ....

a. Fault tolerance

b. Software Fault

c. Fault mitigation

d. Operational assurance

Ans. a. Fault tolerance

(Fault tolerance is the property that enables a system to continue operating properly in the event of the failure of (or one or more faults within) some of its components)

729. ………………….. is commonly built into the network at a routing protocol level.

a. Redundancy

b. Virtualization

c. Cloud computing

d. Hashes

Ans. a. Redundancy

(Redundancy is commonly built into the network at a routing protocol level. The routing protocols are configured so if one link goes down or gets congested, then traffic is routed over a different network link)

730. What is the most important aspect of marking media?

a. Date labeling

b. Content description

c. Electronic labeling

d. Classification

Ans. d. Classification

(Classification is the most important aspect of marking media because it clearly identifies the value of the media and users know how to protect it based on the classification. Including information such as the date and a description of the content isn't as important as marking the classification)

731. What does it mean if a cipher lock has a door delay option?

a. After a door is open for a specific period, the alarm goes off.

b. It can only be opened during emergency situations.

c. It has a hostage alarm capability.

d. It has supervisory override capability

Ans. a. After a door is open for a specific period, the alarm goes off.

(A security guard would want to be alerted when a door has been open for an extended period. It may be an indication that something is taking place other than a person entering or exiting the door. A security system can have a threshold set so that if the door is open past the defined time period, an alarm sounds)

732. An administrator is granting permissions to a database. What is the default level of access the administrator should grant to new users?

a.   Read

b.   Modify

c.   Full access

d.   No access

Ans. d. No access

(The default level of access should be no access. The principle of least privilege dictates that users should only be granted the level of access they need for their job and the question doesn't indicate new users need any access. Read access, modify access, and full access grants users some level of access, which violates the principle of least privilege)

733. A financial organization commonly has employees switch duty responsibilities every six months. What security principle are they employing?

a.   Job rotation

b.   Separation of duties

c. Mandatory vacations

d. Least privilege

Ans. a. Job rotation

(A job rotation policy has employees rotate jobs or job responsibilities and can help detect incidences of collusion and fraud. A separation of duties policy ensures that a single person doesn't control all elements of a specific function. Mandatory vacation policies ensure that employees take an extended time away from their job, requiring someone else to perform their job responsibilities. Least privilege ensures that users have only the permissions they need to perform their job and no more)

734. Which one of the following is not a valid security practice related to special privileges?

a. Monitor special privilege assignments.

b. Grant access equally to administrators and operators.

c. Monitor special privilege usage.

d. Grant access to only trusted employees.

Ans. b. Grant access equally to administrators and operators.

(Special privileges should not be granted equally to administrators and operators. Instead, personnel should be granted only the privileges they need to perform their job. Special privileges are activities that require special access or elevated rights and permissions to perform administrative and sensitive job tasks)

735. An organization is using a Software as a Service (SaaS) cloud-based service shared with another organization. What type of deployment model does this describe?

a. Public

b. Private

c. Community

d. Hybrid

Ans. c. Community

(A community cloud deployment model provides cloud-based assets to two or more organizations. A public cloud model includes assets available for any consumers to rent or lease. A private cloud deployment model includes cloud-based assets for a single organization. A hybrid model includes a combination of two or more deployment models)

736. Which of the following can be a most effective method of configuration management using a baseline?

a. Implementing change management

b. Using images

c. Implementing vulnerability management

d. Implementing patch management

Ans. b. Using images

(Images can be an effective configuration management method using a baseline. Imaging ensures that systems are deployed with the same, known configuration. Change management processes help prevent outages from unauthorized changes. Vulnerability management processes helps to identify vulnerabilities, and patch management processes help to ensure systems are kept up-to-date)

737. Which of the following is not a part of a change management process?

a. Immediately implement the change if it will improve performance.

b. Request the change.

c. Create a rollback plan for the change.

d. Document the change.

Ans. a. Immediately implement the change if it will improve performance.

(Change management processes may need to be temporarily bypassed to respond to an emergency, but they should not be bypassed simply because someone thinks it can improve performance. Even when a change is implemented in response to an emergency, it should still be documented and reviewed after the incident. Requesting changes, creating rollback plans, and documenting changes are all valid steps within a change management process)

738. What is the best form of antivirus protection?

a. Multiple solutions on each system

b. A single solution throughout the organization

c. Antivirus protection at several locations

d. One hundred percent content filtering at all border gateways

Ans. c. Antivirus protection at several locations

(A multipronged approach provides the best solution. This involves having antivirus software at several locations, such as at the boundary between the Internet and the internal network, at email servers, and on each system. More than one antivirus application on a single system isn't recommended)

739. What is a primary goal of change management?

a. Personnel safety

b. Allowing rollback of changes

c. Ensuring that changes do not reduce security

d. Auditing privilege access

Ans. c. Ensuring that changes do not reduce security

(The goal of change management is to ensure that any change does not lead to unintended outages or reduce security. Change management doesn't affect personnel safety. A change management plan will commonly include a rollback plan, but that isn't a specific goal of the program. Change management doesn't perform any type of auditing)

740. Which of the following attacks sends packets with the victim's IP address as both the source and the destination?

a.　Land

b.　Spamming

c.　Teardrop

d.　Ping flood

Ans. a. Land

(In a land attack, the attacker sends a victim numerous SYN packets that have been spoofed to use the same source and destination IP address as the victim's IP address. Spamming attacks send unwanted email. A teardrop attack fragments traffic in such a way that data packets can't be put together. A ping flood attack floods the victim with ping requests)

741. Which is the most common method of distributing malware?

a. Driving downloads

b. Email

c. Rogueware

d. Unapproved software

Ans. b. Email

(Of the choices offered, email is the most common distribution method for viruses of the choices given. Driving downloads isn't a term used in IT security. Rogueware (fake antivirus software) is a common method of tricking users but not the most common method. If users are able to install unapproved software, they may inadvertently install malware, but this isn't the most common method either)

742. .... is a fake network designed to tempt intruders with unpatched and unprotected security vulnerabilities and false data.

a. IDS

b. Honeynet

c. Padded cell

d. Pseudo flaw

Ans. b. Honeynet

(Honeypots are individual computers, and honeynets are entire networks created to serve as a trap for intruders.

They look like legitimate networks and tempt intruders with unpatched and unprotected security vulnerabilities as well as attractive and tantalizing but false data)

743. .... is the technique of segmenting logically sequential data, such as a file, in a way that access of sequential segments are made to different physical storage devices.

a. Bit flipping

b. Data striping

c. Fuzzing

d. Scrubbing

Ans. b. Data striping

(In computer data storage, data striping is the technique of segmenting logically sequential data, such as a file, so that consecutive segments are stored on different physical storage devices. Striping is useful when a processing device requests data more quickly than a single storage device can provide it)

744. Which of the following models provide fully functional applications typically accessible via a web browser?

a. Infrastructure as a Service (IaaS),

b. Platform as a Service (PaaS)

c. Software as a Service (SaaS)

d. People as a service (PaaS)

Ans. c. Software as a Service (SaaS)

(Software as a service (SaaS) is a software distribution model in which a third-party provider hosts applications and makes them available to customers over the Internet. SaaS is one of three main categories of cloud computing, alongside infrastructure as a service (IaaS) and platform as a service (PaaS))

745. The variation in latency between different packets is known as ………..

a. Jitter

b. Scatter

c. Patches

d. Locks

Ans. a. Jitter

(Jitter is defined as a variation in the delay of received packets. The sending side transmits packets in a continuous stream and spaces them evenly apart. Because of network congestion, improper queuing, or configuration errors, the delay between packets can vary instead of remaining constant, as shown in the figure)

746. **Which of the following cloud computing models provide consumers with a computing**

platform, including hardware, an operating system, and applications?

a. Infrastructure as a Service (IaaS),

b. Platform as a Service (PaaS)

c. Software as a Service (SaaS)

d. People as a service (PaaS)

Ans. b. Platform as a Service (PaaS)

(Platform as a Service (PaaS) models provide consumers with a computing platform, including hardware, an operating system, and applications. In some cases, consumers install the applications from a list of choices provided by the CSP. Consumers manage their applications and possibly some configuration settings on the host)

747. If power stays high for a long period of time, it's called as …………..

a. Brownout

b. Surge

c. Sag

d. Spike

Ans. b. Surge

(A surge is a sudden large increase in power that has previously been steady, or has only increased or developed slowly)

748. Which of the following models provide basic computing resources such as servers, storage, and in some cases, networking resources to consumers?

a. Infrastructure as a Service (IaaS)

b. Platform as a Service (PaaS)

c. Software as a Service (SaaS)

d. People as a service (PaaS)

Ans. a. Infrastructure as a Service (IaaS)

(Infrastructure as a Service (IaaS) model provides basic computing resources to consumers. This includes servers, storage, and in some cases, networking resources. Consumers install operating systems and applications and perform all required maintenance on the operating systems and applications. The CSP maintains the cloud-based infrastructure, ensuring that consumers have access to leased systems)

749. Which of the following measures is not concerned with maintaining operations security?

a. Classifying and labeling assets

b. Protecting valuable assets

c. Controlling system accounts

d. Managing security services

Ans. a.   Classifying and labeling assets

(Operations security involves protecting valuable assets, controlling system accounts and managing security services)

750. Which of the following ensures constant redundancy and fault tolerance?

a.   cold spare

b.   warm spare

c.   hot spare

d.   archives

Ans. c. hot spare

(A cold spare is a spare component that is not powered up but is a duplicate of the primary component that can be inserted into the system if needed. Warm spares are those that are already inserted in the system but do not receive power unless they are required Hot spares stay powered on and waiting to be called upon as needed. Archives are data backups stored for historical purposes. To ensure constant redundancy and fault tolerance, hot spare is the best option)

751. Which of the following best describes the three separate functions of CCTV?

a.   Surveillance, deterrence, and evidentiary archives

b. Monitoring, white balancing and inspection

c. Optical scanning, infrared beaming and lighting

d. Intrusion detection, detainment and response

Ans. a. surveillance, deterrence, and evidentiary archives

(Use of CCTV systems for security services include several different functions: Surveillance, assessment, deterrence, and evidentiary archives)

752. A Security Organization Control (SOC) report commonly covers a period of ………..

a. 6 months

b. 12 months

c. 18 months

d. 9 months

Ans. b. 12 months

(A Security Organization Control (SOC) report commonly covers a period of 12 months)

753. Which of the following are computer forensics guidelines?

a. IOCE, SWGDE, and ACPO

b. IOCE, MOM, and SWGDE

c. MOM, SWGDE, and IOCE

d. ACPO, MOM, and IOCE

Ans. a. IOCE, SWGDE, and ACPO

(Like incident response, there are various computer forensic guidelines for example, International Organization for Computer Evidence (IOCE), Scientific Working Group on Digital Evidence (SWGDE) and Association of Chief Police Officers (ACPO))

754. If speed is preferred over resilience, which of the following RAID configuration is the most suited?

a. RAID 0

b. RAID 1

c. RAID 5

d. RAID 10

Ans. a. RAID 0

(In a RAID 0 configuration, files are written in stripes across multiple disks without the use of parity information. This technique allows for fast reading and writing to disk since all of the disks can typically be accessed in parallel. However, without the parity information, it is not possible to recover from a hard drive failure. This technique does not provide redundancy and should not be used for systems with high availability requirements)

755. Which of the following describes why operations security is most important?

a.   An environment continually changes and has the potential of lowering its level of protection

b.   It helps an environment be functionally sound and productive

c.   It ensures there will be no unauthorized access to the facility or its resources

d.   It continually raises a company's level of protection

Ans. a. An environment continually changes and has the potential of lowering its level of protection

(Security operations have the goal of keeping everything running smoothly each and every day. It implements new software and hardware and carries out the necessary security tasks passed down to it. As the environment changes and security is kept in the loop with these changes, there is a smaller likelihood of opening up vulnerabilities)

756. Which of the following antivirus detection methods is the most recent to the industry and monitors suspicious?

a.   Behavior blocking

b.   Fingerprint detection

c.   Signature-based detection

d. Heuristic detection

Ans. a. Behavior blocking

(Of the methods listed, behavior blocking is the most recent evolution in antivirus detection. Behavior blocking allows suspicious code to execute within the operating system and watches its interactions looking for suspicious activities. These activities include writing to startup files or the Run keys in the Registry; opening, deleting, or modifying files; scripting email messages to send executable code; and creating or modifying macros and scripts)

757. What type of software testing tests code passively?

a. Black box testing

b. Dynamic testing

c. Static testing

d. White box testing

Ans. c. Static testing

(Static testing tests code passively. This includes walkthroughs, syntax checking and code reviews. Black box testing gives the tester no internal details: the software is treated as a black box that receives inputs. Dynamic testing tests the code while executing it. White box software testing gives the tester access to program source code, data structures, variables, etc.)

758. Which action is not part of configuration management?

a. Submitting a formal request

b. Operating system configuration and settings

c. Hardware configuration

d. Application settings and configuration

Ans. a. Submitting a formal request

(Submitting a formal request would fall under the change control umbrella. Most environments have a change control process that dictates how all changes will be handled, approved, and tested. Once the change is approved, there needs to be something in place to make sure the actual configurations implemented to carry out this change take place properly. This is the job of configuration management)

759. Which of the following best describes a virtual team?

a. It consists of experts who have other duties within the organization.

b. It can be cost prohibitive to smaller organizations.

c. It is a hybrid model.

d. Core members are permanently assigned to the team

Ans. a. It consists of experts who have other duties within the organization.

(There are three different types of incident response teams. A virtual team is made up of experts who have other duties and assignments within the organization or are outside consultant. A virtual team is commonly developed and used when a company cannot afford to dedicate specific individuals to only deal with incidents)

760. Which of the following is a countermeasure to traffic analysis?

a. Faraday Cage

b. Traffic padding

c. Dumpster Diving

d. Zeroization

Ans. b. Traffic padding

(Traffic padding may be used to hide the traffic pattern, which means to insert dummy traffic into the network and present to the intruder a different traffic pattern. The apparent traffic pattern, which is observed by intruder, is referred to as a cover mode that hides the real operation mode of the system)

761. What is created by combining RAID Level 1 and Level 5?

a. RAID 15

b. RAID 10

c. RAID 3

d. RAID 4

Ans. a. RAID 15

(RAID 15 is created by combining RAID Level 1and Level 5)

762. Which of the following types of attacks uses ICMP protocol for communications between two systems?

a. Land

b. Loki Attack

c. Teardrop

d. Ping flood

Ans. b. Loki Attack

(The use of IDS/IPS is an effective method and many IPS/IDS devices have a signature to detect the presence of LOKI)

763. Maximum Tolerable Downtime (MTD) is comprised of which two metrics?

a. Recovery Point Objective (RPO) and Work Recovery Time (WRT)

b. Recovery Point Objective (RPO) and Mean Time to Repair (MTTR)

c. Recovery Time Objective (RTO) and Work Recovery Time (WRT)

d. Recovery Time Objective (RTO) and Mean Time to Repair (MTTR)

Ans. a. Recovery Time Objective (RTO) and Work Recovery Time (WRT)

(The Recovery Time Objective (RTO, the time it takes bring a failed system back online) and Work Recovery Time (WRT, the time required to configure a failed system) are used to calculate the Maximum Tolerable Downtime.

764. What is the most cost effective alternate site choice?

a. Cold

b. Hot

c. Redundant

d. Warm

Ans. d. Warm

(A warm site is a data center with raised floor, power, utilities, computer peripherals, and fully configured computers; requiring 24-72 hours to become fully operational. Options a, b, and c are incorrect)

765. Which of the following is not an advantage of a hot site?

a. Offers many hardware and software choices

b. Is readily available

c. Can be up and running in hours

d. Annual testing is available

Ans. a. Offers many hardware and software choices

(Hot sites are fully equipped, they do not allow for a lot of different hardware and software choices. The subscription service offers basic software and hardware products and does not usually offer a wide range of proprietary items)

Chapter 15
Software Development Security

766. .... is not a component of the DevOps model?

a. Information security

b. Software development

c. Quality assurance

d. IT operations

Ans. a. Information security

(The three elements of the DevOps model are software development, quality assurance, and IT operations)

767. Which of the following is a valid system development methodology?

a. The spring model

b. The spiral model

c. The production model

d. The Gantt model

Ans. b. The spiral model

(The spiral model is the only valid software development methodology listed. It was developed in 1988 at TRW)

768. Which one of the following is not a valid database management system model?

a. The hierarchical database management system

b. The structured database management system

c. The network database management system

d. The relational database management system

Ans. b. The structured database management system

(The structured database management system model is not a valid type. Four common database types are the hierarchical database management system, the object-oriented database management system, the network database management system, and the relational database management system)

769. A project management tool used to define and group a project's individual work elements in an organized manner is known as ………..

a. Work breakdown structure (WBS)

b. Statement of Work (SOW)

c. Software development life cycle (SDLC)

d. Privacy risk assessment

Ans. a. Work breakdown structure (WBS)

(A work breakdown structure (WBS) is a project management tool used to define and group a project's individual work elements in an organized manner. It is a deliberate decomposition of the project into tasks and subtasks that result in clearly defined deliverables)

770. During which stage of the software development life cycle should security be implemented?

a. Development

b. Project initiation

c. Deployment

d. Installation

Ans. b. Project initiation

(Security should be implemented at the initiation of a project. When security is added during the project initiation phase, substantial amounts of money can be saved. Because the first phase is the project initiation phase, all other answers are incorrect)

771. In the software development life cycle, what is used to maintain changes to development or production?

a. Certification

b. Audit control team

c. Manufacturing review board

d. Change control

Ans. d. Change control

(Change control is used to maintain changes to development or production. Without it, control would become very difficult, because there would be no way to track changes that might affect the product's functionality or security)

772. What form of access control is concerned mainly with the data stored by a field?

a.   Content-dependent

b.   Context-dependent

c.   Semantic integrity mechanisms

d.   Perturbation

Ans. a. Content-dependent

(Content-dependent access control is focused primarily on the internal data of each field)

773. .... is used to enforce referential integrity between database tables

a.   Candidate key

b.   Primary key

c.   Foreign key

d.   Super key

Ans. c. Foreign key

(Foreign keys are used to enforce referential integrity constraints between tables that participate in a relationship)

774. Which one of the following terms cannot be used to describe the main RAM of a typical computer system?

a. Volatile

b. Sequential access

c. Real memory

d. Primary memory

Ans. b. Sequential access

(Random access memory (RAM) allows for the direct addressing of any point within the resource. A sequential access storage medium, such as a magnetic tape, requires scanning through the entire media from the beginning to reach a specific address)

775. What type of reconnaissance attack provides attackers with useful information about the services running on a system?

a. Session hijacking

b. Port scan

c. Dumpster diving

d. IP sweep

Ans. b. Port scan

(A port scanner is an application designed to probe a server or host for open ports. This is often used by administrators to verify security policies of their networks and by attackers to identify network services running on a host and exploit vulnerabilities. Port scans reveal the ports associated with services running on a machine and available to the public)

776. Which of the following technology is used by Java language to minimize the threat posed by applets?

a. Confidentiality

b. Encryption

c. Stealth

d. Sandbox

Ans. d. Sandbox

(The Java sandbox isolates applets and allows them to run within a protected environment, limiting the effect they may have on the rest of the system)

777. Which of the following is not a component of change management process?

a. Access Control

b. Request Control

c. Change Control

d. Release Control

Ans. a. Access Control

(The 3 basic components of change management process are request control, change control, and release control)

778. A program that intelligently analyzes unknown code to identify suspicious commands and code sections is known as …………

a. Heuristic Scanner

b. Vulnerability scanner

c. Security Scanner

d. Network scanner

Ans. a. Heuristic Scanner

(Heuristic analysis is a method employed by many computer antivirus programs designed to detect previously unknown computer viruses, as well as new variants of viruses already in the "wild". Heuristic analysis is an expert based analysis that determines the susceptibility of a system towards particular threat/risk using various decision rules or weighing methods)

779. Which of the following is not a component of configuration management?

a. Configuration Identification

b. Configuration Control

c. Release Control

d. Configuration Audit

Ans. c. Release Control

(The four main components of configuration management are configuration identification, configuration control, configuration status accounting, and configuration audit. While Release Control is a component of change management process)

780. Which of the following correctly describes a database schema?

a. The structure of the database

b. The capability of different versions of the same information to exist at different classification levels within the database

c. An ordered set of values within a row in the database table

d. Something that uniquely identifies each row in a table

Ans. a. The structure of the database

(A database schema is the skeleton structure that represents the logical view of the entire database. It defines how the data is organized and how the relations among them are associated. It formulates all the constraints that are to be applied on the data)

781. What type of malware is considered self-replicating?

a. Boot sector

b. Meme virus

c. Script virus

d. Worm

Ans. d. Worm

(The greatest danger of worms is their capability to self-replicate. Left unchecked, this process can grow in volume to an astronomical amount. For example, a worm could send copies of itself to everyone listed in your email address book, and those recipients' computers would then do the same)

782. Which of the following tool is aimed at supporting one or more software engineering tasks in the process of developing software?

a. CASE tool

b. Traceroute

c. Network tool

d. Usecase tool

Ans. a. CASE tool

(Computer-aided software engineering (CASE) is the domain of software tools used to design and implement applications. CASE tools are similar to and were partly inspired by computer-aided design (CAD) tools used for designing hardware products)

783.. …………….. is the process of exploiting a process or configuration setting in order to gain access to resources that would normally not be available to the process or its user.

a. Buffer overflow

b. Privilege escalation

c. Static analysis

d. Attack surface analysis

Ans. b. Privilege escalation

(Privilege escalation is the act of exploiting a bug, design flaw or configuration oversight in an operating system or software application to gain elevated access to resources that are normally protected from an application or user)

784. Which of the following is the first phase of a software development life cycle?

a. Design

b. Requirements gathering

c. Testing/validations

d.   Release/maintenance

Ans. b. Requirements gathering

(Requirement gathering and analysis is the first stage of any software development life cycle model. This phase is basically the brainstorming phase and often consists of sub-stages like Feasibility Analysis to check how much of the idea can be put into action)

785. Which of the following model uses a linear-sequential life-cycle approach?

a.   Build and Fix Model

b.   Waterfall model

c.   V-Shaped Model

d.   Incremental model

Ans. b. Waterfall model

(The Waterfall model uses a linear-sequential life-cycle approach. Each phase must be completed in its entirety before the next phase can begin. At the end of each phase, a review takes place to make sure the project is on the correct path and should continue)

786. .... is an approach that allows the development team to quickly create a prototype (sample) to test the validity of the current understanding of the project requirements.

a. Evolutionary prototype

b. Operational prototype

c. Throwaway

d. Rapid prototyping

Ans. d. Rapid prototyping

(Rapid prototyping is a group of techniques used to quickly fabricate a scale model of a physical part or assembly using three-dimensional computer aided design (CAD) data. Construction of the part or assembly is usually done using 3D printing or "additive layer manufacturing" technology)

787. A multidisciplinary development team with representatives from many or all the stakeholder populations is called as ……….

a. Integrated product team (IPT)

b. Audit control team

c. Open Web Application Security Project (OWASP)

d. Software configuration management (SCM)

Ans. a. Integrated product team (IPT)

(An integrated product team (IPT) is a multidisciplinary group of people who are collectively responsible for delivering a defined product or process. IPTs are used in complex development programs/projects for review and decision making. The emphasis of the IPT is on involvement of all stakeholders (users, customers, management, developers, and contractors) in a collaborative forum)

788. Which component of the change management process allows developers to prioritize tasks?

a. Release control

b. Configuration control

c. Request control

d. Change audit

Ans. c. Request control

(The request control provides users with a framework to request changes and developers with the opportunity to prioritize those requests)

789. What software development model uses a seven-stage approach with a feedback loop that allows progress one step backward?

a. Boyce-Codd

b. Waterfall

c. Spiral

d. Agile

Ans. b. Waterfall

(The waterfall model uses a seven-stage approach to software development and includes a feedback loop that allows development to return to the previous phase to correct defects discovered during the subsequent phase)

790. What is the most-used type of database management system?

a. The hierarchical database management system

b. The structured database management system

c. The network database management system

d. The relational database management system

Ans. d. The relational database management system

(The relational database management system is the most used type. It is structured such that the columns represent the variables and the rows contain the specific instance of data)

791. Which of the following statements are true with regards to Java applets?

a. They are downloaded from a server

b. They are not restricted in computer memory

c. They are run from the browser

d. They are executed by your system

Ans. b. They are not restricted in computer memory.

(Java is downloaded from the server, executed by the browser, and run on your system. Java has limits placed on what it can do by means of a sandbox and was originally designed with restrictions on what could be done while loaded in memory. Originally their activities were restricted in memory and could not access certain parts of memory or access files or initiate network connections)

792. Which of the following software development methodology uses minimal planning and in favor of rapid prototyping?

a. Spiral Model

b. Rapid application development (RAD)

c. Incremental Model

d. Joint Application Development (JAD)

Ans. b. Rapid application development (RAD)

(Rapid application development (RAD) is a software development methodology that uses minimal planning in favor of rapid prototyping. The "planning" of software developed using RAD is interleaved with writing the software itself. The lack of extensive per-planning generally allows software to be written much faster, and makes it easier to change requirements)

793. Which software development methodology acknowledges the fact that customer needs cannot be completely understood and will change over time?

a. Kanban

b. Scrum

c. Spiral Model

d. Agile model

Ans. b. Scrum

(Scrum is a methodology that acknowledges the fact that customer needs cannot be completely understood and will change over time. It focuses on team collaboration, customer involvement, and continuous delivery)

794. Kanban, a production scheduling system was developed by ....

a. Toyota

b. Netscape

c. Swiss developers

d. Renault

Ans. a. Toyota

(Kanban is a production scheduling system developed by Toyota to more efficiently support just-in-time delivery. Over time, it was adopted by IT and software systems developers)

795. Which of the following method uses a team approach in application development in a

workshop-oriented environment?

a. Exploratory model

b. Joint Application Development (JAD)

c. Reuse model

d. Break and Fix Model

Ans. b. Joint Application Development (JAD)

(JAD (Joint Application Development) is a methodology that involves the client or end user in the design and development of an application, through a succession of collaborative workshops called JAD sessions. Chuck Morris and Tony Crawford, both of IBM, developed JAD in the late 1970s and began teaching the approach through workshops in 1980)

796. A comprehensive, integrated set of guidelines for developing products and software is called as ....

a. Joint Application Development (JAD)

b. Extreme Programming (XP)

c. Capability Maturity Model Integration (CMMI)

d. Pair programming

Ans. c. Capability Maturity Model Integration (CMMI)

(Capability Maturity Model Integration (CMMI) is

a process level improvement training and appraisal program. CMMI is collection of best practices meant for Software Development & Support Companies to improve their products. Administered by the CMMI Institute, a subsidiary of ISACA, it was developed at Carnegie Mellon University (CMU))

797. Code that has been put through a compiler and is unreadable to humans is known as ....

a.   Hamming Code

b.   Python code

c.   Secret code

d.   Compiled code

Ans. d. Compiled code

(Compiled code is code that has been put through a compiler and is unreadable to humans. Most software profits are based on licensing, which outlines what customers can do with the compiled code)

798. Which of the following is considered as a low-level programming language?

a.   Machine languages

b.   Compiled languages

c.   Assembly languages

d.   Interpreted languages

Ans. c. Assembly languages

(An assembly language is considered a low-level programming language and is the symbolic representation of machine-level instructions. It is "one step above" machine language)

799. Which of the following tools convert assembly language source code into machine code?

a. Assemblers

b. Compilers

c. Processors

d. Interpreters

Ans. a. Assemblers

(Assemblers are tools that convert assembly language source code into machine code. Assembly language consists of mnemonics, which are incomprehensible to processors and therefore need to be translated into operation instructions.)

800. The process of classifying objects that will be appropriate for a solution is known as ……….

a. Object-oriented analysis

b. Object-oriented design

c. Object-oriented programming

d. Object-oriented approach

Ans. a. Object-oriented analysis

(Object-oriented analysis (OOA) is the process of classifying objects that will be appropriate for a solution. A problem is analyzed to determine the classes of objects to be used in the application)

801. What acts as a proxy between an application and a database to support interaction and simplify the work of programmers?

a. SDLC

b. ODBC

c. DSS

d. Abstraction

Ans. b. ODBC

(Open Database Connectivity (ODBC) is Microsoft's strategic interface for accessing data in a heterogeneous environment of relational and non-relational database management systems. ODBC acts as a proxy between applications and the backend DBMS)

802. Distributed Component Object Model (DCOM) was developed by ....

a. SAP

b. ORACLE

c. Microsoft

d. Sun Microsystem

Ans. c. Microsoft

(DCOM, or Distributed Component Object Model, is a technology created by Microsoft that allows various software structures to be spread across computers that are networked together)

803. Who developed Distributed Computing Environment (DCE)?

a. National Institute of Standards and Technology (NIST)

b. American National Standards Institute (ANSI)

c. Open Software Foundation (OSF)

d. Object Management Group (OMG)

Ans. c. Open Software Foundation (OSF)

(Distributed Computing Environment (DCE) is a standard developed by the Open Software Foundation (OSF), also called Open Group. It is a client/server framework that is available to many vendors to use within their products)

804. Which of the following standards was developed by Object Management Group (OMG)?

a. DCE

b. DCOM

c. CORBA

d. ORB

Ans. c. CORBA

(Common Object Request Broker Architecture (CORBA) is an open object-oriented standard architecture developed by the Object Management Group (OMG). It provides interoperability among the vast array of software, platforms, and hardware in environments today)

805. Which of the following does not fit in the category of cross-site scripting (XSS) attacks?

a. Nonpersistent XSS

b. Persistent XSS

c. DOM

d. ORB

Ans. d. ORB

(There are three main types of cross-site scripting (XSS) attacks: nonpersistent XSS (exploiting the lack of proper input or output validation on dynamic websites), persistent XSS (attacker loads malicious code on a server that attacks visiting browsers), and DOM (attacker uses the DOM environment to modify the original client-side JavaScript))

806. .... is an XML-based protocol that encodes messages in a web service environment.

a.   Kerberos

b.   SOAP

c.   RADIUS

d.   UDDI

Ans. b. SOAP

(SOAP is an XML-based protocol that encodes messages in a web service environment. It actually defines an XML schema of how communication is going to take place. The SOAP XML schema defines how objects communicate directly)

807. Which of the following is an object-oriented, platform-independent programming language?

a.   Java

b.   SAP

c.   SAS

d.   ORACLE

Ans. a. Java

(Java is an object-oriented, platform-independent programming language. It is employed as a full-fledged programming language and is used to write complete programs and small components, called applets, which commonly run in a user's web browser)

808. The term "data dictionary" is defined as ....

a. A dictionary for programmers

b. A list of databases

c. A virtual table of the rows and tables from two or more combined databases

d. A dictionary used within a database

Ans. b. A list of databases

(A data dictionary contains a list of all database files. It also contains the number of records in each file and each field name and type)

809. Data checks and validity checks are examples of what type of application controls?

a. Preventive

b. Constructive

c. Detective

d. Corrective

Ans. a. Preventive

(Application controls are used to enforce an organization's

security policy and procedures. Preventive application controls include data checks, validity checks, contingency planning, and backups. Answers C and D are incorrect because they are not controls, and answer B is a distracter)

810. Which of the following is not a component of a SQL database?

a. Views

b. Schemas

c. Tables

d. Object-oriented interfaces

Ans. d. Object-oriented interfaces

(The three main components of SQL databases are schemas, tables, and views. Object-oriented interfaces are part of object-oriented database management systems)

811. Which of the following best describes a mobile code?

a. Code that can be used on a handheld device

b. Code that can be used on several different platforms, such as Windows, Mac, and Linux

c. Code that can be executed within a network browser

d. A script that can be executed within an Office document

Ans. c. Code that can be executed within a network browser

(Mobile code is code that can be executed within a network browser. Applets are examples of mobile code. Mobile code is not used on a handheld device, nor is it a script that is executed in an Office document. And although mobile code may run on several different platforms, answer B is an incomplete answer)

812. ………………… is an industry-standard mechanism developed to represent the entire range of over 100,000 textual characters in the world as a standard coding format.

a.　　URL encoding

b.　　Unicode

c.　　Path or directory traversal

d.　　Decoding

Ans. b. Unicode

(Unicode is a computing industry standard for the consistent encoding, representation, and handling of text expressed in most of the world's writing systems. The latest version contains a repertoire of 136,755 characters covering 139 modern and historic scripts, as well as multiple symbol sets)

813. ………… is the standard structure layout that represent HTML and XML documents in

the browser.

a. OOD

b. DOM

c. OOA

d. OOP

Ans. b. DOM

(DOM (Document Object Model) is the standard structure layout to represent HTML and XML documents in the browser. In such attacks the document components such as form fields and cookies can be referenced through JavaScript)

814. A suite of programs used to manage large sets of structured data with ad hoc query capabilities for many types of users is known as ....

a. Database management system (DBMS)

b. Federated identity management system

c. Integrated product team (IPT)

d. Software configuration management (SCM)

Ans. a. Database management system (DBMS)

(A database management system (DBMS) is system software for creating and managing databases. The DBMS provides users and programmers with a systematic way to create, retrieve, update and manage data)

815. Which of the following is not an attribute of DBMS?

a. It provides transaction persistence.

b. It allows the sharing of data with multiple users

c. It provides recovery and fault tolerance

d. Transforms bits to electrical signals

Ans. d. Transforms bits to electrical signals

(DBMS allows for easier backup procedures, ensures consistency among the data held on several different servers throughout the network, provides transaction persistence, provides recovery and fault tolerance, and allows the sharing of data with multiple users)

816. Which of the following does not fit in the category of Database Models?

a. Relational Model

b. Object-oriented model

c. Hierarchical Model

d. Subject-oriented model

Ans. d. Subject-oriented model

(Databases come in several types of models, which include relational, hierarchical, network, object-oriented and object-relational model)

817. A standard programming language that clients use to interact with a database is known as ....

a.   SQL

b.   C

c.   COBOL

d.   FORTRAN

Ans. a. SQL

(Structured Query Language (SQL) is a standard programming language used to allow clients to interact with a database. Many database products support SQL. It allows clients to carry out operations such as inserting, updating, searching, and committing data. When a client interacts with a database, it is most likely using SQL to carry out requests)

818. A set of ODBC interfaces that exposes the functionality of data sources through accessible objects is known as ....

a.   Java Database Connectivity (JDBC)

b.   ActiveX Data Objects (ADO)

c. Object Linking and Embedding Database (OLE DB)

d. Object-relational database (ORD)

Ans. b. ActiveX Data Objects (ADO)

(ActiveX Data Objects (ADO) is an API that allows applications to access back-end database systems. It is a set of ODBC interfaces that exposes the functionality of data sources through accessible objects. ADO uses the OLE DB interface to connect with the database, and can be developed with many different scripting languages)

819. An API that allows a Java application to communicate with a database is ....

a. Java Database Connectivity (JDBC)

b. ActiveX Data Objects (ADO)

c. Object Linking and Embedding Database (OLE DB)

d. Object-relational database (ORD)

Ans. a. Java Database Connectivity (JDBC)

(Java Database Connectivity (JDBC) is an application program interface (API) specification for connecting programs written in Java to the data in popular databases. It provides the same functionality as ODBC but is specifically designed for use by Java database applications)

820. Which of the following database languages

examines data and defines how the data can be manipulated within the database?

a. Data control language (DCL)

b. Data definition language (DDL)

c. Data manipulation language (DML)

d. Ad hoc query language (QL)

Ans. c. Data manipulation language (DML)

(A data manipulation language (DML) is a family of syntax elements similar to a computer programming language used for selecting, inserting, deleting and updating data in a database. Performing read-only queries of data is sometimes also considered a component of DML)

821. What is the function of Data definition language (DDL)?

a. Allow user to view, manipulate, and use the database

b. Defines the structure and schema of the database

c. Enables users to make requests of the database

d. Produces printouts of data in a user-defined manner

Ans. b. Defines the structure and schema of the database

(Data definition language (DDL) defines the structure

and schema of the database. The structure could mean the table size, key placement, views, and data element relationship. The schema describes the type of data that will be held and manipulated, and their properties)

822. A technique used to hide specific cells that contain information that could be used in inference attacks is known as …………..

a.   Partitioning

b.   Perturbation

c.   Cell suppression

d.   Spiral

Ans. c. Cell suppression

(Cell Suppression is a widely-used technique for avoiding disclosure of sensitive information, which consists in suppressing all sensitive table entries along with a certain number of other entries, called complementary suppressions)

823. What type of database is unique because it can possess multiple records that can be either parent or child?

a.   Relational

b.   Hierarchical

c.   Object-oriented

d. Network

Ans. d. Network

(A network database is unique as it supports multiple parent and child records. A relational database uses columns and rows to organize the information. A hierarchical database combines related records and fields into a logical tree structure. An object-oriented database is considered much more dynamic than earlier designs because it can handle not only data but also audio, images, and other file formats)

824. Data that describes other data is called as ....

a. Metadata

b. Nonatomic data

c. Data structure

d. Transaction processing

Ans. a. Metadata

(Metadata is data that describes other data. Non-atomic data is a data value that consists of multiple data values. A data structure is a set of data in memory composed of fields. Transaction processing is a mode of computer operation)

825. Which one of the following is considered a middleware technology?

a. Atomicity

b. OLE

c. CORBA

d. Object-oriented programming

Ans. c. CORBA

(Common Object Request Broker Architecture (CORBA) is vendor-independent middleware. Its purpose is to tie together different vendors' products so that they can seamlessly work together over distributed networks. Atomicity deals with the validity of database transactions. Object Linking and Embedding (OLE) is a proprietary system developed by Microsoft that allows applications to transfer and share information. Object-oriented programming is a modular form of programming)

826. .... is a project-development method that uses pairs of programmers who work off of detailed specifications.

a. Waterfall

b. Spiral

c. Extreme programming

d. RAD

Ans. c. Extreme programming

(Extreme programming, which is an off-shoot of agile,

uses pairs of programmers who work from detailed specifications. Answer A is not correct because waterfall is a classical method. Answer B is not correct because spiral uses iterations that spiral out every 28 days. Answer D is not correct because RAD uses prototypes)

827. .... is a piece of software installed on a system that is designed to intercept all traffic between the local web browser and the web server.

a. Burp Suite

b. Web proxy

c. Session cookie

d. Persistent cookie

Ans. b. Web proxy

(A Web proxy acts as a middleman, or intermediary, between a user accessing the Web and a website. In the context of using the Web, proxies are a way of accessing the Web that provide another layer of anonymity)

828. A field that links all the data within a record to a unique value is known as a ....

a. Candidate key

b. Primary key

c. Foreign key

d. Super key

Ans. b. Primary key

(A primary key, also called a primary keyword, is a key in a relational database that is unique for each record. It is a unique identifier, such as a driver license number, telephone number (including area code), or vehicle identification number (VIN). A relational database must always have one and only one primary key)

829. An operation that ends a current transaction and cancels the current changes to the database is known as ....

a. Jitter

b. Rollback

c. Burp Suite

d. Web proxy

Ans. b. Rollback

(A rollback is the operation of restoring a database to a previous state by canceling a specific transaction or transaction set. Rollbacks are either performed automatically by database systems or manually by users)

830. A process of interactively producing more detailed versions of objects by populating variables with different values or other variables is known as ....

a. Instantiation

b. Polyinstantiation

c. Partitioning

d. Extreme programming

Ans. b. Polyinstantiation

(Polyinstantiation is a computing technique in which multiple instances of a shared resource are created to prevent any single user or process from contaminating the data required by others)

831. What is used when databases are clustered to provide fault tolerance and higher performance?

a. ActiveX Data Objects (ADO)

b. Object Linking and Embedding Database (OLE DB)

c. Object-relational database (ORD)

d. Online transaction processing (OLTP)

Ans. d. Online transaction processing (OLTP)

(Online transaction processing (OLTP) is generally used when databases are clustered to provide fault tolerance and higher performance. OLTP provides mechanisms that watch for problems and deal with them appropriately when they do occur)

832. The process of massaging the data held in the data warehouse into more useful information is known as …………..

a. Instantiation

b. Polyinstantiation

c. Partitioning

d. Data mining

Ans. d. Data mining

(Data mining is a process used by companies to turn raw data into useful information. By using software to look for patterns in large batches of data, businesses can learn more about their customers and develop more effective marketing strategies as well as increase sales and decrease costs. Data mining depends on effective data collection and warehousing as well as computer processing)

833. What is used to carry out phishing attacks, fraudulent activities, identity theft steps, and information warfare activities?

a. Spyware

b. Malware

c. Ransomware

d. Middleware

Ans. b. Malware

(Malware installs key loggers, which collect sensitive financial information for the malware author to use. Also, it is used to carry out phishing attacks, fraudulent activities, identity theft steps, and information warfare activities)

834. A virus that hides its tracks after infecting a system is known as a...............

a. Polymorphic virus

b. Stealth virus

c. Boot sector viruses

d. Macro virus

Ans. b. Stealth virus

(A stealth virus is a hidden computer virus that attacks operating system processes and averts typical anti-virus or anti-malware scans. Stealth viruses hide in files, partitions and boot sectors and are adept at deliberately avoiding detection)

835. Which of the following does not fit in the category of Malware Components?

a. Insertion

b. Deletion

c. Avoidance

d. Eradication

Ans. b. Deletion

(The components of Malware can be composed of up to six main elements. The six elements are Insertion, Avoidance, Eradication, Replication, Trigger, and Payload)

836. Which of the following element of malware uses an event to initiate its payload execution?

a. Insertion

b. Avoidance

c. Replication

d. Trigger

Ans. d. Trigger

(Trigger uses an event to initiate its payload execution; Insertion installs itself on the victim's system, Avoidance uses methods to avoid being detected, and Replication makes copies of itself and spreads to other victims)

837. .... is the most famous computer worms that targets SCADA software and equipment.

a. Stuxnet

b. MSBlast

c. Duqu

d. Flame

Ans. a. Stuxnet

(Stuxnet is a malicious computer worm, first identified in 2010. Stuxnet is the first malware that attacked industrial control systems also known as SCADA (Supervisory Control and Data Acquisition) systems developed by Siemens (Siemens SIMATIC WinCC). These systems monitor and control critical industrial facilities like nuclear power plants, power grids, etc.)

838. What type of malware is covertly installed on a target computer to gather sensitive information about a victim?

a.   Middleware

b.   Spyware

c.   Ransomware

d.   Adware

Ans. b. Spyware

(Spyware is a type of malware that is installed on a computer without the knowledge of the owner in order to collect the owner's private information. Spyware is often hidden from the user in order to gather information about internet interaction, keystrokes (also known as keylogging), passwords, and other valuable data)

839. Software that automatically generates (renders) advertisements is known as ....

a. Malware

b. Spyware

c. Ransomware

d. Adware

Ans. d. Adware

(Adware, or advertising-supported software, is any software package that automatically renders advertisements in order to generate revenue for its author)

840. Malicious programs that run on systems and allow intruders to access and use a system remotely are known as …………..

a. Rootkit

b. Remote access Trojans (RATs)

c. Logic Bombs

d. Botnets

Ans. b. Remote access Trojans (RATs)

(A remote access Trojan (RAT) is a malware program that includes a back door for administrative control over the target computer. RATs are usually downloaded invisibly with a user-requested program -- such as a game -- or sent as an email attachment)

841. In the context of relational databases, which

of the following denotes rows and columns?

a. Rows and tuples

b. Attributes and rows

c. Keys and views

d. Tuples and attributes

Ans. d. Tuples and attributes

(In a relational database, a row is referred to as a tuple, whereas a column is referred to as an attribute)

842. Which one of the following is an example of open vendor-neutral middleware?

a. OOA

b. COM

c. CORBA

d. OOD

Ans. c. CORBA

(CORBA is an open vendor-neutral middleware. Answers a, b, and d are incorrect because COM enables objects written in different languages to communicate, and OOA and OOD are software design methodologies)

843. Which of the following is an example of a 4GL language?

a. OPS5

b. SQL

c. COBOL

d. FORTRAN

Ans. b. SQL

(SQL, CASE and Statistical Analysis System (SAS) are examples of 4GL language. COBOL and FORTRAN are examples of 3GL language while OPS5 is an example of 5GL language)

844. What can be used to help define a data dictionary?

a. DevOps model

b. Entity relationship diagrams

c. Data flow diagrams

d. Database model

Ans. b. Entity relationship diagrams

(An entity relationship diagram (ERD) shows the relationships of entity sets stored in a database. An entity in this context is a component of data. In other words, ER diagrams illustrate the logical structure of databases.)

845. Which one of the following actions is not performed by antimalware software?

a. Opening, deleting, or modifying files

b. Detecting and removing unwanted spyware programs

c. Modifying an executable logic

d. Creating or modifying macros and scripts

Ans. b. Detecting and removing unwanted spyware programs

(Some of the actions that the antimalware software performs include: opening, deleting, or modifying files, modifying an executable logic as well as creating or modifying macros and scripts. While spyware software detects and removes unwanted spyware programs)

846. A set of tools that is placed on the compromised system for future use is known as ....

a. Raking

b. Rootkit

c. Tension wrench

d. Logic Bombs

Ans. b. Rootkit

(A rootkit is a collection of tools (programs) that enable administrator-level access to a computer or computer network. Typically, a cracker installs a rootkit on a computer after first obtaining user-level access, either by exploiting a known vulnerability or cracking a password)

847. What type of virus employs more than one propagation technique to maximize the number of penetrated systems?

a. Stealth virus

b. Companion virus

c. Polymorphic virus

d. Multipartite virus

Ans. d. Multipartite virus

(Multipartite viruses use two or more propagation techniques (for example, file infection and boot sector infection) to maximize their reach)

848. Which of the following programming language(s) can be used to develop ActiveX controls for use on an Internet site?

a. Visual Basic

b. C

c. Java

d. All the above

Ans. d. All the above

(Microsoft's ActiveX technology supports a number of programming languages, including Visual Basic, C, C++, and Java. On the other hand, only the Java language can be used to write Java applets)

849. The spiral model was originally proposed by ……………..

a. IBM

b. Barry Boehm

c. Pressman

d. Royce

Ans. b. Barry Boehm

(Barry Boehm (Boehm, 1988) proposed a risk-driven software process framework (the spiral model) that integrates risk management and incremental development. The software process is represented as a spiral rather than a sequence of activities with some backtracking from one activity to another)

850. The technique of inserting bogus information to confuse the attacker is known as …………..

a. Instantiation

b. Polyinstantiation

c. Partitioning

d. Perturbation

Ans. d. Perturbation

(Perturbation is a technique of inserting bogus information in the hopes of misdirecting an attacker or confusing the matter enough that the actual attack will not be fruitful)

Chapter 16
Preventing and Responding to Incidents

851. The Information Technology Infrastructure Library version 3 (ITILv3) defines an incident as _____.

a. An unplanned interruption to an IT Service or a reduction in the quality of an IT Service.

b. A planned interruption to an IT Service or a reduction in the quality of an IT Service.

c. A computer security incident.

d. The result of malicious or intentional actions on the part of users.

Ans. a. An unplanned interruption to an IT Service or a reduction in the quality of an IT Service.

(An incident is any event that has a negative effect on the confidentiality, integrity, or availability of an organization's assets. Information Technology Infrastructure Library version 3 (ITILv3) defines an incident as "an unplanned interruption to an IT Service or a reduction in the quality of an IT Service.".)

852. The common events that the organization classifies as security incidents _____.

a. Any attempted network intrusion.

b. Any attempted denial-of-service attack.

c. Any unauthorized access of data.

d. All of the above.

Ans.d.All of he above.

(Option A,B,C are all the events that the organization classifies as security incidents.)

853. Which software will often display a pop-up window to indicate when it detects malware _____.

a. Adware.

b. Anti-malware.

c. Spyware.

d. Ransomware.

Ans.b.Anti-malware.

(Anti-malware software, commonly referred to as an on-access or real-time scanner, hooks deep into the operating system's core or kerne land functions in a manner like how certain malware itself would attempt to operate, though with the user's informed permission for protecting the system.

854. A _____ examines the incident to determine what allowed it to happen.

a. System Analysis.

b. Accident Analysis.

c. Root cause Analysis.

d. Failure Analysis.

Ans.c. Root cause analysis.

(Root cause analysis (RCA) is a method of problem solving used for identifying the root causes of faults or problems. A factor is considered a root cause if removal thereof from the problem-fault-sequence prevents the final undesirable event from recurring; whereas a causal factor is one that affects an event's outcome, but is not a root cause. Though removing a causal factor can benefit an outcome, it does not prevent its recurrence with certainty.

855. The attacks that prevent a system from processing or responding to legitimate traffic or requests for resources and objects _____.

a. Man-in-the-Middle Attack.

b. Denial of service attack.

c. Identity Spoofing.

d. Password base attacks.

Ans.b. Denial of service attack.

(a denial-of-service attack (DoS attack) is a cyber-attack where the perpetrator seeks to make a machine or network resource unavailable to its intended users by temporarily or indefinitely disrupting services of a host connected to the Internet.)

856. The attack that manipulates the TCP session is the _____.

a. Smurf attack.

b. TCP reset attack.

c. Fraggle attack.

d. Pink Flood attack.

Ans.b. TCP reset attack.

(TCP reset attack, also known as "forged TCP resets", "spoofed TCP reset packets" or "TCP reset attacks", is a way to tamper and terminate the Internet connection by sending forged TCP reset packet.)

857. An attacker fragments traffic in such a way that a system is unable to put data packets back together is known as _____.

a. Tear drop attack.

b. Ping of death attack.

c. Zeroday exploit.

d. Fraggle attack.

Ans.a. Tear drop attack.

(A teardrop attack is a Denial of service (DoS) attack

that involves sending fragmented packets to a target machine. Since the machine receiving such packets cannot reassemble them due to a bug in TCP/IP fragmentation reassembly, the packets overlap one another, crashing the target network device.)

858. Attack occurs when the attacker sends spoofed SYN packets to a victim using the victim's IP address as both the source and destination IP address is known as _____.

a. Ping of death attack.

b. Fraggle attack.

c. Land attack.

d. SYN flood attack.

Ans.c. Land attack.

(A land attack is a remote denial-of-service (DOS) attack caused by sending a packet to a machine with the source host/port the same as the destination host/port.)

859. The script or program that performs an unwanted, unauthorized, or unknown activity on a computer system is called _____.

a. A drive by download.

b. Malware.

c. Malicious code.

d. Zero-day Exploit.

Ans.c. Malicious code.

(Malicious code is the term used to describe any code in any part of a software system or script that is intended to cause undesired effects, security breaches or damage to a system.)

860. Which code downloaded and installed on a user's system without the user's knowledge.

a. Man in the middle attack.

b. A drive by download.

c. Zero-day Exploit.

d. Ping of death attack.

Ans. b. A drive by download.

(A drive-by download is a program that is automatically installed on your computer when you're visiting a booby-trapped website or viewing a HTML e-mail message.)

861. The attack which occurs when a malicious user is able to gain a position logically between the two endpoints of an ongoing communication is knows as _____.

a. Man in the middle attack.

b. A drive by download attack.

c. Ping of death attack.

d. SYN flood attack.

Ans.a. Man in the middle attack.

(A man-in-the-middle attack (MITM) is an attack where the attacker secretly relays and possibly alters the communication between two parties who believe they are directly communicating with each other.)

862. A criminal act of destruction or disruption committed against an organization by an employee is known as_____.

a. Espionage.

b. Sabotage.

c. Teardrop.

d. Identity Spoofing.

Ans.b. Sabotage.

(Sabotage is defined as deliberate and malicious acts that result in the disruption of the normal processes and functions or the destruction or damage of equipment or information.)

863. The malicious act of gathering proprietary,

secret, private, sensitive, or confidential information about an organization is known as _____.

a. Teardrop.

b. Identity Spoofing.

c. Espionage.

d. IDS Response.

Ans.c.Espionge.

(The practice of spying or using spies to obtain information about the plans and activities especially of a foreign government or a competing company)

864. The individual computers created as a trap for intruders is called _____.

a. Honeypots.

b. Honeynet.

c. Darknets.

d. Pseudo flaws.

Ans.a.Honeypots.

(A honeypot is a computer system that is set up to act as a decoy to lure cyber attackers, and to detect, deflect or study attempts to gain unauthorized access to information systems.)

865. Two or more networked honeypots used together to simulate a network. They look and act like legitimate systems, but they do not host data of any real value for an attacker known as _____.

a. Darknets

b. Pseudo flaws.

c. Honeynet.

d. IDS Response.

Ans.c.Honeynet.

(A honeynet is a network set up with intentional vulnerabilities; its purpose is to invite attack, so that an attacker's activities and methods can be studied and that information used to increase network security.)

866. The false vulnerabilities or apparent loopholes intentionally implanted in a system in an attempt to tempt attackers are called _____.

a. Pseudo flaws.

b. Honeynet.

c. Darknets

d.   IDS Response.

Ans.a.Pseudo flaws.

(Pseudo flaws are false vulnerabilities or apparent loopholes intentionally implanted in a system in an attempt to tempt attackers. They are often used on honeypot systems to emulate well-known operating system vulnerabilities. Attackers seeking to exploit a known flaw might stumble across a pseudo flaw and think that they have successfully penetrated a system.).

867. A _____system is similar to a honeypot, but it performs intrusion isolation using a different approach.

a.   IDS Response.

b.   Darknets

c.   Padded Cells.

d.   Espionage.

Ans.c.Padding Cells.

(A padded cell system is like a honeypot, but it performs intrusion isolation using a different approach. When an IDS detects an intruder, that intruder is automatically transferred to a padded cell. The padded cell has the look and feel of an actual network, but the attacker is unable to perform any malicious activities or access any confidential data from within the padded cell..)

868. _____ provide protection to a network by filtering traffic.

a. Malware.

b. Firewall.

c. Intruders.

d. Antivirus.

Ans.b.Firewall.

(a firewall is a network security system that monitors and controls the incoming and outgoing network traffic based on predetermined security rules.)

869. _____ provides a security boundary for applications and prevents the application from interacting with other applications.

a. Firewall.

b. Intruders.

c. Sandboxing.

d. Anti-malware.

Ans.c. Sandboxing.

(Sandboxing provides a security boundary for applications and prevents the application from interacting with other applications. Anti-malware applications use sandboxing techniques to test unknown applications. If the application displays suspicious characteristics, the sandboxing technique prevents the application from infecting other applications or the operating system..)

870. _____ attack is variant of DoS uses a reflected approach to an attack.

a. DoS.

b. DRDoS.

c. DNS.

d. SYN.

Ans.b. DRDoS.

(A distributed reflective denial-of-service (DRDoS) attack is a variant of a DoS Reflection Denial of Service attacks makes use of a potentially legitimate third party component to send the attack traffic to a victim, ultimately hiding the attackers' own identity. The attackers send packets to the reflector servers with a source Ip address set to their victim's IP therefore indirectly overwhelming the victim with the response packets.)

871. In which attack , the attackers send multiple Synchronize packets but never complete the connection with an Acknowledgement.

a. FIN.

b. SYN.

c. RST.

d. ACK.

Ans.b.SYN.

(In SYN flood attack the attackers send multiple SYN(Synchronize) packets but never complete the connection with an ACK(Acknowledgement).

872. A _____ attack is another type of flood attack, but it floods the victim with Internet Control Message Protocol (ICMP).

a. Fraggle.

b. Smruf.

c. TCP SYN.

d. RST.

Ans.b.Smruf.

(The Smurf attack is a distributed denial-of-service attack in which large numbers of Internet Control Message Protocol (ICMP) packets with the intended victim's spoofed source IP are broadcast to a computer network using an IP broadcast address. Most devices on a network will, by default, respond to this by sending a reply to the source IP address.)

873. The attack which is very effective when launched by zombies within a botnet as a DDoS attack.

a. Botnets.

b. Ping flood attack.

c. Fraggle.

d. Ping of death.

Ans.b.Ping flood attack.

(A ping flood is a simple denial-of-service attack where the attacker overwhelms the victim with ICMP "echo request" (ping) packets. This is most effective by using the flood option of ping which sends ICMP packets as fast as possible without waiting for replies. Most implementations of ping require the user to be privileged in order to specify the flood option.)

874. Botnets are like robots often called _____.

a. Robots.

b. Computers.

c. Machine.

d. Zombies.

Ans. D. Zombies.

(A botnet is a collection of Internet-connected user computers (bots) infected by malicious software (malware) that allows the computers to be controlled remotely by an operator (bot herder) through a Command-and-Control (C&C) server to perform automated tasks, such as stealing information or launching attacks on other computers).

875. The botnet which has infected approximately 4 million computers are also called _____.

a. Simda.

b. Fraggle.

c. DNSChanger.

d. Teardrop.

Ans. c. DNSChanger.

(The Esthost botnet (also called DNSChanger)infected approximately 4 million computers. DNSChanger is still a DNS hijacking Trojan from 2006 until now.[1][2] The work of an Estonian company known as Rove Digital, the malware infected computers by modifying a computer's DNS entries to point toward its own rogue name servers, which then injected its own advertising into Web pages.).

876. _____ is another preventive measure an organization can use to counter attacks.

a. Black-box testing.

b. Gray-box testing.

c. Penetration testing.

d. Performance testing.

Ans.c. Penetration testing.

(A penetration test mimics an actual attack in an attempt to identify what techniques attackers can use to circumvent security in an application, system, network, or organization)

877. A _____ knows nothing about the target site except for publicly available information, such as domain name and company

address.

a. Zero-knowledge team.

b. Full- knowledge team.

c. Partial-Knowledge team.

d. Gray—box testing.

Ans.a.Zero-knowledge team.

(Black-Box Testing by Zero-knowledge Team .A zero-knowledge team knows nothing about the target site except for publicly available information, such as domain name and company address)

878. White Box testing is also called as _____.

a. Full-knowledge team.

b. Partil-knowledge team.

c. Zero-knowledge team.

d. Black-box testing.

Ans.a.Full-knowledge testing

(White-Box Testing by Full-knowledge Team A full-knowledge team has full access to all aspects of the target environment.)

879. A partial-knowledge team that has some knowledge of the target performs _____.

a. Gray-box testing.

b. White-box testing.

c. Black-box testing.

d. Green-box testing.

Ans. a. Gray-box testing.

(Gray-box testing (International English spelling: grey-box testing) is a combination of white-box testing and black-box testing. The aim of this testing is to search for the defects if any due to improper structure or improper usage of applications).

880. The _____ hacker is someone that understands network security and methods to breach security but does not use this knowledge for personal gain.

a. Script Kiddie.

b. White Hat.

c. Ethical.

d. Gray Hat.

Ans.c.Ethical.

(An ethical hacker is someone that understands network security and methods to breach security but does not use this knowledge for personal gain. An ethical hacker will always stay within legal limits.)

881. The process of extracting specific elements from a large collection of data to construct a meaningful representation or summary of the whole is called _____.

a. Audit trials.

b. Monitoring.

c. Clipping levels.

d. Sampling or Data extraction.

Ans.d. Sampling or Data Extraction.

(sampling is a form of data reduction that allows someone to glean valuable information by looking at only a small sample of data in an audit trail.)

882._____ is the form of monitoring that examine the flow of packets rather than actual

packet contents.

a. Egress monitoring.

b. Keystroke monitoring.

c. Traffic analysis.

d. Steganography.

Ans.c.Traffic analysis.

(Traffic analysis and Trend Analysis is sometimes referred to as Network Flow Monitoring. Traffic analysis is the process of intercepting and examining messages in order to deduce information from patterns in communication. It can be performed even when the messages are encrypted and cannot be decrypted. In general, the greater the number of messages observed, or even intercepted and stored, the more can be inferred from the traffic.)

883. The practice of embedding a message within a file is known as _____.

a. Steganography.

b. Cryptography.

c. Encryption.

d. Decryption.

Ans.a.Steganography.

(Steganography (pronounced STEHG-uh-NAH-gruhf-ee, from Greek steganos, or "covered," and graphie, or "writing") is the hiding of a secret message within an ordinary message and the extraction of it at its destination.)

884. The practice of embedding an image or pattern in paper that isn't readily perceivable. It is often used with currency to thwart counterfeiting attempts is called as _____.

a. Water marking.

b. Pattern making.

c. Cryptography.

d. Audit Trails.

Ans.a.Watermarking.

(A watermark is an identifying image or pattern in paper that appears as various shades of lightness/darkness when viewed by transmitted light (or when viewed by reflected light, atop a dark background), caused by thickness or density variations in the paper.)

885. The System that can monitor activity on a single system only is called _____.

a. Host-based monitor.

b. Network –based-monitor.

c. IDS-response.

d. Ips response.

Ans.a. Host-based monitor

(Host-based IDSs (HIDSs) can monitor activity on a single system only A host-based intrusion detection system (HIDS) is an intrusion detection system that monitors and analyzes the internals of a computing system as well as (in some cases) the network packets on its network interfaces (just like a network-based intrusion detection system (NIDS) would do).This was the first type of intrusion detection software to have been designed, with the original target system being the mainframe computer where outside interaction was infrequent).

886. Code review is also known as _____.

a. Peer review.

b. Code review.

c. Overview.

d. None.

Ans.b. code review.

(Code review is systematic examination (sometimes referred to as peer review) of computer source code. It is intended to find mistakes overlooked in software development, improving the overall quality of software. Reviews are done in various forms such as pair programming, informal walkthroughs, and formal inspections)

887. How does a SYN flood attack work?

a.   Exploits a packet processing glitch in Windows systems.

b.   Uses an amplification network to flood a victim with packets

c.   Disrupts the three-way handshake used by TCP.

d.   Sends oversized ping packets to a victim.

Ans.c. Disrupts the three-way handshake used by TCP.

(A SYN flood is a form of denial-of-service attack in which an attacker sends a succession of SYN requests to a target's system in an attempt to consume enough server resources to make the system unresponsive to legitimate traffic)

Chapter 17
Disaster Recovery Planning

888. The occasional fury of our habitat—violent occurrences that result from changes in the earth's surface or atmosphere that are beyond human control is reflected by _____.

a. Human disasters.

b. Natural disasters.

c. Population.

d. Bombingd/explosions.

Ans.b. Natural disasters.

(A natural disaster is a major adverse event resulting from natural processes of the Earth; examples include floods, hurricanes, tornadoes, volcanic eruptions, earthquakes, tsunamis, and other geologic processes. A natural disaster can cause loss of life or property damage, and typically leaves some economic damage in its wake, the severity of which depends on the affected population's resilience, or ability to recover and also on the infrastructure available.)

889. The shifting of seismic plates and can occur almost anywhere in the world without warning this leads to _____.

a. Earthquake.

b. Floods.

c. Storms.

d. Fires.

Ans.a.Earthquake.

(Earthquakes are caused by the shifting of seismic plates. An earthquake (also known as a quake, tremor or temblor) is the shaking of the surface of the Earth, resulting from the sudden release of energy in the Earth's lithosphere that creates seismic waves. Earthquakes can range in size from those that are so weak that they cannot be felt to those violent enough to toss people around and destroy whole cities.).

890. The gradual accumulation of rainwater in rivers, lakes, and other bodies of water that then overflow their banks and flood the community results to _____.

a. Storms.

b. Tsunami.

c. Floods.

d. Earthquake.

Ans.c.Floods.

(Flooding can occur almost anywhere in the world at any time of the year A flood is an overflow of water that submerges land that is usually dry. The European Union (EU) Floods Directive defines a flood as a covering by water of land not normally covered by water. In the sense of "flowing water", the word may also be applied to the inflow of the tide.)

891. Prolonged periods of intense rainfall bring the risk of flash flooding and _____.

a. Floods.

b. Storms.

c. Rain.

d. Earthquake.

Ans.b. Storms.

(A storm is any disturbed state of an environment or astronomical body's atmosphere especially affecting its surface, and strongly implying severe weather.)

892. The ability of a system to suffer a fault but continue to operate is called _____.

a. Error.

b. Mistake.

c. Fault.

d. Bug.

Ans.c. Fault.

(Fault tolerance is achieved by adding redundant components such as additional disks within a redundant array of inexpensive disks (RAID) array, or additional servers within a failover clustered configuration.)

893. _____refers to the ability of a system to maintain an acceptable level of service during an adverse event.

a. RAID.

b. Fault Tolerance.

c. System Resilience.

d. Failover.

Ans.c. System Resilience.

(Resilience is becoming an important service primitive for various computer systems and networks. Resilience is used in many different application domains but the quantification of resilience has not been done well.)

894. If one server fails, another server in the cluster can take over its load in an automatic process called _____.

a. System Resilience.

b. Fault.

c. RAID.

d. Failover.

Ans.d.Failover.

(Failover clusters can include multiple servers (not just two), and they can also provide fault tolerance for multiple services or applications.)

895. A_____ system will default to a secure state in the event of a failure, blocking all access.

a. Failover.

b. Fail-secure.

c. Fail-open.

d. Fail-close.

Ans.b.Fail-secure.

(Fail-secure is a secure state in the event of a failure. The primary use of the term is with regards to security doors and motorized gates. A motor that has "fail-secure" capabilities will, in case of a power outage, be able to be opened by means of a supplied hand crank.)

896. The network capacity available to carry communications is called _____.

a. Force.

b. Bandwidth.

c. Turn-around time.

d. Burst time.

Ans.b.Bandwidth.

(Bandwidth (signal processing) or analog bandwidth, frequency bandwidth or radio bandwidth: a measure of the width of a range of frequencies, measured in hertz).

897. The packets may be lost between source and destination, requiring retransmission is called _____.

a. Packet transfer.

b. Packet gain.

c. Packet Loss.

d. Segments.

Ans.c.Packet Loss.

(Packet loss occurs when one or more packets of data travelling across a computer network fail to reach their destination. Packet loss is typically caused by network congestion. Packet loss is measured as a percentage of packets lost with respect to packets sent.)

898. The time it takes a packet to travel from source to destination _____.

a. Frequency.

b. Bandwidth.

c. Burst time.

d. Latency.

Ans.d.Latency.

(Latency is the delay from input into a system to desired outcome; the term is understood slightly differently in various contexts and latency issues also vary from one system to another.)

899. Electrical noise, faulty equipment, and other factors may corrupt the contents of packets is called _____.

a. Noise.

b. Sound.

c. Interference.

d. Interrupt.

Ans.c. Interference.

(Interference usually refers to the interaction of waves that are correlated or coherent with each other, either because they come from the same source or because they have the same or nearly the same frequency.)

900. The variation in latency between different packets is called _____.

a. Latency.

b. Turn-around time.

c. Latency.

d. Jitter.

Ans.d.Jitter.

(jitter is the deviation from true periodicity of a presumably periodic signal, often in relation to a reference clock signal)

901. A cold site setup is well depicted in the 2000 film _____, which involves a chop-shop investment firm telemarketing bogus pharmaceutical investment deals to prospective clients.

a. Gladiator.

b. Cast away.

c. Boiler Room.

d. Memento.

Ans.c.Boiler Room.

Boiler Room is a 2000 American crime drama film written and directed by Ben Younger, and starring Giovanni Ribisi, Vin Diesel, Nia Long, Ben Affleck, Nicky Katt, Scott Caan, Tom Everett Scott, Ron Rifkin and Jamie Kennedy.

902._____ occupy the middle ground

between hot and cold sites for disaster recovery specialists.

a. Cold sites.

b. Warm sites.

c. Hot sites.

d. Mobile sites.

Ans.b.Warm sites.

(Warm sites avoid significant telecommunications and personnel costs inherent in maintaining a near-real-time copy of the operational data environment.)

903. The nonmainstream alternatives to traditional recovery sites. They typically consist of self-contained trailers or other easily relocated units is called as _____.

a. Hot sites .

b. Cold sites.

c. Mobile sites.

d. Websites.

Ans.c.Mobile sites.

(Mobile sites include all the environmental control systems necessary to maintain a safe computing environment.)

904. Mutual assistance agreements also called _____.

a. Reciprocal agreement.

b. MAAS.

c. Mutual agreement.

d. None of the above.

Ans.a. Reciprocal agreement.

(Reciprocal agreements, are popular in disaster recovery literature but are rarely implemented in real-world practice).

905 The database backups are moved to a remote site using bulk transfers are know as _____.

a. MAAS.

b. Electronic vaulting.

c. Cloud computing.

d. Remote mirroring.

Ans. Electrnic vaulting.

(The remote location may be a dedicated alternative recovery site (such as a hot site) or simply an offsite location managed within the company or by a contractor for the purpose of maintaining backup data.)

906. In which data transfers are performed in a more expeditious manner.

a. Remote mirroring.

b. Cloud computing.

c. Remote journaling.

d. Electronic vaulting.

Ans.c. Remote journaling.

(Remote Journaling is the process of recording the product of a computer application in a distant data storage environment, concurrently with the normal recording of the product in the primary environment.)

907. _____ is the most advanced database backup solution. Not surprisingly, it's also the most expensive!

a. Cloud computing.

b. Remote mirroring.

c. Remote journaling.

d. Electronic vaulting.

Ans.b. Remote mirroring.

(A remote mirror volume is a mirror volume with a source in another cluster. You can use remote mirrors for offsite backup, for data transfer to remote facilities, and for load and latency balancing for large websites. By mirroring the cluster's root volume and all other volumes in the cluster, you can create an entire mirrored cluster that keeps in sync with the source cluster.)

908. _____store a complete copy of the data contained on the protected device.

a. Incremental backup.

b. Full back up.

c. Complete backup.

d. Partial backup.

Ans.b. Full back up.

(Full backup is the starting point for all other backups and contains all the data in the folders and files that are selected to be backed up. Because the full backup stores all files and folders, frequent full backups result in faster and simpler restore operations..)

909._____ store only those files that have been modified since the time of the most recent full.

a. Full backup.

b. Differential backup.

c. Incremental backup.

d. Partial backup.

Ans.c. Incremental backup.

(Only files that have the archive bit turned on, enabled, or set to 1 are duplicated in Incremental backup.)

910._____ store all files that have been modified since the time of the most recent full backup.

a. Full backup.

b. Differential backup.

c. Incremental backup.

d. Partial backup.

Ans..b. Differential backup.

(A differential backup is a type of backup that copies all the data that has changed since the last full backup. For example, if a full backup is done on Sunday, Monday's differential backup backs up all the files changed or added since Sunday's full backup.)

911. A unique tool used to protect a company against the failure of a software developer to provide adequate support for its products or against the possibility that the developer will go out of business and no technical support will be available for the product known as_____.

a. Disk to disk format.

b. Tape Rotation.

c. Restoration.

d. Software escrow arrangement.

Ans.d. software escrow arrangement.

(A software escrow arrangement is a unique tool used to protect a company against the failure of a software developer).

912. The _____ test is one of the simplest tests to conduct, but it's also one of the most critical.

a. Read-through test.

b. Simulation test.

c. Maintenance test.

d. Parallel test.

Ans. Read-through test.

(In Read-through test, you distribute copies of disaster recovery plans to the members of the disaster recovery team for review.)

913. The type of test, often referred to as a table-top exercise, members of the disaster recovery team gather in a large conference room and role-play a disaster scenario is called _____.

a. structured walk-through.

b. Read-through test.

c. Parallel test.

d. Simulation test.

Ans.a. structured walk-through.

(Members of the disaster recovery team gather in a large conference room and role-play a disaster scenario in structured walk-through.)

914. The tests are similar to the structured walk-throughs is called _____.

a. structured walk-through.

b. Read-through test.

c. Parallel test.

d. Simulation test.

Ans.d. Simulation test.

(In simulation tests, disaster recovery team members are presented with a scenario and asked to develop an appropriate response. Over the last few months, quite a few people have asked me to write a bit further explanation about what Simulation Testing even is, and why would you even want to use it. In this post, I'd like to give you a bit more detailed background information on what Simulation Testing is.

In the spectrum of testing, there are two primary axis you can categorize approaches by: scope, and level.)

915. The tests represent the next level in testing and involve relocating personnel to the alternate recovery site and implementing site activation procedures is called _____.

a. structured walk-through.

b. Read-through test.

c. Parallel test.

d. Simulation test.

Ans.c. Parallel test.

(The employees relocated to the site perform their disaster recovery responsibilities just as they would for an actual disaster in Parallel test)

916. The tests operate like parallel tests, but they involve actually shutting down operations at the primary site and shifting them to the recovery site is called _____.

a. structured walk-through.

b. Full-interruption tests.

c. Parallel test.

d. Simulation test.

Ans.b. Full-interruption tests.

(Full-interruption tests are extremely difficult to arrange, and you often encounter resistance from management. In a full interruption test, operations are shut down at the primary site and shifted to the recovery site in accordance with the disaster recovery plan.

This is clearly a very thorough test, but one which is also expensive and has the capacity to cause a major disruption of operations if the test fails.)

917. Which one of the following is an example of a man-made disaster?

a. Tsunami.

b. Earthquake.

c. Power outage.

d. Lightning strike.

Ans.c. Power outages.

(A power outage (also called a power cut, a power blackout, power failure or a blackout) is a short-term or a long-term loss of the electric power to a area.

There are many causes of power failures in an electricity network. Examples of these causes include faults at power stations, damage to electric transmission lines, substations or other parts of the distribution system, a short circuit, or the overloading of electricity mains.)

918. In which one of the following database recovery techniques is an exact, up-to-date copy of the database maintained at an alternative location?

a. Transaction logging.

b. Remote journaling.

c. Electronic vaulting.

d. Remote mirroring.

Ans.b. Remote journaling.

(Remote Journaling is the process of recording the product of a computer application in a distant data storage environment, concurrently with the normal recording of the product in the primary environment.)

919. In the wake of the September 11, 2001 terrorist attacks, what industry made drastic changes that directly impact DRP/BCP activities?

a. Insurance.

b. Tourism.

c. Airline.

d. Insurance.

Ans.C. Airline.

(The attacks on September 11 caused many small

businesses to fail because they did not have business continuity/disaster recovery plans in place that were adequate to ensure their continued viability.)

920. Which one of the following disaster types is not usually covered by standard business or homeowner's insurance?

a. Fire.

b. Flood.

c. Earthquake.

d. Theft.

Ans.b.Flood.

(Most general business insurance and homeowner's insurance policies do not provide any protection against the risk of flooding or flash floods. If floods pose a risk to your organization, you should consider purchasing supplemental flood insurance under FEMA's National Flood Insurance Program.)

921. What disaster recovery principle best protects your organization against hardware failure?

a. Efficiency.

b. Consistency.

c. Redundancy.

d. Primacy.

Ans.c. Redundancy.

(Redundancy is when an employer reduces their workforce because a job or jobs are no longer needed. However, if you lose your job and they get someone in to fill it that is NOT a redundancy…

Protect yourself by doing your research and knowing your rights!)

Chapter 18
Incidents and Ethics

922. The_____ locates information that may be responsive to a discovery request when the organization believes that litigation is likely.

a.   Preservation.

b.   Identification.

c.   Collection.

d.   Processing.

Ans.b. Identification.

(the act of finding out who someone is or what something is the act of identifying someone or something that shows who a person is a document, card, etc., that has your name and other information about you and that often includes your photograph)

923._____ ensures that potentially discoverable information is protected against alteration or deletion.

a.   Preservation.

b.   Identification.

c.   Collection.

d.   Processing.

Ans.a. Preservation.

(Potentially discoverable information is protected against alteration or deletion. Preservation ensures that potentially discoverable information is protected against alteration or deletion.)

924. The collected information to perform a "rough cut" of irrelevant information, reducing the amount of information requiring detailed screening.

a. Identification.

b. Collection.

c. Processing.

d. Preservation.

Ans.d. Preservation.

(Information to perform a "rough cut" of irrelevant information, reducing the amount of information requiring detailed screening.)

925. _____ performs deeper inspection of the content and context of remaining information.

a. Collection.

b. Processing.

c. Analysis.

d. Production.

Ans.c. Analysis.

(Cybersecurity analysts protect websites and networks from cyber threats such as malware, denial-of-service attacks, hacks and viruses.)

926. The information to witnesses, the court and other parties. Conducting Discovery is a complex process and requires careful coordination between information technology professionals and legal counsel is known as _____.

a. Analysis.

b. Production.

c. Presentation.

d. Review.

Ans.c. Presentation.

(Conducting Discovery is a complex process and requires careful coordination between information technology professionals and legal counsel.)

927._____ consists of things that may actually be brought into a court of law.

a. Documentary evidence.

b. Real evidence.

c. Testimonial evidence.

d. Best evidence.

Ans.b. Real evidence.

(This may include items such as a murder weapon, clothing, or other physical objects. In a computer crime case, real evidence might include seized computer equipment, such as a keyboard with fingerprints on it or a hard drive from a hacker's computer system)

928._____includes any written items brought into court to prove a fact at hand. This type of evidence must also be authenticated.

a. Documentary evidence.

b. Real evidence.

c. Testimonial evidence.

d. Best evidence.

Ans.a. Documentary evidence.

(This type of evidence must also be authenticated. For example, if an attorney wants to introduce a computer log as evidence, they must bring a witness (for example, the system administrator) into court to testify that the log was collected as a routine business practice and is indeed the actual log that the system collected.)

929. _____ states that, when a document is used as evidence in a court proceeding, the original document must be introduced.

a. Parol evidence.

b. Testimonial evidence.

c. Real evidence.

d. Best evidence.

Ans.d. Best Evidence.

(Copies or descriptions of original evidence (known as secondary evidence) will not be accepted as evidence unless certain exceptions to the rule apply.)

930._____ states that, when an agreement between parties is put into written form, the written document is assumed to contain all the terms of the agreement and no verbal agreements may modify the written agreement.

a. Best evidence

b. Parol evidence.

c. Testimonial evidence.

d. Documentary evidence.

Ans.b. Parol evidence.

(If documentary evidence meets the materiality, competency, and relevancy requirements and also complies with the best evidence and parol evidence rules, it can be admitted into court.)

931. It is not possible for a witness to uniquely identify an object in court. In those cases, _____ must be established.

a. Chain of evidence.

b. Best evidence

c. Parol evidence.

d. Testimonial evidence.

(This document everyone who handles evidence—including the police who originally collect it, the evidence technicians who process it, and the lawyers who use it in court. The location of the evidence must be fully documented from the moment it was collected to the moment it appears in court to ensure that it is indeed the same item.).

932. Evidence consisting of the testimony of a witness, either verbal testimony in court or written testimony in a recorded deposition is called _____.

a. Best evidence

b. Parol evidence.

c. Testimonial evidence.

d. Documentary evidence.

Ans.c. Testimonial evidence.

(Witnesses must take an oath agreeing to tell the truth, and they must have personal knowledge on which their testimony is based. Furthermore, witnesses must remember the basis for their testimony (they may consult written notes or records to aid their memory). Witnesses can offer direct evidence: oral testimony that proves or disproves a claim based on their own direct observation)

933._____ focus on illegally obtaining an organization's confidential information.

a. Business attacks.

b. Financial attacks.

c. Terrorists attacks.

d. Grudge attacks.

Ans.a. Business attacks.

(This could be information that is critical to the operation of the organization, such as a secret recipe, or information that could damage the organization's reputation if disclosed, such as personal information about its employees. The gathering of a competitor's confidential information, also called industrial espionage, is not a new phenomenon).

934. Attacks are carried out to unlawfully obtain money or services. They are the type of computer crime you most commonly hear about in the news.

a. Business attacks.

b. Financial attacks.

c. Terrorists attacks.

d. Grudge attacks.

Ans.b. Financial attacks.

(The goal of a financial attack could be to steal credit card numbers, increase the balance in a bank account, or place "free" long-distance telephone calls.)

935._____ s are carried out to unlawfully obtain money or services. They are the type of computer crime you most commonly hear about in the news.

a. Business attacks.

b. Financial attacks.

c. Terrorists attacks.

d. Grudge attacks.

Ans.c. Terrorists attack.

(The purpose of a terrorist attack is to disrupt normal life and instill fear, whereas a military or intelligence attack is designed to extract secret information. Intelligence gathering generally precedes any type of terrorist attack)

936. _____ are attacks that are carried out to damage an organization or a person.

a. Grudge attacks.

b. Business attacks.

c. Financial attacks.

d. Terrorists attacks.

(The damage could be in the loss of information or information processing capabilities or harm to the organization or a person's reputation. The motivation behind a grudge attack is usually a feeling of resentment, and the attack)

937. _____ attacks launched only for the fun of it. Attackers who lack the ability to devise their own attacks will often download programs that do their work for them.

a. Financial attacks.

b. Terrorists attacks.

c. Thrill attacks.

d. Business attacks.

Ans.c. Thrill attacks.

(Attackers who lack the ability to devise their own attacks will often download programs that do their work for them. These attackers are often called script kiddies because they run only other people's programs, or scripts, to launch an attack)

938. _____attacks are reconnaissance attacks that usually precede another, more serious attack.

a. Terrorists attacks.

b. Thrill attacks.

c. Business attacks.

d. Scanning attacks.

Ans.Scanning attacks.

(Attackers will gather as much information about your system as possible before launching a directed attack. Look for any unusual activity on any port or from any single address)

939. The person of involvement in a crime and intend to use the information gathered in court, this is called an _____.

a. Restoration.

b. Ethics.

c. interrogation.

d. interview.

Ans.c. Interrogation.

(During your incident investigation, you may find it necessary to speak with individuals who might have information relevant to your investigation. If you seek only to gather information to assist with your investigation, this is called an interview. If you suspect the person of involvement in a crime and intend to use the information gathered in court, this is called an interrogation)

940. In January 1989, _____ recognized that the Internet was rapidly expanding beyond the initial trusted community that created it.

a. Internet Architecture Board.

b. Internet Advisory Board.

c. Internet Security Board.

d. Internet Development Board.

Ans.b. Internet Advisory Board.

(Internet Advisory Board (IAB) recognized that the Internet was rapidly expanding beyond the initial trusted community that created it. Understanding that misuse could occur as the Internet grew, IAB issued a statement of policy concerning the proper use of the Internet.

941. _____ is a branch of computer forensic analysis, involves the identification and extraction of information from storage media.

a. Network analysis.

b. Media analysis.

c. Software analysis.

d. Hardware analysis.

Ans.b. Media analysis.

(Techniques used for media analysis may include the recovery of deleted files from unallocated sectors of the physical disk, the live analysis of storage media connected to a computer system (especially useful when examining encrypted media), and the static analysis of forensic images of storage media).

942. What is the main purpose of a military and intelligence attack?

a. To attack the availability of military systems.

b. To obtain secret and restricted information from military or law enforcement sources.

c. To utilize military or intelligence agency systems to attack other nonmilitary sites

d. To compromise military systems for use in attacks against other systems

Ans.b. To obtain secret and restricted information from military or law enforcement sources .

(Military and intelligence attacks are launched primarily to obtain secret and restricted information from law enforcement or military and technological research sources. The disclosure of such information could compromise investigations, disrupt military planning, and threaten national security.)

943 What is a computer crime?

a. Any attack specifically listed in your security policy Transfer funds from an unapproved source into your account

b. Any illegal attack that compromises a protected computer.

c. Any violation of a law or regulation that involves a computer.

d. Failure to practice due diligence in computer security.

Ans.c. Any violation of a law or regulation that involves a computer.

(A crime is an any violation of law or regulation. The violation stipulation defines the action as a crime. Alternatively referred to as cybercrime, e-crime, electronic crime, or hi-tech crime. Computer crime is an act performed by a knowledgeable computer user, sometimes referred to as a hacker that illegally browses or steals a company's or individual's private information.).

944. What is an incident?

a. Any active attack that causes damage to your system.

b. Any violation of a code of ethics.

c. Any crime (or violation of a law or regulation) that involves a computer.

d. Any event that adversely affects the confidentiality, integrity, or availability of your data.

Ans.d. Any event that adversely affects the confidentiality, integrity, or availability of your data.

(An incident is defined by four security policy. Actions that you define as an incident may not be considered an incident in another organization.)

945. Which one of the following attacks is most indicative of a terrorist attack?

a. Altering sensitive trade secret documents.

b. Damaging the ability to communicate and respond to a physical attack.

c. Stealing unclassified information.

d. Transferring funds to other countries.

Ans.b. Damaging the ability to communicate and respond

to a physical attack.

(The purpose of a terrorist attack is to disrupt normal life and instill fear, whereas a military or intelligence attack is designed to extract secret information. Intelligence gathering generally precedes any type of terrorist attack. The very systems that are victims of a terrorist attack were probably compromised in an earlier attack to collect intelligence.)

946. Which of the following would not be a primary goal of a grudge attack?

a. Disclosing embarrassing personal information.

b. Launching a virus on an organization's system.

c. Sending inappropriate email with a spoofed origination address of the victim organization.

d. Using automated tools to scan the organization's systems for vulnerable ports.

Ans. d. Using automated tools to scan the organization's systems for vulnerable ports

(Grudge attacks are attacks that are carried out to damage an organization or a person. The damage could be in the loss of information or information processing capabilities or harm to the organization or a person's reputation)

947. What is the main purpose of a military and intelligence attack?

a. To attack the availability of military system.

b. To obtain secret and restricted information from military or law enforcement sources

c. To utilize military or intelligence agency systems to attack other nonmilitary site

d. To compromise military systems for use in attacks against other systems.

Ans.b. To obtain secret and restricted information from military or law enforcement sources

(Military and intelligence attacks are launched primarily to obtain secret and restricted information from law enforcement or military and technological research sources.)

948. What is the most important rule to follow when collecting evidence?

a. Do not turn off a computer until you photograph the screen.

b. List all people present while collecting evidence.

c. Never modify evidence during the collection process.

d. Transfer all equipment to a secure storage location.

Ans.c. Never modify evidence during the collection process.

(The most important rue is to modify or taint evidence, if you modify evidence it becomes inadmissible I court.).

949. What would be a valid argument for not immediately removing power from a machine when an incident is discovered?

a. All the damage has been done, Turning the machine off would not stop additional damage.

b. There is no other system that can replace this one if it is turned off.

c. Too many users are logged in and using the system.

d. Valuable evidence in memory will be lost.

Ans.d. Valuable evidence in memory will be lost.

(The most compelling reason for not removing power from a machine is that you will lose the contents of memory.)

950. If port scanning does no damage to a system, why is it generally considered an incident?

a. All port scans indicate adversarial behavior

b. Port scans can precede attacks that cause damage and can indicate a future attack.

c. Scanning a port damages, the port.

d. Port scanning uses system resources that could be put to better uses.

Ans.b. Port scans can precede attacks that cause damage and can indicate a future attack.

(Some port scans are normal. An unusual high volume of port scan activity can be reconnaissance activity preceding a more dangerous attacks, When you see port scanning, you should always investigate.)

951. What type of incident is characterized by obtaining an increased level of privilege?

a.	Compromise

b.	Denial of service

c.	Malicious code

d.	Scanning.

Ans.a. Compromise

(Anytime an attacker exceeds their authority, the incident is classified as a compromise.)

952. What is the best way to recognize abnormal and suspicious behavior on your system?

a.	Be aware of the newest attacks. Configure your IDS to detect and report all abnormal traffic.

b.	Configure your IDS to detect and report all abnormal traffic.

c.	Know what your normal system activity looks like.

d. . Study the activity signatures of the main types of attacks.

Ans.c. Know what your normal system activity looks like.

(When you know what the activity on your computer looks like in a normal day. Then you can immediately detect any abnormal day)

953. If you need to confiscate a PC from a suspected attacker who does not work for your organization, what legal avenue is most appropriate?

a. Consent agreement signed by employees.

b. Search warrant.

c. No legal avenue is necessary.

d. Voluntary consent.

Ans.b. Search warrant.

(In this case you need search warrant to confiscate equipment without giving the suspect time to destroy evidence).

954. Why should you avoid deleting log files daily?

a. An incident may not be discovered for several days and valuable evidence could be lost

b. Disk space is cheap, and log files are used frequently.

c. Log files are protected and cannot be altered.

d. Any information in a log file is useless after it is several hours old.

Ans.a. An incident may not be discovered for several days and valuable evidence could be lost

(A log file usually contains large volume of generally useless information. In computing, a log file is a file that records either events that occur in an operating system or other software runs, or messages between different users of a communication software.[citation needed] Logging is the act of keeping a log. In the simplest case, messages are written to a single log file.)

955. What are ethics?

a. Mandatory actions required to fulfill job requirements

b. Laws of professional conduct

c. Regulations set forth by a professional organization

d. Rules of personal behavior

Ans.d. Rules of personal behavior

(Ethics are simply rules of personal behavior. Many professional organizations establish formal codes of ethics to govern their members, Ethics are personal rules , individual rules use to guide their lives)

956. According to the (ISC) 2 Code of Ethics, how are CISSPs expected to act?

a. Honestly, diligently, responsibly, and legally.

b. Honorably, honestly, justly, responsibly, and legally.

c. Upholding the security policy and protecting the organization.

d. Trustworthy, loyally, friendly, courteously

Ans.b. Honorably, honestly, justly, responsibly, and legally.

(The second canon of(ISC)2Code of ethics states how a CISSP should act, which is honorably, honestly, justly, responsibly and legally).

957. Which of the following actions are considered unacceptable and unethical according to RFC 1087, "Ethics and the Internet"?

a. Actions that compromise the privacy of classified information.

b. Actions that compromise the privacy of users.

c. Actions that disrupt organizational activities

d. Actions in which a computer is used in a manner inconsistent with a stated security policy

Ans.b. Actions that compromise the privacy of users.

(RFC 1087 does not specially address the statement in A,C OR D Although each type of activity is unacceptable only the activity identified in option b is identified RFC 1087.)

Chapter 19
Malicious Code and Application Attacks

958. Which object s include a broad range of programmed computer security threats that exploit various network, operating system, software, and physical security vulnerabilities to spread malicious payloads to computer systems.

a. Master boot record.

b. Malicious payload.

c. Virus.

d. Malicious code.

Ans.d. Malicious code.

(Malicious code objects, such as computer viruses and Trojan horses, depend on irresponsible computer use by humans to spread from system to system with any success.)

959. The malicious individual who doesn't understand the technology behind security vulnerabilities but downloads ready-to-use software (or scripts) from the Internet and uses them to launch attacks against remote systems is called _____.

a. Trojan Horse.

b. Virus.

c. Kiddie

d. Internet Worm.

Ans.c.kiddie

(The trend gave birth to a new breed of virus-creation software that allows anyone with a minimal level of technical expertise to create a virus and unleash it upon the Internet. This is reflected in the large number of viruses documented by antivirus experts to date)

960. Which is one of the virus attack the portion of bootable media (such as a hard disk, USB drive, or CD/DVD) that the computer uses to load the operating system during the boot process.

a. Trojan Horse.

b. Virus.

c. Kiddie.

d. MBR.

Ans.d.MBR.

(The master boot record (MBR) virus is one of the earliest known forms of virus infection. These viruses attack the MBR—the portion of bootable media (such as a hard disk, USB drive, or CD/DVD) that the computer uses to load the operating system during the boot process.)

961. _____ viruses use more than one

propagation technique to penetrate systems that defend against only one method or the other.

a. Stealth viruses.

b. Multipartite viruses.

c. Trojan viruses.

d. Macro viruses.

Ans.b. Multipartite viruses.

(Multipartite viruses use more than one propagation technique is an attempt to penetrate systems that defend against only one method or the other. For example, the Marzia virus discovered in 1993 infects critical COM and EXE files, most notably the command.com system file, by adding 2,048 bytes of malicious code to each file.)

962. The viruses hide themselves by actually tampering with the operating system to fool antivirus packages into thinking that everything is functioning normally are called _____.

a. Trojan viruses.

b. Macro viruses.

c. Stealth viruses.

d. Polymorphic viruses.

Ans.c. Stealth viruses.

(Stealth boot sector virus might overwrite the system's master boot record with malicious code but then also modify the operating system's file access functionality to cover its tracks.)

963. Which viruses modify their own code as they travel from system to system is called_____.

a. Macro viruses.

b. Stealth viruses.

c. Polymorphic viruses.

d. Encrypted viruses.

Ans.c. Polymorphic viruses.

(The virus's propagation and destruction techniques remain the same, but the signature of the virus is somewhat different each time it infects a new system. It is the hope of polymorphic virus creators that this constantly changing signature will render signature-based antivirus packages useless.)

964._____ viruses use cryptographic techniques, such as those to avoid detection.

a. Polymorphic viruses.

b. Encrypted viruses.

c. Multipartite viruses.

d. Hoaxes.

Ans.b. Encrypted viruses.

(Encrypted viruses are actually quite similar to polymorphic viruses—each infected system has a virus with a different signature. However, they do not generate these modified signatures by changing their code; instead, they alter the way they are stored on the disk).

965. Encrypted viruses use a very short segment of code, known as_____.

a. Encrypted viruses.

b. Decrypted viruses.

c. Virus decryption routine.

d. Stealth viruses.

Ans.c. Virus decryption routine.

(Encrypted viruses use a very short segment of code, known as the virus decryption routine, which contains the cryptographic information necessary to load and decrypt the main virus code stored elsewhere on the disk. Each infection utilizes a different cryptographic key, causing the main code to appear completely different on each system.)

966. _____ are malicious code objects that infect a system and lie dormant until they are triggered by the occurrence of one or more conditions such as time, program launch, website logon, and so on.

a. Hoaxes.

b. Trojan.

c. Logic bombs.

d. Melissa virus.

Ans.c. Logic bombs.

(The vast majority of logic bombs are programmed into custom-built applications by software developers seeking to ensure that their work is destroyed if they unexpectedly leave the company)

967. A software program that appears benevolent but carries a malicious, behind-the-scenes payload that has the potential to wreak havoc on a system or network is called _____.

a. Hoaxes.

b. Kiddies.

c. Internet worms.

d. Trojan horses.

Ans.d. Trojan Horses.

(Trojans differ very widely in functionality. Some will destroy all the data stored on a system is an attempt to cause a large amount of damage in as short a time frame as possible. Some are fairly innocuous)

968. Which virus infects a target machine and then uses encryption technology to encrypt documents, spreadsheets, and other files stored on the system with a key known only to the malware creator.

a. Internet worms.

b. Trojan horses.

c. Ransomware.

d. Melissa worm.

Ans.c. Ransomware.

(The user is then unable to access their files and receives an ominous pop-up message warning that the files will be permanently deleted unless a ransom is paid within a short period of time. The user then often pays this ransom to regain access to their files)

969. One of the most famous ransomware strains is a program known as _____.

a. Melissa worm.

b. Hoaxes.

c. Kiddies.

d. Cryptolocker.

Ans.d. Crypto locker.

(The Crypto Locker ransomware attack was a cyberattack using the Crypto Locker ransomware that occurred from 5 September 2013 to late-May 2014. The attack utilized a trojan that targeted computers running Microsoft Windows, and was believed to have first been posted to the Internet on 5 September 2013)

970. A collection of computers (sometimes thousands or even millions!) across the Internet under the control of an attacker known as the_____.

a. Botmaster.

b. Macro virus.

c. Mega virus.

d. Botnets.

Ans.a. Botmaster.

(The botmaster of this particular botnet used the systems on their network as part of a denial of service attack against a website that he didn't like for one reason or another. He instructed all the systems in his botnet to retrieve the same web page repeatedly, in hopes that the website would fail under the heavy load)

971._____ contain the same destructive potential as other malicious code objects with an added twist—they propagate themselves without requiring any human intervention.

a. Virus.

b. Worms.

c. Errors.

d. Malware.

Ans.b. Worms.

(The Internet worm was the first major computer security incident to occur on the Internet. Since that time, hundreds of new worms (with thousands of variant strains) have unleashed their destructive power on the Internet.)

972. Which worm received a good deal of media attention in the summer of 2001 when it rapidly spread among web servers running unpatched versions of Microsoft's Internet Information Server (IIS).

a. RTM Worm.

b. Internet Worm.

c. Code Red Worm.

d. Computer Worm.

Ans.c .Code Red Worm.

(Code Red performed three malicious actions on the systems it penetrated: It randomly selected hundreds of IP addresses and then probed those addresses to see whether they were used by hosts running a vulnerable version of IIS.

It defaced HTML pages on the local web server,

It planted a logic bomb that would initiate a denial of service attack against the IP address 198.137.240.91, which at that time belonged to the web server hosting the White House's home page.)

973._____ monitors your actions and transmits important details to a remote system that spies on your activity.

a. Malware.

b. Adware.

c. Ransomware.

d. Spyware.

Ans.d. Spyware.

(Spyware might wait for you to log into a banking website and then transmit your username and password to the creator of the spyware. Alternatively, it might wait for you to enter your credit card number on an ecommerce site and transmit it to a fraudster to resell on the black market).

974._____ uses a variety of techniques to display advertisements on infected computers. The simplest forms of adware display pop-up ads on your screen while you surf the Web.

a. Ransomware.

b. Spyware.

c. Adware.

d. Malware.

Ans.c Adware.

(Adware and malware authors often take advantage of third-party plug-ins to popular Internet tools, such as web browsers, to spread their malicious content.)

975. One of the simplest techniques attackers use to gain illegitimate access to a system is to learn the username and password of an authorized system user is called as _____.

a. Password guessing.

b. Password attack.

c. Password crackers.

d. Dictionary attacks.

Ans.b. Password attack.

(Once they've gained access as a regular user, they have a foothold into the system. At that point, they can use other techniques, including automated rootkit packages, to gain increased levels of access to the system.)

976._____ is one of the most effective tools attackers use to gain access to a system.

a.   Cornerstone.

b.   Social Engineering.

c.   Counter measure.

d.   Content filter.

Ans.b. Social Engineering.

(A social-engineering attack consists of simply calling the user and asking for their password, posing as a technical support representative or other authority figure who needs the information immediately)

977._____ vulnerabilities exist when a developer does not properly validate user input to ensure that it is of an appropriate size.

a.   Cornerstone.

b.   Social Engineering.

c.   Content filter.

d.   Buter overflow.

Ans.d. Buter overflow.

(Input that is too large can "overflow" a data structure to affect other data stored in the computer's memory)

978. The _____ is a timing vulnerability that occurs when program checks access permissions too far in advance of a resource request.

a. Time-of-check-to-time-of-use (TOCTTOU).

b. Time of check (TOC).

c. Time of use (TOU).

d. None

Ans.a. Time-of-check-to-time-of-use (TOCTTOU).

(if an operating system builds a comprehensive list of access permissions for a user upon logon and then consults that list throughout the logon session, a TOCTTOU vulnerability exists. If the system administrator revokes a particular permission, that restriction)

979. Which attacks occur when web applications contain some type of reflected input?

a. Sql injection attack.

b. Cross-site scripting.

c. Privilege attack.

d. Dictionary attack.

Ans.b Cross site scripting.

(For example, consider a simple web application that

contains a single text box asking a user to enter their name. When the user clicks Submit, the web application loads a new page that says, "Hello, name.")

980. Which attacks are even riskier than XSS attacks from an organization's perspective?

a. Cross-site scripting.

b. Privilege attack.

c. Dictionary attack.

d. Sql injection attack.

Ans.d.Sql Injection attack.

(As with XSS attacks, SQL injection attacks use unexpected input to a web application. However, instead of using this input to attempt to fool a user, SQL injection attacks use it to gain unauthorized access to an underlying database.)

981. _____are often the first type of network reconnaissance carried out against a targeted network.

a. Ip Probes

b. reconnaissance

c. Dumpster Diving.

d. vulnerability scan.

Ans.Ip Probes.

(In telecommunications generally, a probe is an action taken or an object used for learning something about the state of the network. For example, an empty message can be sent simply to see whether the destination exists. Ping is a common utility for sending such a probe.)

982. The malicious individual simply reconfigures their system so that it has the IP address of a trusted system and then attempts to gain access to other external resources is called _____.

a. Dumpster Diving.

b. reconnaissance

c. Ip Probes.

d. Ip Spoofing.

Ans.d.Ip Spoofing.

(In an IP spoofing attack, the malicious individual simply reconfigures their system so that it has the IP address of a trusted system and then attempts to gain access to other external resources)

983. _____attacks occur when a malicious individual intercepts part of the communication between an authorized user and a resource and then uses a hijacking technique to take over the session and assume the identity of the authorized user.

a. reconnaissance

b. Ip Probes.

c. Ip Spoofing.

d. Session Hijacking.

Ans.d. Session Hijacking.

(Session hijacking attacks occur when a malicious individual intercepts part of the communication between an authorized user and a resource and then uses a hijacking technique to take over the session and assume the identity of the authorized user.)

984. What is the most commonly used technique to protect against virus attacks?

a. Signature detection .

b. Heuristic detection .

c. Data integrity assurance.

d. Automated reconstruction.

Ans.a.Signature Detection.

(Signature Detection mechanisms use known description of viruses to identify malicious code resident a system.)

985. You are the security administrator for an e-commerce company and are placing a new web server into production. What network zone should you use?

a. Internet

b. DMZ

c. Intranet

d. Sandbox.

Ans.b.DMZ.

(The DMZ (Demilitarized zone) designed to house systems web servers that must be acceptable from both intenal and external servers)

986. Which one of the following types of attacks relies on the difference between the timing of two events?

a. Smurf

b. TOCTTOU

c. Land

d. Fraggle.

Ans.b. TOCTTOU

(The time-of-check to Time-of-use(TOCTTOU) attack relies on the timing of the execution of two events)

**987. Which of the following techniques requires that administrators identify appropriate applications for an environment?

a. Sandboxing.

b. Control signing.

c. Integrity monitoring.

d. Whitelisting.

Ans.d. Whitelisting.

(Application whistling requires that administrator specifies approved applications, and then the operating uses this list to allow only known good applications to run.)

988. What advanced virus technique modifies the malicious code of a virus on each system it infects?

a. Polymorphism

b. Stealth

c. Encryption

d. multipartism

Ans.a. Polymorphism.

(In an attempt to avoid detection by signature –based antivirus software packages, Polymorphic viruses modify their own code each time they infect a system.)

989. Which one of the following tools provides a solution to the problem of users forgetting complex passwords?

a. LastPass.

b. Crack.

c. Shadow password files.

d. Tripwire.

Ans.a.LastPass.

(A last pass is tool that user to create unique strong passwords each services they use without the burden of memorizing them all)

990. What type of application vulnerability most directly allows an attacker to modify the contents of a system's memory?

a. Rootkit

b. Back door

c. TOC/TOU

d. Buffer overflow.

Ans.d. Butterflow.

(Butter overflow attacks allow an attacker to modify the contents of system memory by writing beyond the sources allocated for variable.)

91. Which one of the following passwords is least likely to be compromised during a dictionary attack?

a. Mike

b. elppa

c. dayorange

d. fsas3alG.

Ans.d.fsas3alG.

(Option D is simply a random string of characters that a dictionary attack would not uncover.)

992. What file is instrumental in preventing dictionary attacks against Unix systems?

a. /etc/passwd.

b. /etc/shadow

c. /etc/security

d. /etc/pwlog

Ans.d./etc/pwlog.

(Shadow password files moves encrypted password from the publicly readable /etc/passwd file to the protected /etc/shadow file.)

993. What character should always be treated carefully when encountered as user input on a web form?

a. !

b. *

c. &

d. '

Ans.d.'.

(The single quote character used in SQL queries and must be used carefully on webforms to protect against Sql injection attacks.)

994. What database technology, if implemented for web forms, can limit the potential for SQL injection attacks?

a. Triggers.

b. Stored procedures.

c. Column encryption.

d. Concurrency control.

Ans.b.Stored Procedures.

(Developers of web applications should leverage database stored procedures to limit the applications ability to execute arbitrary code. With stored procedures sql statements resides on the database servers and may only be modified by database administrators.)

995. What type of reconnaissance attack provides attackers with useful information about the services running on a system?

a. Session hijacking

b. Port scan

c. Dumpster diving

d. IP sweep.

Ans.b.Port scan.

(Ports scans reveals the ports associated with the services running on a machine and available to the public. A port scan is a series of messages sent by someone attempting to break into a computer to learn which computer network services, each associated with a "well-known" port number, the computer provides. Port scanning, a favorite approach of computer cracker, gives the assailant an idea where to probe for weaknesses.)

996. What condition is necessary on a web page for it to be used in a cross-site scripting attack?

a. Reflected input

b. Database-driven content

c. .NET technology

d.   CGI scripts.

Ans.a. Reflected input.

(Cross size scripting is successful only against web applications that uses reflected input. Cross-Site Scripting (XSS) attacks are a type of injection, in which malicious scripts are injected into otherwise benign and trusted web sites. XSS attacks occur when an attacker uses a web application to send malicious code, generally in the form of a browser side script, to a different end user. Flaws that allow these attacks to succeed are quite widespread and occur anywhere a web application uses input from a user within the output it generates without validating or encoding it.)

997. What type of virus utilizes more than one propagation technique to maximize the number of penetrated systems?

a.   Stealth virus

b.   Companion virus

c.   Polymorphic virus

d.   Multipartite virus.

Ans.d. Multipartite virus.

(Multipartite virus use two r more propagation techniques to maximize their reach. A multipartite virus is a computer virus that infects and spreads in multiple ways. The term was coined to describe the first viruses that included

DOS executable files and PC BIOS boot sector virus code, where both parts are viral themselves. Prior to the discovery of the first of these, viruses were categorized as either file infectors or boot infectors. Because of the multiple vectors for the spread of infection, these viruses could spread faster than a boot or file infector alone)

998. What is the most effective defense against cross-site scripting attacks?

a.   Limiting account privileges

b.   Input validation

c.   User authentication

d.   Encryption

Ans.b.Input validation.

(Input validation prevents cross site scripting attacks by limiting user input to predefined range This prevents the attacker from including the html <SCRIPT> tag in the input)

999. What worm was the first to cause major physical damage to a facility?

a.   Stuxnet

b.   Code Red

c.   Melissa

d.   Rtm.

Ans. a. stuxnet.

(Stuxnet was a highly sophisticated worm designed to destroy nuclear enrichment centrifuges attached to siemens controllers. Stuxnet is a malicious computer worm, first identified in 2010 but thought to have been in development since at least 2005, that targets industrial computer systems and was responsible for causing substantial damage to Iran's nuclear program.)

1000. What technology does the Java language use to minimize the threat posed by applets?

a. Confidentiality

b. Encryption

c. Stealth

d. Sandbox.

Ans. d. Sandbox.

(The java sandbox isolates applets and allows them to run within a protected environment, limiting the effect they may have on the system. In computer security, a sandbox is a security mechanism for separating running programs, usually to mitigate system failures or software vulnerabilities from spreading. It is often used to execute untested or untrusted programs or code, possibly from unverified or untrusted third parties, suppliers, users or websites, without risking harm to the host machine or operating system.)

Glossary

Business Continuity Planning 45

Communication and Network Security 193

Cryptography and Symmetric Key Algorithms 97

Disaster Recovery Planning 523

History of CISSP Certification 8

How will it work? 5

Identity and Access Management 261

Incidents and Ethics 545

Introduction 1

Introduction to CISSP 7

Launch of Computerized Adaptive Testing (CAT) for CISSP Exams 5

Laws, Regulations, and Compliance 55

Malicious Code and Application Attacks 569

Ongoing certification 12

Personnel Security and Risk Management Concepts 33

Physical Security Requirements 147

PKI and Cryptographic Applications 111

Preventing and Responding to Incidents 498

Principles of Security Models, Design, and Capabilities 125

Protecting Security of Assets 74

Security Assessment and Testing 337

Security Governance Through Principles and Policies 13

Security Operations 371

Security Vulnerabilities, Threats, and Countermeasures 147

Software Development Security 449

The CISSP Exam 11

Topical Domains 10

Made in the USA
Lexington, KY
11 June 2018